Democratic Peace: A Political Biography

The Democratic Peace Thesis holds that democracies rarely make war on other democracies. Political scientists have advanced numerous theories attempting to identify precisely which elements of democracy promote this mutual peace; many of these academics agreed that Democratic Peace could be the final and ultimate antidote to war. However, as the theories were taken up by political figures, the immediate outcomes were war and the perpetuation of hostilities.

In *Democratic Peace: A Political Biography*, political theorist Piki Ish-Shalom sketches the origins and early development of the Democratic Peace Thesis and reveals that the so-called ivory tower is not—and never has been—isolated from real-world politics. He then focuses on the ways in which various Democratic Peace Theories were used by Bill Clinton and George W. Bush both to shape and to justify U.S. foreign policy, particularly the United States' stance on the Israeli-Palestinian situation and the war in Iraq. In the conclusion, Ish-Shalom boldly confronts the question of how much responsibility theoreticians must bear for the political uses—and misuses—of their ideas.

Piki Ish-Shalom is Associate Professor of International Relations at the Hebrew University of Jerusalem.

Democratic Peace
A POLITICAL BIOGRAPHY

Piki Ish-Shalom

University of Michigan Press
Ann Arbor

First paperback edition 2015
Copyright © by the University of Michigan 2013
All rights reserved

This book may not be reproduced, in whole or in part, including illustrations, in any form (beyond that copying permitted by Sections 107 and 108 of the U.S. Copyright Law and except by reviewers for the public press), without written permission from the publisher.

Published in the United States of America by the
University of Michigan Press
Manufactured in the United States of America
♾ Printed on acid-free paper

2018   2017   2016   2015   6   5   4   3

A CIP catalog record for this book is available from the British Library.

Library of Congress Cataloging-in-Publication Data

Ish-Shalom, Piki.
    Democratic peace : a political biography / Piki Ish-Shalom
      pages   cm
    Includes bibliographical references and index.
    ISBN 978-0-472-11876-2 (cloth : alk. paper) — ISBN 978-0-472-02915-0 (e-book)
    1. Democracy.   2. Peace.   I. Title.

JC423.I84   2013
303.6'6—dc23

                                                            2012047394

ISBN 978-0-472-03629-5 (pbk. : alk. paper)

This book is dedicated to my parents, Rina and Alex Ish-Shalom, who lovingly and caringly made my own biography possible.

CONTENTS

Acknowledgments — ix

A Note to the Reader — xiii

    Introduction — 1

1. Theory as a Hermeneutical Mechanism: A Theoretical Model — 14

2. Democratic Peace as Theoretical Constructions — 39

3. Democratic Peace as a Public Convention — 68

4. Word-Lords: The Israeli Right's Mobilization of the Rhetorical Capital of Democratic Peace — 85

5. The Civilization of Clashes: The Neoconservative Reading of Democratic Peace — 112

6. The Three Free World Theories — 142

7. Theorizing and Responsibility — 171

    Conclusions: Zooming In, Zooming Out — 204

Notes — 219

References — 231

Index — 259

ACKNOWLEDGMENTS

It has taken awhile. It has taken way longer than I planned or expected, and having taken such a while, the political biography of the democratic peace has become a key part of my own biography. And like any biography, it is interwoven with the biographies of so many others. Any piece of academic writing, including a single-authored one, is, in many ways, a collective endeavor, and this book is no different. Accordingly, I offer my gratitude to many people.

My first thanks go to those known by the professional title of "anonymous reviewers." And as such, they are "us" in the broadest sense; in the amorphous way that academia is a community. I often go through my incoming emails with a certain amount of trepidation, first because I'm anxiously awaiting a reply from a journal, fearing that all-too-common rejection, and second because I'm dreading seeing another invitation in my inbox asking me to review a manuscript. And those invitations keep on coming, piling up alongside so many other assignments which we academics have: teaching, writing, administration (in this or that order). And when an invitation does come, for a moment I mentally scramble for an excuse to send the managing editor. But then I (usually) remember that I too await reviews (quick, reasoned, and helpful) of my own work, and so I accept the invitation and review the manuscript. Probably we are all in this situation, and most of us occasionally don the reviewer's mask of anonymity, and do so with all our intellectual capabilities, and hopefully with some compassion too. My gratitude, then, is to all of us, but especially to those many anonymous reviewers who met this project in its article and book forms, reviewed it, commented on it, and pushed me to improve my arguments and make the book what it is (though of course all the mistakes still in it are my own personal intellectual property).

But there are also those whom I know by name—the members of my more tangible academic community, who in various ways have helped me in writing this book. First, then, I offer my thanks to Noa Levanon, who very skillfully assisted me with the research. Other students also helped me in less structured ways, by discussing democratic peace ideas in my classes at the Hebrew University of Jerusalem from 2006–2009. They include Viki Auslender, Shaiel Ben-Ephraim, Michal Gershon, Daniela Huber, Or Israeli, Lior Lehrs, Adi Livni, Mor Mitrani, Yaron Schneider, Anna Skorik, and Elad Strohmayer.

And then there are my colleagues—some of whom read parts of the manuscript, many of whom interacted with me in different ways, to help me become the academic I am. I am indebted to Asma Abbas, Emanuel Adler, Shlomo Avineri, Dan Avnon, Dorit Barak, Oren Barak, Uri Bialer, Nick Biziouras, Lothar Brock, Christian Büger, Rachela Caspy, Avner de-Shalit, Tali Dingott Alkopher, Dalia Gavriely-Nuri, Anna Geis, Jeff Goldfarb, Stefano Guzzini, Chris Hobson, Arie Kacowicz, Markus Kornprobst, Anna Leander, Nava Löwenheim, Oded Löwenheim, Elzbieta Matynia, Omar McDoom, Steve Miller, Dan Miodownik, Assaf Moghadam, Harald Müller, Lien-Hang Nguyen, Ido Oren, Rodger Payne, Martín Plot, David Plotke, Galia Press-BarNatan, Thomas Risse, Steve Rosen, Dani Schwartz, Avi Segal, Shlomi Segall, Avraham Sela, Mark Sheetz, Shaul Shenhav, Sasson Sofer, Raanan Sulitzeanu-Kenan, Tony Smith, Steve Walt, and Jonas Wolff.

Parts of the book have been published as articles in various journals: "Theory as a Hermeneutical Mechanism: The Democratic Peace and the Politics of Democratization," *European Journal of International Relations* 12, no. 4 (December 2006): 565–98; "The Rhetorical Capital of Theories: The Democratic Peace and the Road to the Roadmap," *International Political Science Review* 29, 3 (June 2008): 281–301; "The Civilization of Clashes: Misapplying the Democratic Peace in the Middle East," *Political Science Quarterly* 12, no. 4 (Winter 2007–2008): 533–54, (Reprinted in Robert Jervis and Loren Kando, eds., *The Future of U.S. Foreign Policy*, New York: The Academy of Political Science, 2008); "Theorizing Politics, Politicizing Theory, and the Responsibility that Runs Between," *Perspectives on Politics* 7, no. 2 (June 2009): 303–16; and "Theorization, Harm, and the Democratic Imperative: Lessons from the Politicization of the Democratic-Peace Thesis," *International Studies Review* 10, no. 4 (December 2008): 680–92. I am indebted to all the publishing houses and journals for letting me use material originally published in their pages.

The research for this book was supported by grants from the Davis

Institute for International Relations, the Hebrew University of Jerusalem (2003–2004), the Belfer Center for Science and International Affairs, Harvard University (2004–2005), the John M. Olin Institute for Strategic Studies, Harvard University (2005–2006), the Israel Foundations Trustees (2008–2010), the Faculty of Social Sciences at the Hebrew University of Jerusalem (2007–2008), and the Peace Research Institute Frankfurt (2012). I am thankful for their generous support, which allowed me the necessary time and financial resources to complete this book.

I am also grateful to Ruth Freedman who during the last couple of years painstakingly, professionally, and caringly edited my texts, improving and refining each and every word in them (including these very ones), and rescuing English from me. I am thankful also to Melody Herr from the University of Michigan Press who found merit in the manuscript and expertly and empathetically helped me make a book out of it. I wish all editors were like her.

Happily, my biography is not just academic, and is a life enriched by my family—by my parents Rina and Alex, who made my own biography possible; by my sister, Neta, and my brother, Yoni; by my in-laws, Heny and Marcus Vainroj, who are responsible for the next name on the list—my wife, Katty, to whom my love and life belong, and by our three marvelously rewarding kids who were born into this project: Noga, Shahaf, and little Inbar, and because of whom writing this book has gained a meaning beyond text.

And finally, my gratitude to the birds who kept me company while I worked, for letting me watch them, and for keeping me sane throughout this long project.

A NOTE TO THE READER

The book discusses a variety of subjects which are usually studied separately and by different communities of scholars. Though the chapters all reinforce each other and cohere into a single set of arguments, some readers may like to focus on specific subjects that they find interesting. To them, I'd like to suggest the following road map:

Readers interested in theoretical arguments should seek them in chapter 1: "Theory as a Hermeneutical Mechanism: A Theoretical Model." Critical theoreticians may wish to focus on chapter 2, "Democratic Peace as Theoretical Constructions," a conceptual chapter which uses a hermeneutical and critical interpretation to analyze and interpret democratic peace theories and discuss their normative foundations. Readers interested in the story of the democratic peace thesis in general should skip the first two chapters and focus on chapters 3 to 6: "Democratic Peace as a Public Convention," "Word-Lords: The Israeli Right's Mobilization of the Rhetorical Capital of Democratic Peace," "The Civilization of Clashes: The Neoconservative Reading of Democratic Peace," and "The Three Free World Theories." These four chapters present the case studies and examine the actual political effects of the democratic peace thesis (and other theoretical constructions). And for those interested in normative theory, I would suggest chapter 7, "Theorizing and Responsibility," and the concluding chapter, "Conclusions: Zooming In, Zooming Out," which takes my normative analysis and proposal a step further.

INTRODUCTION

Childless though he was, Immanuel Kant is the towering (or assumed) father of many offspring, one of which is the subject of this book: the theories of democratic peace; those theories that try to explain the absence (or near absence) of war between consolidated democracies. And just as Kant's hometown of Königsberg changed hands and names throughout its history, so the theories of democratic peace have gone through transformations, assuming different incarnations, or different sorts of idea structures. This book is about the political biography of those theories, and it will analyze the complex sociopolitical process by which they migrated outside academia and had various affects on the political realities of the day. These affects are clearly shown with respect to presidents Bill Clinton and George W. Bush, who were different in many ways yet converged on a peculiar, sometimes alarming, adherence to the democratic peace theories. Both used them in shaping, executing, and also legitimating their policies. The same can be said of leading Israeli politicians such as Benjamin Netanyahu and Natan Sharansky, and also of American pundits—especially those in the neoconservative camp. The theories, so it seems, appear to have influenced decision makers, or at least their rhetoric—which contravenes the common understanding of academe as an ivory tower.[1]

But this alleged influence is unsettling in one sense at least; namely, that it is not in line with what the democratic peace theoreticians had in mind when conceiving their theories. In some crucial cases, it even runs counter to what the theoreticians had in mind. Suffice it to read the title of Dean Babst's 1964 preliminary article on democratic peace: "Elective Government—A Force for Peace" in order to understand that, although a criminologist by training, for Babst the phenomenon and theory of democratic peace could well have been the Rosetta Stone of international relations studies—namely, the final and ultimate antidote to war. This same hopeful disposition guides much of the democratic peace literature, usually implicitly and in the background, yet often bursting explicitly into the open in the articles' last paragraph.[2] However, the real-world ramifications of the theories were quite inverse, serving the rationalization and legitimation of the Iraq War, and putting obstacles in the way of the tortured peace process between Israelis and Palestinians. Karl Marx's insight may be useful here, when he wrote in a different context and on other matters, "Men make their own history, but they do not make it just as they please; they do not make it under circumstances chosen by themselves (1969:15)." The theories similarly made history, but not under circumstances chosen by their theoreticians, and consequently, not as intended by them. So, although the political biography of democratic peace indeed contravenes the common and positivist understanding of academe as an ivory tower, it does not necessarily confirm the naivety of many critical theoreticians regarding the political powerfulness of academe.[3]

This book confronts this startling phenomenon of the discrepancy between hopes, expectations, and intentions, on the one hand, and actual real-world ramifications on the other hand. It deals with it theoretically, offering a model of theory as a hermeneutical mechanism; theory that migrates outside academia with the help of interested political agents, making its way to the public and political worlds, evermore politicized in the process. As is explained and demonstrated, it is there in the public and political arenas, that the theory's political metamorphosis is completed, where it is stripped of its academic robe and translated into public and political representations and misrepresentations that only slightly resemble its academic origin, yet carry grave real-world ramifications.

No less important, this book confronts the phenomenon ethically. It concludes by raising the issue of the responsibilities of theoreticians for those real-world ramifications, political harms, and moral wrongs that theories cause; ramifications, political harms, and moral wrongs that more often than not are not controlled by the theoreticians. The study indicates how politically influential theories can be, and yet how politically insignificant theoreticians at times are. Absurd as this assertion seems to be, it is painfully true. Politics play an important role in the migration of theories, and no less than truth speaks to power—it is power that shapes truth. To be true to themselves, theoreticians should be aware of this political entanglement.

Writing the political biography of theories in general and those of democratic peace theories in particular, I ask how the theories were conceived in the serene halls of academia, and how they gained a life—a political life—independent from their academic authors. I further ask how theoreticians ought to address the political entanglement of theory and the real world, what are the moral implications of this political entanglement, and additionally, how can theoreticians assume some control of the their theories' political fortunes.

Methodology and Rationale

My aim in this book is not to offer a process tracing of the transformation of ideas into policies. Rather, I offer what can be termed discourse tracing—analyzing the process whereby one kind of discourse was transformed into another, and how the academic and theoretic discourse of democratic peace became a public and political discourse that shaped the understanding of world politics and framed the selection of acceptable policies. As such, this book fits in well within the extensive theoretical International Relations (IR) literature that studies the role of ideas, concepts, norms, and meanings in bringing change, and particularly with the constructivist literature and constructivist assertion that knowledge is a foundation of the social construction of reality.[4]

However, the interest and aims of this book are broader than the existing literature, at least in one sense. This book does not limit itself to studying the influence of ideas and theories on reality, but also explores the impact reality has on ideas and theories. It takes very seriously both mundane factors such as power and political considerations, and ideal factors such as ideology. All these factors interact with theories, with their public acceptance, and with their ability to affect reality. As argued earlier, theories do not affect reality on their own terms, by their original formulations, or even according to their theoreticians' intentions. The process of affecting reality is much more complex and involves tainting theories with power, politics, and ideology. Theories as well as reality change in their mutual encounter.

My methodology reflects the aim of discourse tracing by critically interpreting several kinds of texts: the academic and theoretic literature of democratic peace, and the writings and speeches of the relevant political entrepreneurs. This methodology enables tracking of the discursive changes in theoretical assertions en route to becoming political assertions of the type that can motivate political action. By studying several categories of material—academic theoretical literature, publicist writings, political addresses and declarations, and policy papers—it is possible to trace how a theory becomes altered and, at times, perverted, becoming both the frame of a political mindset and a useful political and rhetorical tool of manipulation.

Accordingly, the sources encompass the conventional theoretical academic literature, semi-academic journals the likes of *Commentary* and the *National Interest*, partisan publications such as the *Weekly Standard*, publicist writings and op-eds in major newspapers, presidential addresses, and policy papers. This book's treatment of these texts eludes the traditional categories of primary versus secondary sources as most are Janus-like and can be presented as both. They are secondary in that they offer interpretations of other texts but they are also primary since this study analyzes and interprets them as politically and normatively informed writings that affect reality and require additional critical interpretation.

Book Structure

This book has four dimensions. The first is theoretical, developing the theoretical model of theory as a hermeneutical mechanism. The second dimension is conceptual, and employing hermeneutical and critical interpretation it analyzes and interprets various theories of democratic peace, disclosing their normative foundation. The third dimension is historical and empirical, describing both the process of the theories' migration, and the actual affects they had on the world outside academia. The fourth dimension is normative, addressing the issue of theoreticians' responsibility for the real-world ramifications of their theories. The dimensions are arranged in seven different chapters, plus an additional chapter of conclusions.

Chapter 1, "Theory as a Hermeneutical Mechanism: A Theoretical Model," develops the theoretical framework with which I analyze the political biography of theories, and their migration outside academia. This migration is theoretically conceptualized as a hermeneutical mechanism. It is a three-stage model depicting the transformation theory undergoes while migrating. The theoretical model is inspired by Michael Freeden and Antonio Gramsci. Freeden provides the theoretical incentive to focus on the internal structure of theory. I understand theory to be a political thought, similar to the way Freeden understands ideology (1996). Thus, theory is conceptualized as an idea entity, and moreover as a political thought: a configuration of decontested political concepts that are arranged together, each conferring meaning on the others and being lent meaning by them. Accordingly, theory is termed theoretical construction, emphasizing the aforementioned internal structure of decontested concepts. Being a sort of political thought (though not an ideology), theory presents us with meaningful political concepts, and its function—explicitly or implicitly, predominantly or partially—is to motivate us to political action. This accounts for the political potentiality of theories—a political potentiality whose actualization is told, using case study illustrations, in the political biography.

For this potentiality to be actualized, the theoretical construction has to migrate outside academia and in the process undergo metamorphosis into public convention and political conviction. Public convention is where Gramsci's theory of hegemony comes to the fore (Gramsci 1957, 1971, 1992, 1996, 2007), informing my theoretical framework and infusing it with the political dimension so crucial in the hermeneutical mechanism. Public convention is defined as general background knowledge about the world that is taken for granted and shapes the commonsensical codes of thinking and behavior. Whereas the theoretical construction of democratic peace seeks methodologically to verify and explain the relation between democracy and peace, the public convention of democratic peace takes for granted the (theoretically contested) assertion that democracies are peaceful polities. Political conviction is defined as specific knowledge engendering a strong, opinionated view that necessitates political action. The political conviction arising from the theoretical construction of democratic peace is that, because democracies bring stability and peace, promoting democracy is a vital interest, and democratization a matter of national security. The idea entities of public conventions and political convictions are respectively the second and third stages in the hermeneutical mechanism, and they are in essence the public and political representations (and misrepresentations) of the theoretical construction. As such they are simplified versions of the theory, and in the third stage, that of political conviction, they are also a politicized and dogmatized version that speaks in absolute terms of yes and no.

Furthermore, politicization and dogmatization also carry certain discursive changes in the genres via which the three different idea entities are conveyed. Theoretical constructions are conveyed by theoretical explanatory vernacular; that is, meticulous claims of the relations between different phenomena, articulated to deliver the subtlest minutia of a theory's contentions as established through strict and careful theorization. It functions to convey theoretical discoveries and the logic of explanation and verification. Public conventions are circulated via the discursive genre of commonsensical descriptive vernacular; that is, the loose expression of unreflective accounts that unfold the narratives in which the world is captured and figured out by the public common sense. It functions so as to affirm and reaffirm the commonsensical depiction of reality. Political convictions are conveyed through the discursive genre of political avowal vernacular; that is, forceful declarations rhetorically uttered in slogan-like fashion to confirm and convey political stands. This discursive genre functions to justify and legitimize ideological beliefs and political actions. Evident in the discursive changes is again the politicization and dogmatization that theories undergo in the process of the hermeneutical mechanism, and hence the argument made earlier and substantiated in this book, that in as much as theory changes reality, reality also changes theory throughout the process. The affects, that is, are mutual.

Lastly, the theoretical chapter introduces the concept of rhetorical capital, defined as the aggregate persuasive resources inherent in entities, including theories. The rhetorical capital of theories is what attracts politicians to use, misuse, and abuse them to advance ideological sectarian agendas. In the theoretical chapter, I examine the different persuasive resources. Suffice it here to say that there are several specific resources in each theory although there is also a general resource shared by most theories. The general resource is the structural duality of accessibility and incomprehensibility overlaid with the prestige of objectivity. The disparity between the relative accessibility of theories to the public at large and the incomprehensibility of the technicalities of theorization facilitates the politicization of theory. It buttresses the entrance of politicians and ideologues into the gap between accessibility and incomprehensibility and they work to simplify and politicize the theories, making them more amendable to public consumption and more vulnerable to political misuse and abuse. This is especially the case as theoreticians themselves are allegedly shielded from the obligation to bring their theories to the public by the ethos and prestige of objectivity and by the belief in the separation of fact and value, researcher and researched. The assumed objectivity of theoreticians leads them to abandon their theories to their political fate while politicians use this relative disregard to harness the theories to their political and ideological interests, using the rhetorical capital of theories. We return to these themes repeatedly throughout the book.

We find this in chapter 2, "Democratic Peace as Theoretical Constructions," which questions the assumed separation of fact and value. It is a conceptual chapter in that it analyzes hermeneutically and critically the concepts used in the different theories of democratic peace. Chapter 2 examines in this manner the preliminary 1964 article by Dean Babst, and then proceeds to other seminal articles from the 1980s onward. By employing hermeneutics and critical interpretation, it is possible to explore in depth the democratic peace theories as theoretical constructions: configurations of decontested political concepts. Accordingly, it will be possible to identify the difference in normative groundwork that provides the real, yet implicit, driving force for the separation of the democratic peace into two families or paradigms—one cultural-normative, and the other structural. The former is more liberal and founded on conceptualizing democracy as a participatory and deliberative sociopolitical project; the latter is more conservative and founded on a structural understanding of democracy as a regime founded on contest between political elites overruling the polity. It is this fundamental normative difference, rather than mere differences in the explanatory mechanism, that divides the different theories. The analysis also demonstrates theories as political thoughts: inclusive understandings of the phenomena they seek to explain. Thus they can equip us with political road maps to navigate the world.

Yet, in order for a theoretical construction to actualize this political potentiality and act as forceful road map in the real world, it must first migrate outside academia and transform into its public and political representations; that is, into public conventions and political convictions. The focus of chapter 3, "Democratic Peace as a Public Convention," is tracing the first phase of migration and analyzing the process by which theoretical constructions overtook the common sense, and gained the status of public conventions; namely, a partial and transitory framing of the common sense à la Gramsci. This analysis focuses on the political context facilitating the migration; that is, the end of the Cold War, and even more so Clinton's 1992 presidential campaign, in which he embraced the dictates of the democratic peace theories, politically enrapturing the neoconservatives, and successfully building a political power base. It was this moment that marked the first milestone in the transformation of democratic peace as a theoretical construction into public convention. Chapter 3 analyzes the commonalities of Clinton and the neoconservatives that drove them together, as well as the differences that shortly thereafter drove them apart. Those differences will help us also to understand the variances between the Clinton and George W. Bush administrations. The early 1990s saw similar processes in the transatlantic liberal milieu of Clinton, and the chapter explores this with particular reference to Tony Blair.[5]

Following the Clinton presidency, the ground was fertile for the third stage of the hermeneutical mechanism: the transformation of public conventions into political convictions—a transformation that was carried through by political entrepreneurs and ideological agents. Two chapters are devoted to this transformation, each focusing on another group of political entrepreneurs. The first group is the Israeli right, and the second the American neoconservatives. The case of the Israeli right will be examined in chapter 4, "Word-Lords: The Israeli Right's Mobilization of the Rhetorical Capital of Democratic Peace." It mainly focuses on Benjamin Netanyahu and Natan Sharansky, and how they politically employed the rhetorical capital of the democratic peace theories to secure their political agendas. Both were united by their struggle against the Oslo accords of the 1990s, yet they diverged on their aim and tactic. Netanyahu conducted politics of postponement, hoping to postpone the negotiations so the Israeli terms of negotiations would improve, and the size of territorial concessions to the Palestinians would be reduced. Sharansky conducted politics of avoidance, hoping to steer clear of any true negotiations that may lead to territorial concessions. Sharansky, that is, was whole heartedly committed to the idea of Greater Israel. Both politicians made a shrewd and successful rhetorical mobilization of the theories, relying on the status of the theories as public conventions in American policy elites. This chapter shows that their success in mobilizing the rhetorical capital of the theories resulted in Bush's road map of June 24, 2002. In the road map, Bush both committed the United States to a Palestinian sovereignty and conditioned the peace process on Palestinian democratization. The result was a sort of a vicious circle that put a halt to the peace process (tortured as it was before),[6] enabling the Israelis to strengthen their grip on the occupied territories. This was a paradigmatic case of a successful misuse and abuse of the rhetorical capital embedded in the theories of democratic peace.

Chapter 5, "The Civilization of Clashes: The Neoconservative Reading of Democratic Peace," studies the involvement of the American neoconservatives with the democratic peace theories. This case is not simply one of rhetorical abuse of the theories. The interaction between the neoconservative creed and the theoretical constructions had several manifestations, and the theoretical constructions played several political roles. First, various prominent neoconservatives—foremost among them, Joshua Muravchik—were the leading political entrepreneurs involved in initiating the hermeneutical mechanism and bringing the thesis into the public realm during the early 1990s. This aspect of the involvement is covered mainly in chapter 3. Nonetheless, the same public conventions of the democratic peace the neoconservatives were so instrumental in creating gradually came to frame their own thinking on world politics, up to the point where relatively weak public conventions were transformed into forceful political convictions. In this capacity, political convictions were a dominant factor in shaping the neoconservative grand strategy of promoting democracy at gunpoint. This strategy was most evident in the Bush Doctrine, with its emphasis on democracy and freedom promotion, unilateralism and preemption (implemented, however, as prevention), which served as the basis for the Iraq War. Additionally, the rhetorical capital of the democratic peace was used to rationalize and legitimize the war to the American public, especially once the American armed forces failed to find weapons of mass destruction. Hence, we can see that the democratic peace theories, and they were mostly the structural theories, played multifunctional roles in the neoconservative creed and had various kinds of interactions with the neoconservative political worldview and grand strategy. This chapter analyzes all those roles and interactions, establishing the political salience and prominence of political convictions originating in the theoretical world.

Chapter 5 pursues two further tasks. The first is to offer an analysis of efforts by the realist theoreticians Stephen Walt and John Mearsheimer to rehabilitate realism as public convention and political conviction (a status it had during the Cold War). In their battle against the impending Iraq War, Walt and Mearsheimer sought to present the American public with a theory-grounded alternative grand strategy to that of Bush and the neoconservatives. This chapter presents and analyzes their efforts. I end the chapter by offering an internal critique of the Bush Doctrine and the neoconservative grand strategy, based on the conceptual analysis offered throughout the chapter.

By the end of chapter 5, we are ready to embark on a normative discussion about the responsibilities of theoreticians and how they should be discharged. However, before undertaking this discussion, chapter 6, "The Three Free World Theories," explores two other cases of theories going through hermeneutical process: soft power and the capitalist peace theory. Those two additional cases will help me by fulfilling two tasks. The first is to demonstrate that the hermeneutical mechanism model not only applies to democratic peace theories, but is generalizable and applicable to other cases. The second task is to explore variances in implementation and realization of the hermeneutical mechanism model. As is the case with political biographies of persons, so is the case with political biographies of theories: the life stories are never identical, and they are cut differently depending on the circumstances and contingencies involved. A book that offers not only the political biography of one theory, but also introduces a novel theoretical framework on the migration of theories in general, should examine possible differences in the realization of the model, and this is the second task of the chapter. However, to retain coherence of structure and theme I have chosen not to stray far from the democratic peace theories—hence the focus on analyzing two additional free world theories—namely, soft power and capitalist peace theory. Both of these theories (or conceptual frameworks), along with the democratic peace theories, make up the family of contemporary liberal theories of international relations. Examining the actual migration of these theories gives us a better understanding of the relations between democracy and academia. However, there is one fundamental difference between soft power and capitalist peace theory and the democratic peace theories, and that is the active role their theoreticians took in initiating the process of migration and translating the theoretical constructions into public conventions and political convictions: Joseph Nye Jr. in the case of soft power, and Erik Gartzke in the case of the capitalist peace theory. This is a crucial and fundamental theoretical difference, which, in addition, carries with it also certain normative implications that we will explore later. Yet, notwithstanding the differences, a simple fact still remains: both soft power and capitalist peace theory migrated to the political world and have several real-world ramifications. Soft (and smart) power came to dominate the discourse of Barack Obama's administration on strategic matters, while capitalist peace theory was mobilized rhetorically by Netanyahu, and replaced democratic peace in his politics of postponement. These real-world ramifications make it important to discuss the normative issue of the theoretician's responsibility, which are discussed in the final chapter.

Chapter 7, "Theorizing and Responsibility," tackles head-on the problematic issue of the theoreticians' responsibilities for the real-world ramifications of their theories—real-world ramifications that engender political harms and moral wrongs, both by stifling democratic deliberation, and helping to actualize and legitimize large-scale violence. The normative discussion is problematic for two reasons. The first is the highly controversial conclusions that will be inferred from it. The second reason is the meandering sociopolitical process in the migration of theories and the metamorphosis they undergo, both of which are usually quite independent of their originators—the theoreticians. It is almost as if the theories are sometimes hijacked from their original creators. The result is real-world ramifications that are not necessarily in-line with the normative and political intensions of the theoreticians, and at times are even their opposite. Since theoreticians have neither intentionality nor effective agency, it is wrong to ascribe moral blame responsibility to them, as we sometimes find. However, as intelligent and original authors of theories, it is also wrong to acquit theoreticians of all responsibility. Accordingly, I will steer a midcourse between blame and acquittal, and ascribe theoreticians with collective scholarly, political, and social task responsibilities for the real-world ramifications, political harms, and moral wrongs of their theories. Social task responsibility burdens theoreticians with searching for the root cause of the recurring pattern of politicization that theories undergo, which results, as it does, in the moral harms previously mentioned.

As becomes clear in the chapter, the root cause is the structural duality that endows theories with rhetorical capital: the structural duality of accessibility and incomprehensibility, overlaid with the prestige of objectivity. This structural duality generates the rhetorical capital of theories that is useful as a resource to be mobilized by politicians and ideologues, trying to advance their political and ideological agenda. To discharge their social task responsibility and counteract the theories' vulnerability to political misuse and abuse, theoreticians need to renounce the principle of objectivity, adopt instead a normative ethics of the social sciences, and be explicit about the normative groundwork that informs and constitutes their theories. Discharging the other two types of responsibility—the scholarly and the political—theoreticians should take an active stance in democratic deliberations. They ought to take upon themselves the role of theoretician-citizens, and be active in the public sphere and through civil society. In this manner they can bring their theoretical insights to the public sphere, and improve policies, but more importantly, also improve the policy-making process by invigorating the political faculties of citizens and public deliberations. Thus, they can help to realize the democratic ideal of deliberation and participation.

This being argued, this book reaches its concluding chapter, "Conclusions: Zooming In, Zooming Out." Here, I take the normative conclusions a step further and suggest how normative ethics can be operationalized individually in theory making. The way to operationalize normative ethics is by a strategy I call *Zooming in, Zooming out*. This strategy binds together three principal themes of the book: the centrality of political concepts in the internal structure of theory (or theoretical constructions), the essential contestedness of political concepts, and the normative underscoring of the theoreticians' responsibilities. Zooming in, Zooming out is a dual movement where we at once zoom into the internal components of theoretical constructions; that is, political concepts, and seek to define them normatively by applying moral sensitivity and an eye to their real-world ramifications: to their effects on the society outside academia (zoom out).

The Zooming in, Zooming out strategy requires a willingness and ability to morally justify the definitions with which we delineate the political concepts we employ in our theories. As I explain in this book's conclusion, the act of defining is an act of social construction of social categories, and as such it is infused with moral and political substances and implications. Zooming in, Zooming out means to set free the theoreticians' moral commitments and political convictions from the clutch of the conventional definitional criteria of exhaustiveness, exclusiveness, and operationalization; moral commitments and political convictions that covertly rule the act of defining and render the political concepts' essential contestedness. These moral commitments and political convictions must be set free and given a dominant and explicit role in the act of defining. This way, the moral commitments and political convictions of theoreticians, which are usually left hidden and unacknowledged, would rise to the fore and become explicit to the theoreticians themselves, to the scholarly community as a whole, and to the public at large outside the world of academia. Subsequently, theoreticians would be able to engage critically and reflexively with the workings of their moral commitments and political convictions in shaping their theory making. Then, and only then, can we move ahead with the theoretical task of seeking explanatory mechanisms constructed on the shoulders of the political concepts. And since the explanatory mechanisms would be explicitly founded and grounded on morally-defined political concepts, the resulting theories would also be justifiable morally.

In terms of the democratic peace, I propose an explanatory theory centering on the political concepts of deliberation and participations. I argue that these two political concepts should act as both an explanatory and normative core of the proposed democratic peace theory. Combing a moralized theory and an active stance as theoretician-citizens in the public sphere and civil society would be a substantial step forward in discharging the obligations arising from the normative ethics of the social sciences.

Admittedly, there is an inbuilt tension in this book—a tension that is an offshoot of the epistemological middle ground with which I approach the political biography of theory and which also informs my conclusions.[7] On the one hand, I argue against a presumption of objectivity in the social sciences, but on the other, I criticize relativism. Likewise, I challenge both the naive positivist belief in foundationalism, and also the poststructuralist radical call for anti-foundationalism. And to top it all, while exposing the ubiquitousness of power politics, I express trust in the emancipatory promises of ethics. Throughout this book, I aim to defend the epistemological middle ground and infer ethical propositions in which morality takes center stage, normative ethics replaces the conventional ethics of objectivity, and morality is the appropriate foundation for social sciences. Often, it can be more agreeable to follow a tension-free road; it is more comfortable to take the path well-trodden. However, in this case, it is both more justified and more rewarding to take the less-traveled road, along with its accompanying tension. I hope to convince those readers who follow me down the length of the road that, though it is indeed less traveled, it is nevertheless sound and well founded.

I

THEORY AS A HERMENEUTICAL MECHANISM
A Theoretical Model

This chapter sets out the theoretical model for the book: a model explaining the conditioned power of theories. In order to establish my theory, I aim to use hermeneutics—though with a slight twist. Hermeneutics is usually understood as the art of reading and interpreting texts. I want to stress, however, the dual nature of hermeneutics. Although hermeneutics indeed interprets texts, it is also a more active intellectual endeavor of interpreting reality once reality is conceived as an unwritten text. That is not to say that reality is nothing but a text or even to claim it is a text at all. Rather, I wish to make the more modest assertion that the social and political reality studied by theoreticians encompasses narratives, practices, habits, rules of conduct, modes of behavior, norms, ideas, ideals, and so on. It is these social entities that can be envisaged as an unwritten text. Interpreting reality as an unwritten text involves attaching meaning to reality, which is effected through the use of concepts. In the realms of politics and international politics, it is political concepts that serve as the vehicle for attaching meaning.

To explain the power of theories, I will present a three-stage model in which theoretical constructions transform into public conventions and then into political convictions. Once we understand theory as the first stage of a three-stage hermeneutical mechanism, it becomes clear how the theories of democratic peace can influence decision makers, or at least their rhetoric. Moreover, it also becomes clear that it is not the academic theories per se that affect the shaping of the political agenda and its implementation. What affects the political agenda and its implementation are configured theories, and sometimes distorted configurations of theories: theories as the public conceives them—in other words, the public and political representations of these theories. An additional element of this process concerns interested political entrepreneurs who introduce theories to the public by trivializing and sometimes distorting them instrumentally.

Accepting the three-stage model may appear to undermine the force of theory, as it is neither theory nor theoreticians that affect politics. One ought to remember, however, that theories as theoretical constructions are the origins of the politically configured and reconfigured influential public conventions and political convictions, and as such play an important role in political campaigning when ideas are debated and communicated, and receive legitimation. Furthermore, the way politicians use academic theories is an indication of the theories' political capital, and no less important, it also shows the rhetorical capital of the theories.

There are two important reasons why politicians might use theories. The first is that theories persuade politicians so that their strategic thinking becomes framed by them—or more precisely, by the theories' political representation. As this book maintains, this is what happened in the case of the neoconservatives and their advocacy of grand strategies of forced democratization for the Middle East. In the neoconservatives' case, the theories were powerful drivers of the politicization process that the theories themselves underwent later, resulting in political convictions which were the framers of strategic thinking.

The second reason politicians might turn to theories is that they believe theories carry rhetorical capital and are powerful mechanisms for political persuasion. So, the politicians' reasoning continues, it is politically expedient to utilize theories to legitimize what they perceive ideologically as warranted policies. As I argue later, this was the case with prominent Israeli right-wing politicians like Benjamin Netanyahu and Natan Sharansky, who, from the mid-1990s, used the democratic peace thesis' rhetorical capital to convey their ideological objectives of safeguarding Israel against territorial concessions to the Palestinians.

The theoretical framework offered here fits in well within the extensive theoretical International Relations (IR) literature that studies the role of ideas, concepts, norms, and meanings in effecting change, and mainly with the constructivist literature and constructivist assertion that knowledge is a foundation for the social construction of reality (see, e.g., Adler 1992; Adler and Haas 1992; Checkel 1997; Finnemore and Sikkink 1998; Guzzini 2000, 2001; Haas 1992; Keck and Sikkink 1998; Klotz 1995; Kratochwil 1989; Price 1995; Risse, Ropp, and Sikkink 1999).[1] However, this book's interest and aims are broader than the existing literature, at least in one sense—that I do not limit myself to exploring how ideas and theories influence reality—I also explore how reality impacts on ideas and theories.[2] I take both mundane factors such as power and political considerations and ideal factors such as ideology very seriously. All these factors interact with theories and their public acceptance and ability to affect reality. In other words, theories do not affect reality on their own terms, through their original formulations, or even according to their theoreticians' intentions. The process of affecting reality is much more complex and involves the theories being tainted by power, politics, and ideology. Or, stated differently, it is their socially and politically altered configurations, their representations (and misrepresentation) as public conventions and political convictions, which affect reality. Both theories and reality change on encounter. And it is that reciprocal change which warrants a political biography of theory and the study of the political life cycle of theory—in this case, a political biography of the democratic peace theories—the most salient IR theories of the post–Cold War era.

Theoretical Overview and Framework

The purpose of the theoretical chapter is to explore two theoretical approaches and use them to construct a single, coherent framework for understanding theory as a hermeneutical mechanism for attaching meaning to political concepts. The first approach is Michael Freeden's view of ideology as political thought (1996). This approach informs the first stage of the model—theoretical construction. The second approach involves a Gramscian-inspired modification of constructivism. This chapter discusses certain shortcomings of constructivism, focusing on constructivism's underestimation of the mechanisms of politics. It then reconstructs constructivism into a Gramscian-inspired sociopolitical theory, which supports this book's conceptualization of public conventions. This new approach to constructivism is helpful in depicting how public conventions are transformed into political convictions that subsequently drive political action.

Theory as Theoretical Constructions

Freeden, who draws on the literature of essentially contested concepts propounded in the 1950s by W. B. Gallie (1956), defines ideology as "configurations of *decontested* meanings of political concepts, when such meanings are ascribed by methods at least partly foreign to those employed in currently predominant approaches of scientists, philosophers, linguists, or political theorists" (1996:7). This definition encapsulates Freeden's discussion of the essence of ideology. For Freeden, ideology is one form of political thought, and political thoughts are the assembling together of political concepts; the latter being the basic building blocks of every mode of political thought, such as political philosophy, political theory, and ideology (1996:2).

The core of Freeden's analysis is functionality: what is the function of political thought, and how does political thought perform this function.[3] The implication is that the function of any political thought is to persuade people and motivate them to political action, by assigning meaning to political concepts. Political concepts are by their very nature contested; they embody manifold flexibility of meaning, which needs to undergo a process of interpretation (1996:4). For example, freedom can be conceived as freedom from compulsion, or, alternatively, freedom to aspire, act, and achieve. Likewise, equality can mean, for example, equality of outcomes or opportunities, political equalities, or economic equalities. Each of these meanings provides a different menu of political praxis. Hence, persuading people to accept one meaning rather than another leads them into one political practice rather than another. For example, if by equality we mean an economic egalitarianism based on equal results, we will strive politically for a somewhat socialist organization of society. Conversely, if by equality we mean political equality that ensures equal opportunity, we will strive for a somewhat liberal organization of the state.

As Freeden points out, there is yet another important issue to understand: no single political concept has a viable meaning in itself. It gains meaning, viability, and political significance only in the context of a complete configuration of political concepts (1996:75–91). That is precisely what political thought offer us: a configuration of decontested political concepts that are being arranged together so that each concept confers meaning on the others and receives meaning from them in return. Thus, political thought such as ideologies, political philosophy, and social science theories (the focus of this book), present us with meaningful political concepts whose function—explicitly or implicitly, originally or derivatively, primarily or secondary, predominantly or partially—is to motivate us to political action.

Following Freeden's discussion of ideologies, I suggest understanding theories in a much more holistic sense than usual. Theories as political thoughts offer much more than mere explanations: they offer comprehensive readings of the phenomena under investigation, an entire worldview of political phenomena. Like any other form of political thought, theories take the political concepts investigated and used in the process of theorization, and decontest and endow them with meanings. However, it should be stressed that even though theories are a kind of political thought, it does not make them ideologies. As political thought, theories and ideologies indeed share various features. However, they also diverge on certain critical points, making them two distinct idea entities. Both decontest concepts, though they do that differently—as I argue and demonstrate, both decontest concepts based among other things on normative groundwork. But, unlike ideologies, theories are constrained by methodological and epistemological rules (later described as the four requisites for sound theorizing), and it is those rules which differentiate theory from ideology.

Since theories are configurations of political concepts endowed with meanings, I identify and conceptualize them as theoretical constructions, which stresses their complex structure and intricate function. By presenting us with meaningful political concepts, theories act as the preliminary stage of the hermeneutical mechanism. But before the theoretical concepts can actually motivate political action and function effectively in the world of politics, they need to migrate outside academe and into the public sphere—in other words, they must be transformed into public conventions. This brings us to the second approach—the Gramscian-inspired modification of constructivism.

Theory as Public Conventions and Political Convictions

It is more than a decade since—with a touch of irony—Stefano Guzzini declared constructivism to be a success story and "the officially accredited contender to the established core of the discipline" (2000:147). Guzzini went on to describe a situation whereby "'The social construction of . . .' is littering the title pages of our books, articles, and student assignments" (2000:147). Yet, after all these years and many more contributions to the constructivist literature, it seems that, as a whole, constructivism cannot free itself from the accusation that by focusing on the social construction of reality (or the construction of social reality), it ignores the harsh facts of political reality, and is therefore idealist, utopist, or simply too "soft." Indeed, by concentrating on the deep causes of social processes and by claiming to be a theory of the *"constructing of social reality"* (2000:149), constructivism exposes itself to these charges by undervaluing the shorter-term processes in which mundane politics; that is, politics with its own sets of reasons, interests, and maneuvers, play a major role.

Related to this problem are other shortcomings of the constructivist school. First is the inadequate analysis of the agent and, in the case of the political world, the political entrepreneur. Second, there is an inbuilt weakness in studying plural societies, which, for example, modern democratic societies are. In such societies it is difficult to identify a common meaning that can provide a foundation for constructing a social reality. I try to address these shortcomings by introducing the political dimension into constructivism, and thus converting it from being simply a social theory of the constructing of social reality to being a political theory of the constructing of sociopolitical reality as well.

The departure point is the same as for constructivism: it is the dual interest in the *"social construction of meaning (including knowledge), and of the construction of social reality"* (2000:149).[4] It is a view of the social as being governed by meaningful action constituted by the shared and intersubjective knowledge of reality. It is the claim that material factors also play a fundamental part in constructing sociopolitical reality as they both constrain and enable the production of knowledge that in turn endows the material world with the meaning on which actions are based. From this is derived the constructivist contention of the constitutional nexus between ideal and material factors, and the role this nexus plays in constructing social reality. Positioning themselves between positivists and postmodernists, the constructivist "middle ground" (Adler 1997) maintains that our knowledge is about something that is real, yet requires our interpretation of it to really matter.

What is important to explicate, and mostly is unappreciated, is that this intersubjective knowledge is mostly unreflective and unaware of itself. Consequently, those who know (and the Greek term *doxa* may be more appropriate here) barely engage in evaluating and criticizing the validity and sources of their knowledge. By stressing the unreflective nature of shared knowledge (i.e., the constitutive foundation of the sociopolitical world), I introduce the Gramscian notion of hegemony into constructivism, albeit in a very cautious manner (See also Weldes 1996). Bringing Gramsci into constructivism will also help me introduce politics into it, as the Gramscian program, which is ideological, is also—more importantly for present purposes—political in essence (Gramsci 1957, 1971, 1992, 1996, 2007; for secondary sources, see Adamson 1980; Bates 1975; Boggs 1976; Cammett 1967; Davidson 1977; Femia 1981; Ghosh 2001; Ives 2006; Nemeth 1980).

Antonio Gramsci (1891–1937) was one of the leading Marxist thinkers of the interwar years. Orthodox Marxism of the period offered a deterministic and somewhat vulgar interpretation of Marx, stressing the materialistic aspects of his thought and highlighting the brutal mechanisms by which capitalism protected its financial interests. According to this orthodox Marxism, the capitalist bourgeoisie use political society—the state's institutions—and its monopoly on coercion to forcefully subdue the proletariat and safeguard its own sectarian interests. Gramsci took a different course, stressing the less material aspects of Marxism. At the center of political and social inquiry, he placed what might today be termed "soft power."[5] While not ignoring the use of force in society, Gramsci claimed that the key to protecting the capitalist economy and bourgeois society from collapse lies elsewhere—in the domain of civil, rather than political society. In other words, brute force is not what maintains the social order, but rather sophisticated control over the proletariat's thinking, by using the uncritical common sense with which the proletarians think about their world. The social institutions of civil society—such as schools, churches, cultural establishments, and other modes of socialization—easily construct the proletariat's uncritical and unreflective thought. In this process, common sense is manipulated into accepting the social order as given, as a natural law, and as safeguarding the common interest. This mechanism is called hegemony; that is, soft power over the common people's way of thinking, and thence their behavior—it "stupidifies" them into a horde that does not question the capitalist economy and bourgeoisie order. This is the perfect mechanism by which social stability is almost effortlessly maintained.

Thomas Bates defines Gramsci's hegemony as "political leadership based on the consent of the led, a consent which is secured by the diffusion and popularization of the world view of the ruling class" (1975:352). Highlighted here is Gramsci's Marxism, which led to a view of society as divided along class lines and to assess the state's socialization mechanisms as bourgeoisie controlled and extremely powerful. Consequently he understood hegemony in totalistic terms, as an appropriation of the common sense of an entire public, including the proletariat. Gramsci also understands hegemony as a "stupidifying" mechanism that prevented the proletariat from questioning the capitalist economy and bourgeois order. This reading by Bates is indeed correct, and these points are crucial to understanding Gramsci the ideologue as well as his shortcomings.

Here, however, I wish to call attention to Gramsci's description of four different aspects of hegemony that showcase his merits as a political theoretician. The first is the fundamental importance of ideal factors in framing the commonsensical thinking; these form a "worldview" that secures the consent of the led. It is the populace's view of the world that informs their everyday behavior. Second, these ideal factors never operate by themselves; they are united with material factors by what Gramsci calls "historical block." Ideal factors and material factors constitute each other and together foster the emergence of hegemony. These two aspects of hegemony are what relate Gramsci to constructivism, making it easy to construct a common ground between the two schools of thought. Yet it is in the third and fourth aspects of hegemony where his contribution to constructivism may reside. The third aspect is Gramsci's focus on politics, on the mechanisms of ruling, and of distributing resources in society. It is this political interest of Gramsci that can inform constructivism, making it a political theory as well as a social one—a theory of the political construction of sociopolitical reality. The fourth aspect is the "doxic" nature of knowledge—whether individual or shared knowledge about the world. Doxic knowledge may turn out to be false (as Gramsci points out), or true. But more importantly, doxic knowledge is unestablished knowledge, and goes unchallenged and unreflected upon. What is highlighted here is this "doxic" nature of knowledge, which makes knowledge amenable to political mobilization and opens the way to reconstructing constructivism as a political theory. To highlight the differences between the Gramscian ideological and political understanding of hegemony, instead of hegemony, let us consider the notion of public conventions, defined as general background knowledge about the world that is taken for granted and shapes the commonsensical codes of thinking and behavior.

Public conventions as a potential remedy to the nonpolitical nature of constructivism are closely tied to the focus of this book: IR theories and political reality's relations of mutual influence. If we apply the Gramscian and constructivist assertion that public conventions are based on ideal factors it seems that public conventions may well stem from social science theories, which are ideal factors. And in this case, contrary to Gramsci's reading of hegemony, the theoreticians' agenda need not be a hidden political agenda to advance certain sectarian interests. Rather, it might involve a sincere quest for some universal truth in the overall service of humanity. Nevertheless, the result might be public conventions. The theoreticians themselves might continuously challenge their own theories (or more realistically, their colleagues'). However, one result of theories migrating to the public and political spheres would be the loss of the academic culture of questioning, and a consequent uncritical and unreflective belief in theories as truth. In other words, theoretical constructions could become public conventions.

Understanding how public conventions undergo the final, third stage of theory as hermeneutical mechanisms requires introducing human agency into the three-staged model. At this stage, purposeful human agents intentionally transform public conventions into political convictions—in other words, into specific knowledge that engenders a strong, opinionated view that necessitates political action. The human agent can also be understood in terms of Gramsci's organic intellectual or by the more contemporary theoretical concept of political entrepreneur.[6] Like the concept of agency,[7] both allude to a purposeful attempt by politically motivated individuals to change their political environment and innovate policies according to a well-deliberated agenda. The best tactic for politically motivated individuals, especially when battling well-established alternatives, is to exploit existing public conventions, transforming them into political convictions suitable to their political needs. A successful use of existing public conventions will lower opposition to innovation and open the way to political change with relative ease. Generating supportive political convictions from public conventions will strongly motivate people toward the desired political action. Later, this book's empirical chapters offer a plethora of examples of such agency and entrepreneurship, in the shape of President Clinton, American neoconservatives, or Israeli politicians.

Theory as a Hermeneutical Mechanism of Attaching Meaning to Political Concepts

The two theoretical approaches can be amalgamated into a single framework of understanding theory as a hermeneutical mechanism for attaching meaning to political concepts. First, there is Freeden's conceptualization of political thought, which points to the crucial role of political concepts in theory and conversely to the role of theory in political concepts: decontesting the concepts' meanings and constructing comprehensive configurations; namely, theoretical constructions, from them. Once we understand theory as a configuration of decontested political concepts, we can better understand how theory influences political practice. By decontesting political concepts' meanings and constructing a set of comprehensive theoretical constructions from them, theory can infuse the concepts with meaning and induce individuals to understand them in a specific fashion. And as our understanding of political phenomena rests on concepts, attaching meaning to concepts allows us to frame our understanding of phenomenon. Then, once our understanding is framed, we act on this understanding. Thus, theory as political thought can motivate individuals to political action, and hence is a hermeneutical mechanism.

Although hermeneutics is usually understood as the art of interpreting already-written texts, I wish to introduce a further meaning for it—one that implies more active interpretation. The idea is that once reality is conceived as an unwritten text, we can understand theorization as a hermeneutical process of understanding reality. That is not to say reality is nothing but a text, nor even to claim it is a text at all. But once we accept that the core subject matter of social science theories consists of social entities such as narratives, social practices, habits, rules of conduct, modes of political behavior, norms, ideas, and ideals, we can refer to reality as unwritten texts that are constantly being composed and recomposed by human agents and human societies, or, as Paul Ricoeur metaphorically describes it, "*documents of human action*" (1991:153). The process of studying these unwritten texts by theorizing is the process of understanding them; that is, the process of interpreting them hermeneutically. And if, as already argued, the building blocks of any mode of political thought—including theories as theoretical constructions—are political concepts, then theorizing reality amounts to and results in attaching meaning to political concepts.

A second way to understand theory as a hermeneutical mechanism is to recognize that hermeneutics (in the more conventional sense of interpreting written texts) is never a one-way undertaking. To interpret is to derive meanings from texts, but once meanings are derived, they linger with the interpreter to be accepted or rejected. This again indicates that hermeneutics is not only a passive process, but also involves the active element of influence affecting the interpreters. That is what Hans-Georg Gadamer, following Martin Heidegger's hermeneutical phenomenology, meant by "fusion of horizons": the interpreter who use hermeneutics never remain the same after encountering a text (1989:306). Her understanding of a text, even a text written long ago, infuses her life with new meanings, and thus influences her understanding of the present.

The same is true of decontesting—attaching meaning—to political concepts. This can never be a passive act; it invariably affects our understanding of the world—understanding achieved through meaning-laden concepts—in other words, meaningful concepts. Hence, theoretical constructions have the potential to frame both our understanding and our political action. To put it differently, concepts are not merely passive signifiers; they frame political behavior. Gadamer's hermeneutics is instructive once again. For Gadamer understanding is a locus of action since he conceives application as dovetailed with understanding. As Alan How writes concerning Gadamer, "In understanding something, we implicitly apply it to our own situation" (2007:14). When theory actually frames our understanding and political action, it uses what I describe as the hermeneutical mechanism—the active aspects and implications of hermeneutics—the art of interpretation.

The hermeneutical mechanism can be especially effective because in a sense, the political is a state of flux, and politics, or the political act, is an attempt to fixate the flux in order to gain political dividends. The political is the arena where individuals compete, deliberate, and cooperate so as to allocate resources and shape institutions and policies, where individuals have visions of what should be done and how it should be done. In other words, people are trying to fixate the flux according to their vision. Now one effective method of achieving this is to attach meaning to political concepts, thus framing the common sense of the everyman, and driving him to the desired political action. Stated differently, framing the common sense by attaching meaning to political concepts is a very efficient and extremely cost-effective mode of power. It is political art and the political act par excellence.

The question then arises, when does a theory fulfill its potential of effectively influencing political action via the hermeneutical mechanism. It is here that constructivism comes back into the picture. Theory is just one type of political thought among many, such as ideology and political philosophy, and usually several theories vie to explain the same phenomenon. Hence, we need to understand why one theory, rather than other theories or types of political thought, manages to assert its influence by attaching meaning to political concepts. A theory mainly succeeds in this way when it becomes a public convention, and following the constructivist argument advanced earlier, a public convention results from a combination of objective, material, and structural conditions (material factors) that undergo subjective or intersubjective processes of analyzing, understanding, and evaluating these conditions (ideal factors). Another lesson we can take from constructivism is the crucial part identity and collective identity play in mediating the intersubjective understanding of material conditions (see, for example, Hansen and Wæver 2002; Katzenstein 1996; Weldes 1996; Wendt 1992). A basic part of how people analyze and understand the material and structural conditions in which they find themselves concerns their self-understanding, the collective norms they follow, and their self-definition vis-à-vis others. In the present context, identity is the axis around which material factors and ideal factors converge to create a public atmosphere conducive to transforming specific theoretical constructions into public conventions. It is this axis that determines the public and political fate of theories.

However, in democratic states and pluralistic societies, socializing mechanisms are relatively weak, and cleavage lines, as well as collective identities, are manifold and crosscutting. In these cases, contrary to Gramsci's theory of hegemony and the nonpolitical theory of constructivism, public conventions will not be absolute, and they will not be embedded across the public at large. There will probably also be no public convention exclusively framing the common sense of all. In modern, pluralistic, democratic societies, the public and political spheres engender a plethora of ideas and public conventions that rival each other and coexist comfortably and uncomfortably, in an often transient fashion. And it is this restricted, partial, and transient status exhibited by public conventions that we should expect theories and other political thoughts to assume.

Nevertheless, despite their restricted, partial, and transient nature, public conventions still have political importance and affect reality, and do so mainly in the setting of two different political scenarios. The first is when competent political entrepreneurs decide to mobilize them and their political and rhetorical capital in the expedient and manipulative service of their agenda. Rhetorical capital is defined as the aggregate persuasive resources inherent in entities, be they material ones, or abstract and ideal ones, such as theories. Introducing the concept of rhetorical capital allows us to ask what a theory has that attracts and enables the rhetorically minded politician to use it to her rhetorical advantage. Put differently, there is something inherent in theory that encourages the process by which politicians exploit it. Thus, pointing out the expedient nature of the political use of theory does not render theory politically useless; it simply demonstrates an absurd yet painfully true fact: theories can be politically influential though theoreticians can be politically insignificant. Later in the book I deal with this disturbing argument, and suggest a number of remedies.

The second political scenario is when public conventions are so intrinsic in influential sectors—such as policy elites—that the conventions frame the thinking on world affairs, and eventually affect policy planning and implementation. This is the tension between the abuse of theory for political expediency that minimizes the independent power and agency of theory (the first scenario), and theory as a powerful ideal factor, which drives political action (second scenario) by functioning as an unreflected-upon conventional wisdom. However, the tension between the two scenarios is not as stark as it first may seem, and it is certainly not the tension between conscious and unconscious political behavior. A theory's attractiveness to politicians and their ability to abuse it stems from the theory's political and rhetorical capital, which among other things, arises from its character as a public convention. On the other hand, theory's translation from unreflected-upon public convention into concrete policy is mediated by much reflected-upon political processes; this translation involves strategic calculations to devise warranted policies, rhetorical persuasion campaigns on the merits of the desired policies, and political campaigning to legitimize the policies pursued.

Moreover, no matter how competent the entrepreneurs who decide to mobilize the political conventions may be, their capabilities are not unlimited and their political maneuverability has its constraints. Public conventions are a major factor in these constraints, as they both limit and enhance political entrepreneur efficacy. Public conventions are among the factors that influence the public's view of what is acceptable and unacceptable, legitimate and illegitimate, normative and nonnormative. To some extent, public conventions also affect what political entrepreneurs themselves see as acceptable, legitimate, normative, or not. These entrepreneurs themselves are embedded in the social structures they wish to influence and in the public conventions they seek to mobilize. Hence, their capacity to lead, mobilize, and shape is restricted by the same sets of public conventions, norms, and understandings that they wish to affect. In other words, the political decision to mobilize a specific public convention is only a free political act up to a point.

To summarize, public conventions affect reality both on their own terms and on political entrepreneurs' terms. They do this both spontaneously by being general background knowledge about the world that is taken for granted, and by shaping the commonsensical codes of thinking and behavior—and they do this intentionally—by being mobilized instrumentally and politically. They also do this both as undercurrents of protracted social processes and as short-term political maneuvers—as theorized by the social theory of constructivism and by the political theory of politically reconstructed constructivism.

The hermeneutical mechanism is by no means a one-way route. At the same time as theoretical constructions are translated into public conventions framing the public understanding of world affairs, public conventions also have some power over the theoretical process of formulating theoretical constructions. For example, it may well be that the widespread public convention and political conviction among the American public (including American theoreticians) that democracy is morally, politically, and economically superior to other sorts of political institutionalization has created a supportive academic climate for theorizing the phenomenon of democratic peace which may indicate that democracy is superior to other forms of political institutionalization also in strategic terms. The same applies to the relationship between the second and third stages. As has been discussed, determined and competent political entrepreneurs can mobilize public conventions and translate them into effective political convictions, and at the same time have political convictions that are predisposed by the public conventions that influence their outlook. In other words, public conventions and political convictions are mutually constitutive.

Before concluding this section, I wish to address one possible criticism. Some critics may embrace the political phase of the hermeneutical mechanism, insisting on secluding theory in the ivory tower. They may claim that theories are nothing but instruments in the hands of instrumentalist politicians; that the use of academic theories is nothing but political expediency. They may consequently offer an alternative explanation: that what truly lies behind the book's case studies are the hidden interests of politicians who utilized the theories to their own ends. This is certainly true, especially in the case of the Israeli right. However, it misses the more essential issue of the political and rhetorical capital of theories. Therefore, my response to this criticism is twofold. First, I would argue that political expediency does not operate in a void: it is usually a response to political cause. So-called hidden interests are themselves predisposed to causes by, among other things, public conventions, and in the case of the American neoconservatives' grand strategy of forced democratization, by the public convention originated and verified by the theories (or more accurately, their misrepresentations) that democracies do not fight each other. Second, if the theories were as devoid of political significance as such critics maintain, they would neither be useful as political expedients, nor mobilized politically. Something within the theories invites their use and abuse by politicians. That factor is their rhetorical capital, and it is this capital that attracts politicians to utilize theories. Pointing to the instrumental uses of theories is not an alternative explanation or proof of the powerlessness of theories: it is a complementary explanation that highlights the political incentives behind the processes that drive the translation of public conventions into political convictions.

Rhetorical Capital

The concept of rhetorical capital has already been mentioned. Introducing it contributes to the theoretical literature of rhetoric by enabling researchers to study not only the rhetor's skills, but also the assets available to him or her. It allows us to ask what it is—say, in a theory—that enables the rhetor to use it to her rhetorical advantage. Consideration of the rhetorical capital element enables us to study theories from the point of view of their rhetoric without falling into the postmodernist relativism so common among adherents of the rhetoric of science. For our purposes, the question I wish to ask is: what in theories comprises their rhetorical capital? In other words, what are the features of theories that render them vulnerable to political and rhetorical abuse? These features comprise the general features that most theories share; namely, the structural duality of accessibility and incomprehensibility overlaid with the prestige of objectivity, as well as other features specific to particular theories. In the case of democratic peace theories, which are explored more extensively in chapter 4, their rhetorical capital is comprised of four such specific features. First, the status of the democratic peace thesis among policy elites as a public convention—as a law-like phenomenon governing the realm of world politics. Second, the existence of two distinct theories—the structural and the normative—that try to explain the phenomenon while each delivering a different political message. Third, the policy implications of subscribing to the conclusions of the democratic peace thesis; namely, the ensuing political commitment urging the democratization of nondemocratic states for the sake of national security. Fourth, the long and prestigious heritage of the thesis, which is ascribed, rightly or wrongly, to Immanuel Kant.

It was Aristotle who defined rhetoric as "the faculty of discovering in every case the available means of persuasion" (1909:5). And since the days of ancient Greece, rhetoric has evolved further into the art of persuasion as we know it today. As the practice of rhetoric has developed, so has the theory of rhetoric, which has emerged into a vast and sophisticated body of scholarship specifying the terms and means of persuasion. Rhetorical capital as defined above conforms nicely to the theory of rhetoric, and may also contribute to the literature by allowing researchers to shift their focus from the *rhetors*' skills to the rhetorical assets available to them.[8] For example, it can augment William Riker's discussion of rhetoric and heresthetics—the art of setting up situations to compel political adversaries to support one's purpose (1996; see also Riker 1986). Rich as Riker's discussion of political ingenuity in heresthetics may be, it leaves us with a scant understanding of the persuasive tools employed. This lack can be rectified using the concept of rhetorical capital.

Rhetorical capital not only relates to the literature of rhetoric, it is also indebted to and informed by a vast literature dealing with social capital and its conceptual kindred, including economic capital, cultural capital, symbolic capital, human capital, and political capital (Bourdieu 1986). A brief discussion of social capital allows us to develop the concept of rhetorical capital and understand its analytical merits and limitations more fully. Social capital has become a catchall concept with multiple definitions serving assorted scholarly and political agendas. Alejandro Portes grasped this multidimensional nature and function of the concept by aptly dubbing it "a cure-all" (1998). Thus, he sees it as a somewhat loose concept; able to be evaluated both positively—as enabling contributions to different research fields, and negatively—in it potential to leave too much out. It should be supplemented with other theoretical apparatuses to be able to produce conclusive theories.[9] Without supplementary theoretical apparatus, the looseness of the concept of social capital precludes researchers from the possibility of producing conclusive theories: it can only supply them with functionalist analysis pointing to some feasible explanatory model.

The multidimensional nature of the concept is also evident from the varied entities attributed with social capital. Pierre Bourdieu uses the term social capital mostly as an attribute of membership, applying it to individuals in a group (1986:248–49). However, Robert Putnam, attributes social capital to social networks. Putnam's analysis led to two relocations of social capital: social capital is no longer the attribute of individuals, but of groups or collectives (2000). And, no less important, it is no longer the attribute of concrete subjects or entities. Social networks are abstract constructs, theoretical fictions with heuristic value. Putnam's analytical move/relocation supports my claim that rhetorical capital also applies to nonhuman abstract entities, such as theories.[10]

As the locus of social capital, social networks can also help us analogously to move beyond the formal definition of rhetorical capital—as an aggregate of the persuasive resources inherent in entities—and understand the internal constitution of rhetorical capital more fully. Rhetorical capital is an attribute of entities generated by various features of those entities. Certain features may act as persuasive resources all by themselves; in other words, they can stand alone rhetorically. Other features serve as persuasive resources when they form a set of relations—a network—with other features of the same entity. This involves internal networking in which internal features of the entity interrelate. Still, other features of the entity are resources of persuasion only on the background of external structure that frames the entity. This involves external networking in which the internal features of the entity relate it to some external, broader, and more encompassing entities. Let us take a poem for example. A poem can have both internal-to-the-text and external-to-the-text resources of persuasion. Rhymes, for example, are internal-to-the-text features that can act as resource of persuasion; resources that an able rhetor can use to convey her message fluidly and gracefully. Yet the rhetor can do even better if he or she chooses a poem whose rhyme joins the poem's rhythm in engendering a calming or confrontational mood to augment his or her persuasive resources—rhymes and rhythm being internal-to-the-text features networked together to produce augmented persuasive resources. And of course our rhetor will fare best by choosing a well-known poem—which is constituted culturally as a national symbol with connotations of martyrdom, heroism, or piety—or whatever the cause requires. In this case, the poem as a well-known and national symbol, is an external-to-the-text cultural structure that further augments the poem's internal features as assets of persuasion: resources of rhetorical capital. Thus, rhetorical capital is an attribute generated by features, some internal to an entity, some external to it, and most—though not all—relational, constituting sets of relations that serve as persuasive assets, persuasive assets that come alive not by themselves, but in the hands of able *rhetors*.

To summarize, rhetorical capital is a loose analytical concept.[11] It cannot establish theoretical explanations alone, yet it has ample heuristic value to think functionally about the persuasive resources that are available to rhetors. It can be supplemented, for example, by such theoretical apparatuses as Riker's heresthetics, Alan Finlayson's Rhetorical Political Analysis (2007), or the analytic triad of classical rhetoric: pathos, ethos, and logos. Using these complementary theoretical apparatuses, researchers can develop fuller explanatory theories of the art of persuasion which describe the available persuasive resources, the techniques for mobilizing them, how they work, the best political conditions under which they function, and finally, the political goals they serve to secure.

Introducing rhetorical capital allows me to open a space to study theories in terms of their rhetorical function without falling into the postmodernist relativism so common among adherents of the rhetoric of science. The rhetoric of science or, as it is also known, the rhetoric of inquiry, evolved following the postmodernist and poststructuralist critique (see, for example, Nelson, Megill, and McCloskey 1987; Prelli 1989; Simon 1990, 1989; Megill 1994; Gross and Keith 1997; Lyne 1998; specifically for the study of IR theory, see Beer and Hariman 1996), and together with them contests the foundationalist view of science.[12] The rhetoric of science disputes two different philosophies. First, it opposes positivism by challenging objectivism with relativism and argues that scientific inquiry is governed by the logic of rhetoric cloaked by the semblance of objectivity and so-called rigorous methodology. Science, we are told by scholars of the rhetoric of science, is oriented toward persuasion, not toward discovering truth. Scientists pursue prestige and financing by approaching their colleagues, the public, and the decision makers with their rhetoric.

Second, as a particular branch of the more general study of rhetoric, the rhetoric of science questions Habermasian philosophy of the public sphere. It rejects envisioning public deliberation as rational by highlighting the centrality of political manipulation in the public sphere and the public sphere's nonrational, even irrational, qualities. It is not rational and power-free ideal speech that guides the public discourse, but rhetorical devices, which overtake the public discourse by triggering the public's nonrational faculties. The rhetoric of science is specifically interested in how theories engage with the public sphere. Scientists would like to think that the objective and, more importantly, the rational nature of theories make them perfect facilitators of ideal speech situations in which arguments are clarified, and interest and values elucidated, en route to a public and rational understanding and agreement. However, rhetoric of science scholars would argue that objectivity and rationality are just a convenient myth used by both theoreticians and politicians as a rhetorical device to realize their ideological and political aims. Accordingly, it is not in the service of truth and general interests that theories are used, but in the service of ideologies and narrow interests.

In both these critiques, we can identify the traditional conflict between rhetoric and philosophy: the former with its emphasis on the transient, stylish, and witty, the later with its emphasis on the Absolute, Essence, and Wisdom. Philosophy and social science, different as they are, do share an interest in the three jurisdictions of Absolute, Essence, and Wisdom (though sometimes applied differently) that places them on the same side in the long-standing intellectual feud with rhetoric.[13]

Although the rhetoric of science literature does provide some insightful lessons on the inner mechanisms of science, its conclusions are far too sweeping. Rhetoric of science's scholars immerse themselves in what is, after all, a marginal and minor area of scientific work, mistaking it for the core and essence of science. Of course scientists engage in rhetoric, which they use to convey the soundness of their findings to colleagues and sometimes to the wider public, and indeed, some are very skilled rhetors. However, the rhetoric comes into play, so to speak, once the scientists have finished with the science and, convinced of the accuracy of their findings and merit of their theories, use rhetoric to try to persuade their colleagues. It is here that I diverge from the rhetoric of science and its relativism and antifoundationalism. My argument is not that science is inherently rhetorical or irrational,[14] but rather that science outputs (theories) are vulnerable to rhetorical abuse since, although the theories are accessible to the public, they are at the same time technically overwhelming, which renders them incomprehensible. It is this structural duality of accessibility and incomprehensibility, overlaid with the prestige of objectivity, which constitutes the core of the rhetorical capital of theories. Additionally, as the next section explores, it is this structural duality that produces the requisiteless version of theory—in other words, its misrepresentation as both public convention and political conviction. At the same time, specific features of particular theories might add to their rhetorical capital.

In later chapters, the notion of rhetorical capital helps me to demonstrate the rhetorical use of the democratic peace thesis by Benjamin Netanyahu and Natan Sharansky in their attempts to secure their political goals.

The Four Requisites for Sound Theorizing

What happens to the theoretical constructions when they are transformed into public conventions and political convictions? Or, in other words, what happens to theory when it migrates to the public and political spheres? In broad terms, theory becomes politicized and simplified—processes that are hard to distinct but involve slightly different kinds of changes. Politicization refers mainly to changes in how theory is perceived and approached; simplification refers mainly to the disregard for the epistemic procedural rules that apply to theories—namely, the four requisites for sound theorizing. To answer the question of what happens to the migrated theory more specifically, a distinction should be drawn between theory as product and theorizing as the producing process. As a product, theory migrates well and is potentially at least accessible to the wider public, which can learn about the theories and their contentions. The public essentially has access to the contentions of theory, and in the case of the democratic peace thesis, has been exposed to the theoretical contention that democracies do not fight each other. However, theorizing as the producing process does not migrate well. Theorization is incomprehensible to an untrained public. It is overburdened with technicalities, subtleties and jargon, rendering it beyond the grasp of the average layperson, even the typical college-educated citizen. This structural duality of accessibility and incomprehensibility facilitates the stripping away from the migrated theory four essential requisites for sound theorizing.

The first requisite of theorizing that is lost in migration is the academic culture of cautiousness, self-reflection, and self-criticism. This culture guarantees that academic endeavor is an open project aimed at overcoming prejudices and obstacles in the path of establishing theoretical truth. It is not that theoreticians have a limitless capacity for self-reflection and a boundless capacity for self-criticism. Various factors get in the way of such competences. First, public conventions are at work whenever theoreticians collect data, analyze data, and construct theories from this data. Public conventions are part of the social and historical situation which, as Karl Mannheim argued in 1968, is so important in knowledge production.[15] Thus, for example, Ido Oren has shown how American public conventions and perceived strategic interests have shaped American political science for decades (2003). Also, Susan Carroll and Linda Zerilli show how political science as a discipline has been dominated by masculine conventions (1993). Second, positivism limits self-reflection and self-criticism. As this book (and especially the next chapter) shows, by adhering to the positivist confidence in objectivity and neutrality, theoreticians have blinded themselves from recognizing and acknowledging the moral groundwork that informs their theories. Third, as mainly noted by feminist epistemologists, blind spots protect theoreticians from recognizing the personal and collective prejudices that bias theory construction (Hawkesworth 1996).

The three factors are at work and hinder self-reflection and self-criticism. Yet they do not hamper these processes fully, especially not if we view self-reflection and self-criticism as a communal practice and asset, conducted collectively by the theoreticians as a community. Think of the academic exchange of ideas, the evaluation and refutation of theories, and the peer-review system which oversees the process of publishing new theories. Consider the impact of critical thinking, exemplified by scholars such as Oren, or Carroll and Zerilli, and the awareness that their thinking has raised regarding the blinding effects of conventions, and which has helped to break the latter's spell. The aforementioned practices are all crucial aspects of the academic culture, and while they may not all be part of every theoretician's repertoire (being blinded by the three factors), they are nevertheless dependably undertaken at the collective level by theoreticians as a community. Hence, although blinded at times by public conventions, positivist confidences, and blind spots in individuals, the academic world is well equipped to confront these obstacles and prejudices on a gradual basis.

Thus, without undermining Thomas Kuhn's 1962 claims—or devaluing the self-reflexivity and self-criticism built into the democratic political culture—there is evidently much more criticism and reflexivity in academic discourse than in political discourse, and it ensures ongoing evaluation of new and existing theories. When propounded by politicians and ideologues democratic peace is regarded as a well-known, undisputed, and uncontested fact. Hence, peace among democracies is taken for granted. This, for instance, is how George W. Bush sees the phenomenon of peace among democracies, "We know from history that free nations are peaceful nations. We know that democracies do not attack each other" (2006b). The phenomenon, according to President Bush, is uncontested; there is no need for a complicated and subtle theoretical apparatus to infer conclusions from compound reality. We can simply induce from history observation and obviate academic caution.

Second, theories lose their terms of conditionality in migration. Most theories are explicit about the conditions of their validity. For example, according to most democratic peace theoreticians, peaceful democratic relations are dyadic and valid only within pairs of democracies. But the general agreement among theoreticians is not translated to a consensual agreement (consensus that runs the risk of becoming an ossified theoretical convention). A number of researchers hold the monadic view that democracies are generally less aggressive than other forms of government (Oneal and Russett 1997; Ray 1995, 1997; Reiter and Stem 2002, 2003; Rummel 1983). Two points are notable in the monadic/dyadic discussion. The first is that it is vital for theoreticians to establish the conditionality of their theories. The second relates to the way the theoretical discussion about conditionality is conducted, the type of arguments which are involved, and the general theoretical approach to data. But I will say more on this in a moment, when I introduce the different vernaculars used to convey information.

A second conditionality was established by Edward Mansfield and Jack Snyder, who skillfully showed that the transition to democracy is dangerously prone to destabilization (2005).[16] Put differently, democratization might lead to both domestic and international violence, and, accordingly, democratic peace is possible only within pairs of *consolidated* democracies. Such conditionalities disappear in the political sphere where theoretical claims become totalistic assertions. Max Boot, for example, the prolific neoconservative pundit, defines the democratic peace theory as "the notion that liberal democracies are unlikely to use weapons of mass destructions, sponsor terrorism, and undertake other activities that threaten their neighbors and the United States" (2003:27). Similarly, Benjamin Netanyahu—the prominent Israeli politician and Israeli prime minister—learns from history that "modern democracies do not initiate aggression. This has been the central lesson of the 20th century" (1996). Outside academia, it seems, democracies are peaceful—not only among themselves (if at all peaceful), but peaceful overall, and that they are so is a matter of uncontested fact.

Third, theories lose their probabilistic nature and become absolute, law-like statements. Jack Levy infamously declared democratic peace to be "as close as anything we have to an empirical law in international relations: (1989:270). It is important to note that even Levy did not declare it a law, only a semi-law. Yet, politicians and ideologues consider the theory differently. We see this, for example, in the pronouncement by Lawrence Kaplan and William Kristol—another two neoconservative pundits—that democratic peace is "a truth of international relations" (2003:104). The aforementioned statements by Bush and Netanyahu exude a similar absolute and law-like quality. They do not deal with probabilities: democracies are not less likely than other regimes types to be involved in war; democracies do not initiate war, period.

Fourth, and again related to this question of conditionality, is the role of the laws of logic, which stipulate what is validly inferred from a theory and what is not. When there are no terms of conditionality, the rules of deducing conclusions from theory, and more relevant to the public arena, deducing policy guidelines from theory, can hardly function. For example, we cannot infer from the theory which states that consolidated democracies never (or rarely) fight each other, that other kinds of dyads (e.g., democracy vs. nondemocracy, or nondemocracy vs. nondemocracy) are necessarily war-prone. Thus, we cannot deduce—as did the neoconservatives, and which was used to legitimize the war in Iraq—that democratizing Iraq will bring immediate regional stability—at least not as long as we are unwilling to democratize the rest of the region. And even if we did democratize the rest of the region, we may still face a long period of regional destabilization while the newly democratized states struggle through the long and arduous process of consolidating their democracies.

Discarding the four requisites for sound theorizing results in a simplistic yes-no reading of theories that is highly amenable to the trivialization of theories and the political mobilization of their rhetorical capital; theory transmogrifies into public and political representations.[17] Or, stated differently, the idea entity of theoretical constructions is reconfigured into the idea entities of public conventions and political convictions. It generates yet another change, this time a discursive one. To communicate their findings (their theoretical constructions), theoreticians use the discursive genre of theoretical explanatory vernacular; that is, meticulous claims of the relations between different phenomena, articulated to deliver the subtlest minutia of a theory's contentions as established through strict and careful theorization. Public conventions, on the other hand, are circulated via the discursive genre of commonsensical descriptory vernacular; that is, the loose expression of unreflective accounts that unfold the narratives in which the world is captured and figured out by the public common sense. The former discursive genre functions to convey theoretical discoveries and the logic of explanation and verification. The latter discursive genre functions to affirm and reaffirm the commonsensical depiction of reality. Political convictions are conveyed through the discursive genre of political avowal vernacular—forceful declarations rhetorically uttered in slogan-like fashion to confirm and convey political stands. This discursive genre functions to justify and legitimize ideological beliefs and political actions.

Discarding the four requisites and alternating the discursive genres through which the three different types of idea entities are communicated results in what can concisely be summarized as follows: the theoretical construction of democratic peace seeks methodologically to verify and explain the relations between democracy and peace. As such, it involves an ongoing theoretical discussion that goes to the heart of contestation and meticulously argues about both data and theory. This is how we should understand (and appreciate), for example, the ongoing discussion about the monadic versus dyadic nature of democratic peace. Though most theoreticians regard the democratic peace as dyadic, there are those, including Bruce Russett in his later writings, who have kept the discussion alive and open-ended by presenting a growing body of fresh data that supports the monadic view and argues against the dyadic view (which was established and verified by the earlier Russett, among others). The public convention relating to democratic peace takes the (theoretically contested) assertion for granted that democracies are peaceful polities. The political conviction arising from the democratic peace thesis is that promoting democracy is of vital interest, and that democratization is a matter of national security. The political conviction conveyed by political avowal vernacular, puts a stop to deliberation and ossifies theoretical constructions into nonestablished and unexamined truth; that is, into doxa. In their transition from one idea-entity to another, theoretical contentions become less reticent, cautious, and flexible, and more totalistic, rigid, and dogmatic in character.

Both the surrender of the four requisites for sound theorizing and the discursive changes are evident in the democratic peace theories' political mobilization, and will be explored in subsequent chapters.

Conclusions

As we have seen, there are three stages to attaching meaning to political concepts in the process of theorizing as a hermeneutical mechanism, three stages conforming to three different types of idea entities, and three different kinds of discursive genres. In the first stage, the theoretician assigns political concepts meaning by constructing a theory. This is the academic stage, and although it is an instance of attaching meaning to political concepts, it is not in itself an accomplished case of theory as an hermeneutical mechanism: it does not involve driving people to political action as it only produces theoretical constructions. To motivate political action, the theory must migrate from academe to the public sphere. In other words, the academic-theoretic discourse must be transformed into social discourse, the discursive genre of theoretical explanatory vernacular must be alternated into the discursive genre of commonsensical descriptory vernacular, and theoretical constructions must be reconfigured into public conventions. This is the second or sociopolitical stage: the process of fixating the meanings of political concepts in the common sense of important segments of society, especially policymakers and foreign policy pundits. Although relatively rare, when it does occur it is the most profound level of theory as a hermeneutical mechanism—it succeeds in attaching specific meanings to specific political concepts and infusing these meanings into the common sense. Thus, a theory succeeds in framing the understanding of some publics—it succeeds in creating public conventions. A theory of this kind, albeit in an altered configuration—its public representation—is extremely powerful and open to the third stage. This is the political stage, when political entrepreneurs make a conscious or partially conscious effort to utilize a theory's public representation for their political and ideological needs, and translate the public conventions into political convictions, conveyed by the discursive genre of political avowal vernacular. Here we witness most clearly the political utilization, and sometimes manipulation or abuse, of the theoretical constructions. The next five chapters of this book provide an empirical examination of the three stages of the theoretical model—of theory as a hermeneutical mechanism.

2

DEMOCRATIC PEACE AS THEORETICAL CONSTRUCTIONS

In 1964 we saw the revival of the Kantian republican peace, and the start of a process that epitomizes the first stage of theory as a hermeneutical process as depicted and analyzed in this book—in other words, the stage when meaning becomes attached to political concepts through academic discourse. A relatively obscure and neglected article by Dean Babst, published in 1964, predated the later flowering of the democratic peace research agenda. Babst's theoretical observation was revived during the 1970s and 1980s, when a growing number of researchers reaffirmed an interesting empirical phenomenon: that democracies never—or, as the qualified and academically held version maintained, rarely—go to war with each other.[1] Although this claim was harshly criticized over the years (see, for example, Lane 1994; Spiro 1994; Farber and Gowa 1995; Oren 1995; Gowa 1999; Gaubatz 1999; Cohen 1994; Rosato 2003; Gat 2005), it steadily gained support and a theoretical thesis emerged according to which democracies do not fight each other because they are democracies. This was followed by a further theoretical phase in which several theories attempted to explain the phenomenon and the thesis and to identify those characteristics of democracy which produce peace—in other words, they tried to develop an explanatory mechanism. The theories that tried to explain the phenomenon and the thesis crystallized into two theoretical families or paradigms. The first explains the democratic peace phenomenon by focusing on the structural dimensions of democracy, claiming that the division of power, checks and balances, and leaders' accountability to the public make the decision-making process complex and slow, allowing the decision makers of democratic states to resolve conflicts peacefully. By postulating leaders' universal desire to remain in office, the more sophisticated versions of structural explanation demonstrate—for example, by formal game modeling—that the democratic structure drives leaders to resolve disputes with other democracies before escalation to war (e.g.,

Fearon 1994; Bueno de Mesquita, Morrow, Siverson, and Smith 1999). The second family of theories highlights the normative dimensions of democratic societies, arguing that the norms of tolerance and openness within these states extend into the relations between them, producing greater willingness to use conflict-resolution techniques and to reach compromises, so that conflicts are settled peacefully (e.g., Maoz and Russett 1993; Dixon 1994).

The different democratic peace theories, which are generically and collectively known as the democratic peace thesis (and referred to as such throughout this book), are the most successful recent case of theory as a hermeneutical mechanism. This chapter analyzes the first stage of the hermeneutical mechanism to which this thesis was subjected; namely, the academic task of attaching meaning to political concepts. I argue that the debate between these two families of theories, the structural and the normative-cultural, encompasses the range of meanings attached to the democratic peace phenomenon, and further show how the different concepts are decontested and configured in concert—in other words, the theoretical debate is about the essence of democratic peace. Following a hermeneutic reading and critical interpretation of some of the seminal works of the democratic peace, and by exploring the concepts used in those articles, I establish that the theories seeking to explain the democratic peace phenomenon are in fact competing configurations of decontested meanings of political concepts—in other words, theoretical constructions. No less importantly, the hermeneutical analysis and critical interpretation of these articles reveals that these theories are derived from different ideological and moral convictions and commitments.

The Concepts of War and Peace

What is peace? Is it really a contested political concept? Do we all understand peace in the same theoretical way? A short survey of the literature reveals several definitions of peace. The realist conception of peace is that peace is the absence of war (Waltz 1959:1). For realists, the absence of war is temporary. Since peace is the opposite of war, and since war is a common and unavoidable feature in international relations, peace is no more than a spasmodic hiatus between wars. Hence, realists warn us not to be fooled by the joys of peace, which can veil the inevitable dangers lurking beneath the relations between states, and lead to complacency and lack of preparation for the next inevitable outbreak of war. Peace, in other words, is dangerous.

Yet, more is at stake here than just the dangers of peace. If peace is defined by the absence of war, then war must be a crucial concept in democratic peace theories. War is also a contested political concept that theories try to decontest. War too has several definitions and explanations. For instance, Seyom Brown defines international war as "violence between organized political entities claiming to be sovereign nations" (Brown 1994:1). Clearly, this definition contains several more contested concepts, such as "violence," "political," "nations," and perhaps the most contested, "sovereignty." Without delving into these concepts, it is clear that we are caught in an unending path. If we try to use the realist definition to configure peace we face dealing with many more concepts and an abundance of potential configurations for decontested political concepts.

Additionally, the realist definition of peace is far from the only definition of peace. Kenneth Boulding would see this realist view of peace as "unstable peace"; in other words, not real peace. For Boulding, real peace equals "stable peace"—"a situation in which the probability of war is so small that it does not really enter into the calculations of any of the people involved" (1979:13). This is fundamentally different from the realist definition of peace as the absence of war. For Boulding, peace is much more than simply the absence of war: it is a kind of peace whose degeneration one need not fear, which eliminates the necessity to be perpetually prepared for war. When stable peace of this kind exists, as it does between the United States and Canada, few resources are invested to ensure military protection against the stable peace partner and a pluralistic security community can be achieved.

Yet, as with the realist definition of peace, this definition implicates many more political concepts, such as expectations, calculations, and rationality. Moreover, the concepts of legitimacy, mutual legitimacy, or bonding interests, are also likely to be relevant. Karl Deutsch's idea of the "security community offers another plausible explanation of stable peace" (Deutsch et al. 1957),[2] which, in turn, invokes the concept of a common identity, or "we-feeling."

There are other options too for defining and explaining the concept of peace. For example, peace can be perceived as something utopian, entailing the total absence of conflict. It could also involve mutual disregard (peace of indifference), or cooperation and commerce. It would be Sisyphean to try and list the multitude of definitions of "peace," or reconfigure the many contested concepts that any of these configurations would imply.

The Concepts of Democracy and Democratization

The second concept—democracy—takes us to yet another realm of analysis. Here, too, we encounter serious problems of contested meanings. Generally speaking, there are two broad paradigms of democratic theory. The first paradigm is elitist, structural, formal, and procedural. It tends to understand democracy in a relatively minimalist way (see, for example, Schumpeter 1962; Lippmann 1955; Przeworski 1999). A regime is a democracy when it passes a certain structural threshold and has free and open elections, autonomous branches of government, division of power, and checks and balances. This precludes a tyrannical concentration of power in the hands of an elite. Once this structure is in place, we can call the regime a democracy.

The second paradigm, which relates to what we term "normative," "cultural," "deliberative democracy," and "participatory democracy,"[3] tends to focus on other issues beside structure and to demand much more of democracy (see, for example, Pateman 1970; Mansbridge 1970; Barber 1984; de-Shalit 1997; Elster 1998; Habermas 1998; Dryzek 2002). First, it emphasizes society and the individual citizens[4]—not the political system and the regime. Second, it also demands democratic norms and a democratic culture. This implies—among other things—political rights, tolerance, openness, participation, and a sense of civic responsibility.

What, then, do we mean by democracy? Do we mean a political system governed by elections? Or do we mean a society with a set of embedded norms and cultures? Choosing between the two paradigms means choosing between two paths, since the paradigms stem from two radically different worldviews. The first is conservative in nature; the second is liberal or socialist (or "progressive," to use nineteenth-century terminology).

The minimalist structural definition of democracy stems from a conservative skepticism regarding human faculties. According to this view, it is not rationality that drives human action, but a mixture of perennial desires, instincts, and communal traditions. This mixture is extra rational and drives humans to strive for power. There are two major consequences to this. First, because everyone seeks power, social and political organizations are in perpetual danger of destabilization. Second, there is the opposite consequence—the constant danger of a dictatorial concentration of power in the hands of those individuals who succeed in gaining power. The conservative solution to these two dangers is minimal, structural democracy. On the one hand, by holding regular elections, democracy guarantees that no power will last forever and prevents the concentration of power in the hands of a dictator. On the other hand, by confining political participation to elections, democracy precludes political and social destabilization.

The normative and cultural definition of democracy is more far-reaching and is based on an optimistic, liberal view of human rationality. Human beings are rationally driven creatures. It is not that they lack emotions, desires, instincts, or communal bonds, but these are all controlled to a large extent by rationality and by rational calculations, including controlled political behavior. The rational individual is also seen as the locus of indivisible civic rights. This normative and cultural definition of democracy therefore centers on participation and rights, seeking to widen the scope of citizens' political participation, and thus extend the meaning of democracy. According to this view, there is little fear of destabilizing the polity because political participation is rationally based.

These two fundamentally different paradigms correspond to the two previously mentioned theories of democratic peace: the structural theory and the normative-cultural theory. The resemblance is not accidental. In fact, the democratic peace theories do not "resemble" the paradigms of democracy but, rather, follow them. As we will see, those who believe democracy is defined mainly by structure will seek to explain consequences of democracy; that is, democratic peace, in terms of the core concept of democratic structure. Conversely, those who see democracy as based mainly on political culture and notions of morality will take these factors to be the explanatory variables of democratic peace.

Moreover, these theories are configurations of decontested concepts, which endow each other with meaning. Thus, democracy endows peace with meaning, and vice versa. This mutual lending of meaning, however, results in totally different understandings of democratic peace. In the structural theory of democratic peace, democracy is decontested minimally and structurally—democracy is just a configuration of elections, checks and balances, and the principle of accountability. Moreover, this meaning of democracy endows peace with a specific, minimal meaning—probably not the realist definition of peace, but also not the fully stable peace of Boulding, or the peace of Deutsch's security community. The reasons are quite simple. If democracy is a structure, it is relatively easy to build, but also relatively easy to dismantle. Hence, peace might be secured between democracies as defined by structure, but the stability of such peace is questionable. Decision makers and the public cannot fully trust their counterparts in the other democracy, since the stability of democracy is not guaranteed; they will still have to be prepared for war.

Conversely, in the normative variant, democracy is far more stable and comprehensive. Once a society has been socialized into a set of democratic norms, these norms become embedded in the behavior and functioning of individuals and society. Democratization is a long and arduous process, but once completed and consolidated it is very difficult to reverse (see also Ericson 2000). Consequently, two democratic polities can trust each other and maintain long-term peaceful relations. This is all the more so because the peace between them relies directly on the norms of peaceful coexistence and mutual respect. The stability of these norms, their embeddedness in the minds and behavior of citizens, ensures respect for the citizens of the other democracy. All this leads closer to Boulding's stable peace and to Deutsch's security community.

These alternative paradigms exist not only in the realm of the abstract: each also leads to a discrete policy. Once one accepts that democracies do not fight each other, the policy implication should be to support democratization abroad. Allegedly, each state that becomes a democracy ceases to be a security threat to other democracies. To enlarge the number of democracies is to enlarge the zone of peace.

But how can other countries and societies be democratized? Broadly speaking, democratization policies can be divided into two types, derived directly from the definitions of democracy. If democracy means having a structure including elections, division of powers, and checks and balances, democratization implies *building this structure*; in other words, it emphasizes the formal, the procedural, and the structural. It also means investing efforts in the state apparatus, in the "old" or institutional politics. If, on the other hand, democracy is taken to mean the kind of culture and morality that produces a civic community, then democratization implies *constructing this community*. It means the socialization and dissemination of democratic values to foster a democratic society and culture, mainly by facilitating domestic agents of political and social transformation in the target country. It means investing efforts on the social and individual levels, trying to construct a civil society of informed, involved, and participating citizens.

The Different Theoretical Constructions

Here, I want to focus on articles that typify the two paradigms of democratic peace. However, before I do so, I would like to analyze several articles that can be classified as preliminary writing on the subject, and serve as important signposts in the development and maturation of the democratic peace theories. First, I dwell briefly on the article that brought the democratic peace to life after a century and a half in which it was known only as Kant's Republican Peace. For a seminal article, it has remained quite anonymous, unread, and less quoted than other articles on the democratic peace. It was published as early as 1964, not by an International Relations scholar but rather by a criminologist: Dean Babst. Furthermore, the venue of publication was not one of the prestigious International Relations journals, but rather a less widely circulated sociological journal, the *Wisconsin Sociologist*. The article is a mere six pages in length, and as Babst himself admits, it is only "a preliminary test of this hypothesis" (1964:9); the hypothesis that "freely elected governments of independent countries, the borders of which are firmly established," would be less disposed to "make war against each other" (1964:9). As a preliminary test, it indeed utilizes very simplistic and rudimentary statistical tools, but then again, exploratory articles can probably suffice with just that (and being just six pages long).

Babst established the observation that democracies do not make war against each other, and he believed his results were robust enough to call them (as seen from the title of the article)—"a force for peace," and to conclude the article with the following prescriptive conclusion, "The rapid increase in the number of elective governments since World War II is an encouraging sign. Diplomatic efforts at war prevention might well be directed toward further accelerating this growth" (1964:14). Yet the article remained almost forgotten until 1972, when Babst published a second version, which was shorter and more popular. This time the tidings were more widely circulated and Babst's message began to spread: there was apparently something theoretically interesting and normatively attractive about the subject of freely elected democratic governments. A decade later, the seeds that criminologist Babst planted were reaped by International Relations scholars.

1983 was the year two influential articles were published that contributed substantially to the development of the democratic peace theories. One was R. J. Rummel's "Libertarianism and International Violence," which appeared in the *Journal of Conflict Resolution*. The other, by Michael Doyle, was the mammoth, two-part article, "Kant, Liberal Legacies, and Foreign Affairs," which appeared in *Philosophy and Public Affairs*. These two articles differ in more than one way: Rummel's work is a piece of empirical quantitative research, while Doyle's article is more philosophical and seeks to revive Kant's *Perpetual Peace* and update it to the twentieth century. Rummel makes a forceful monadic assertion, whereas Doyle's article is more subtle and puts forward a dyadic argument. Both, however, share the rudimentary characteristics of exploratory pieces. In neither does the term "democratic peace" appear. Moreover, each article focuses on a unit of analysis other than democracy. Rummel hails the libertarian state, and Doyle acclaims liberal society. Although both entities are parallel to democracy, and congruent with it to a degree, neither is democracy per se. Consequently, neither offers what a decade later became known as the "democratic peace." These articles mark an historical phase in the resurgence and coming to age of the democratic peace theories as they were nascent articles which held many, yet not all, of the necessary democratic peace ingredients. However, returning to what set them apart, we can identify a deeper cleavage between the two, in the sense that each article has a different moral and ideological framework. Rummel is influenced by right libertarianism, and Doyle by left welfarism.

For Rummel, the key to the absence of official violence between states is the extent of freedom exercised within them. The unit of analysis is the state, the explanatory variable is the extent of freedom exercised in the state, and the correlation between the two is inverse: the more freedom is exercised internally, the less official violence the state will employ externally. The libertarian state is the ideal state with respect to official violence (or better still, the lack of it). In the libertarian state, the freedom exercised limits the elites, allowing and encouraging exchange between individuals. That exchange in turn creates an interlocking balance of powers that restrains conflicts and violence. In Rummel's words,

> libertarian states comprise social fields in which the actions of groups and individuals respond to many divergent and opposing social and psy-

chological forces. These forces spontaneously resolve into interlocking and nested balances of powers and associated structures of expectations. These define the social order. Such systems (like the free market) tend to be self-regulating and to isolate and inhibit conflicts and violence when they occur. They tend to encourage exchange, rather than coercive and violent solutions, in conflict between groups and individuals. (1983:28)

But this basic theoretical assertion has a more fundamental moral foundation, which we can identify once we focus on Rummel's concepts and definitions.

For Rummel, freedom consists of two mutually empowering factors.

By theory, libertarian will have two meanings, one a limited version of the other. The first is *political freedom*, involving civil liberties and political rights—what we usually mean by a democratic, open system. Second, there is *freedom* in a more expansive sense, which includes not only political freedom, but also the freedom of groups and individuals to pursue their socioeconomic interests free from government coercion. The latter reflects the classical-liberal idea of limited and minimal government. (1983:30)

Reading these lines, it becomes clear that freedom according to Rummel is mainly the kind of negative liberty Isaiah Berlin endorses (1969), in the sense of freedom from external and arbitrary intervention in a person's life. The state Rummel supports is a minimalist state stripped to its bare necessities—the state as "night watchman," which is responsible mainly for public order and security, which together ensure the stability necessary for personal autonomy and a successful free market economy. Rummel's definitions bring to mind Robert Nozick's *Anarchy, State, and Utopia* (1974), the book so admired by the American right, following its sanctification of individual liberty and its enshrinement in personal property. Nozick's vision is of a society marked mainly by economic relations based on voluntary exchanges—or, as Rummel puts it, "Freedom is best measured by the degree to which governmental power is decentralized and limited and society is based on exchange" (1983:30). This is indeed the epitome of right libertarianism, and according to Rummel, the liberty exercised in social-democratic states is far from sufficient, "While political freedom is consistent with a large, democratic-socialist government, as in Sweden or Denmark, I argue that such centralized, semi-socialist governments introduce a considerable measure of coercion that contributes to foreign violence" (1983:30). Because of their social-democratic nature, Sweden and Denmark cannot enjoy the full benefits of the libertarian peace. Not, according to Rummel, to the degree enjoyed by states like Botswana.

Rummel himself admits this moral and ideological foundation toward the end of his article. He raises several possible challenges to his theoretical framework.

> all studies of conflict have some explicit or implicit normative premises or point of view. Often these are ideological, as are those defining social justice and positive peace as equality or those that use the value-laden concept of structural violence. Regardless, one should not try to eliminate any of this, but rather to make normative assumptions explicit and honest by incorporating them into a clear theory, and insofar as is possible, make them part of whatever empirical testing is done. (1983:67–68)

If this is indeed the case, and I do agree with Rummel on this point, the strong libertarian commitment found in his theory should come as no surprise. Nor is it surprising that Rummel enthusiastically supported the Bush Doctrine and its implementation in Iraq. In his personal blog, he gave arguments supporting the war, based on his interpretations of the democratic peace theory. Thus, for example, on November 2, 2005, Rummel wrote, "So, why are we fighting in Iraq and fostering democratic freedom there and elsewhere? The answer is to promote an end to war, and democide, and to minimize internal political violence. In other words, it is to foster global human security. Surely, this is worth fighting for" (2009).

The same holds true for Doyle, albeit from a different moral and ideological groundwork. For Doyle, the issue in question is the "liberal peace" (1983a:222), and rather than offering social science research, he offers us a journey into the history of philosophy. Truths are not to be discovered anew by some sophisticated methodology borrowed from science. Truths, or rather the Truth, can be attained by philosophical reasoning and analytical theorizing assisted by a close familiarity with the corpus of philosophical literature and its history—in this case, Kant's *Perpetual Peace* (1903:122–23). Latter in his mammoth, two-part article, Doyle indeed closely follows Kant's three definitive articles and elaborates on why they were right in Kant's lifetime, and why they are still so relevant.

The theoretical bottom line is similar to Rummel's in that it is quite rudimentary and sketchy. Doyle does not propose a theory in the sense of a parsimonious explanatory schema. Rather, he offers a multifaceted theoretical framework, which resembles a philosophical treatise more than a social science theory. However, the theoretical framework is somewhat similar to Rummel's. Liberty is the key to international peace by establishing mutually beneficial exchanges between states that is free of arbitrary interference by state institutions—interference that, at times, can lead to violent international relations. Doyle asserts that "When states respect each other's rights, individuals are free to establish private international ties without state interference. Profitable exchanges between merchants and educational exchanges among scholars then create a web of mutual advantages and commitments that bolsters sentiments of public respect" (1983a:213).

But any resemblance between Doyle and Rummel is superficial. On a deeper level, their definitions of freedom are very different. For Rummel, freedom is mainly negative—the freedom from arbitrary interferences. For Doyle, negative freedom is necessary, but not sufficient. Negative liberty must be accompanied by the positive form of liberty—the liberty that enables, even assures, that citizens can enjoy their negative liberty. As Doyle puts it, "Liberalism calls for freedom from arbitrary authority, often called 'negative freedom,' which includes freedom of conscience, a free press and free speech, equality under the law, and the right to hold, and therefore to exchange, property without fear of arbitrary seizure. Liberalism also calls for those rights necessary to protect and promote the capacity and opportunity for freedom, the 'positive freedoms'" (1983a:206–7). As welfarists like to stress ironically, negative liberty by itself may guarantee one's prospects for freely dying of hunger unaided by others. And therefore, for welfarists, positive liberty needs to be established on the shoulders of negative liberty to guarantee that free citizens can also use their freedom to pursue personal goals and achieve happiness. This means that (positive) freedom encompasses social and economic rights that guarantee at least equality of opportunity: "Such social and economic rights as equality of opportunity in education and rights to health care and employment, necessary for effective self-expression and participation, are thus among liberal rights" (1983a:207).

Moreover, Doyle does not suffice with these two concepts of liberty, arguing instead that liberalism demands a third set of rights—the political rights of participation: "A third liberal right, democratic participation or representation, is necessary to guarantee the other two. To ensure that morally autonomous individuals remain free in those areas of social action where public authority is needed, public legislation has to express the will of the citizens making laws for their own community" (1983a:207). Understood thus, liberalism is no longer the Nozickian-like libertarianism endorsed so enthusiastically by Rummel, but rather the liberalism of John Rawls, the leading philosopher of American welfarism, who constructed his theory of justice around the concept of fairness and obligation to benefit all members of society (Rawls 1999). Liberalism for Doyle, who follows Rawls, is a political set of ideas and norms. And the entity that he explores is not the state but rather society, and society is responsible through the state to provide all individuals with three sets of rights in the form of negative freedoms, positive freedoms, and political participation. The prescribed state is not the "night watchman," but rather the welfare state, fashioned as to universally provide its citizens (and mostly the least well-off) with their needs; a state that is based on and guaranteed by a society bound together in solidarity.

Doyle maintains that a society that guarantees and universally ensures these rights will enjoy liberal peace, but only with other liberal societies. Unlike Rummel, he contends that liberal peace is a dyadic, rather than a monadic phenomenon. And indeed, the second part of Doyle's article provides an in-depth exploration of the other side of the phenomenon (1983b): what was later dubbed "the dark side of democratic peace" (Geis, Lothar, and Müller 2006); in other words, how liberal societies wage war, carry out democratic crusades, and even exploit non-liberal societies economically. For Doyle, the mutual expectations of liberal states and societies are what engender liberal peace: "In short, domestically just republics, which rest on consent, presume foreign republics to be also consensual, just, and therefore deserving of accommodation. The experience of cooperation helps engender further cooperative behavior when the consequences of state policy are unclear but (potentially) mutually beneficial" (1983a:30:230; see also Doyle 1986:1161). This theoretical reliance on mutual expectations for accommodation brings Doyle, as we see shortly, very close to the normative theories of democratic peace.

However, before we explore the normative theories of democratic peace, I wish to raise another issue that Doyle highlighted, further examined later; namely, the role and responsibilities of social science theorists.

Of course, this pacific calculus further assumes that, as Kant required in his "Second Supplement," a "Secret Article" be included in the treaty for a Perpetual Peace: "The maxims of the philosophers concerning the conditions of the possibility of public peace shall be consulted by the states which are ready to go to war." To this proviso, we need add that the greater complexity of international relations today calls for economists, political scientists, sociologists, and psychologists as well as natural scientists to add their advice to that of the philosophers. (1983b:352–53)

This theme is later explored in depth. For now, however, let us note that for Doyle, the liberal peace carries with it certain crucial benefits, and that it is within the reach of academics to help their societies attain this benevolent state of affairs and harvest its fruits. As we see later, although I share this normative interest with Doyle, I am far from convinced that it is so straightforward to secure this involvement by academics.

To summarize: even though Rummel's and Doyle's articles do bear several superficial resemblances, mainly in that they are exploratory and sketchy, they are separated by certain fundamental differences that are driven by normative and ideological disagreements. Rummel's theory is based on right libertarianism that focuses on voluntary and private exchanges between minimal states. Doyle's philosophy, on the other hand, is founded on left welfarism, focusing on a robust conceptualization of societies.

A decade later, in 1993, the democratic peace thesis truly came of age. In an oft-quoted article, Zeev Maoz and Bruce Russett injected the democratic peace into the lifeblood of International Relations. They did so in the very prestigious journal that has continued to publish quantitative articles on the democratic peace, the *American Political Science Review*. In the skilled hands of Maoz and Russett there was no questioning that the phenomenon under study is peace between democracies, and not some other kind of peace—say between libertarian states or liberal societies. Additionally, the article contributed greatly to the recognition that, indeed, there were two distinct families of theory out there, rivaling each other to explain the democratic peace—the normative theory and the structural theory. Moreover, theirs was no exploration, but the thing itself: the state of the art of positivist social science using highly sophisticated methodologies. However, as shortly becomes clear, even in this citadel of scientism there was no escape from the normative assumptions that lie at the foundation of the research.

An outstanding and innovative feature of the article was its consistent and persistent use of the term democratic peace, including in the title itself. The term democratic peace had already surfaced and started to circulate in academic publications around 1992; for example, in a special section titled "Democracy, War and Peace" in the *Journal of Peace Research*,[5] and in Maoz and Russett's presentation of their article at the 1992 annual conference of the International Studies Association. But until 1993, the academic use of the term was quite sporadic. Through their continuing use of it, Maoz and Russett, along with Russett's 1993 book *Grasping the Democratic Peace*, contributed to establishing the term and gaining its embrace by academic circles.

Maoz and Russett began their article by declaring that "Recognition of the democratic-peace result is probably one of the most significant nontrivial products of the scientific study of world politics. It may also be the basis of far more important insights into the workings of the international political world in modern times" (1993:624). In that declaration they were following in the footsteps of Jack Levy, who was one of the first to declare the absence of war between democracies as the closest thing to a law. In 1988, Levy argued, "This absence of war between democracies comes as close as anything we have to an empirical law in international relations" (1988:662). It is rightly pointed out by James Lee Ray that Levy made this declaration without any comprehensive statistical analysis (2003:211). At the time, he was basing this powerful conclusion mainly on Babst. Moreover, in 1988, it was too early to use the term democratic peace. In 1994, Levy revisited his 1988 conclusion and repeated it more forcefully, this time under the explicit title of the democratic peace, "the idea that democracies almost never go to war with each other is now commonplace. The skeptics are in retreat and the proposition has acquired a nearly law-like status" (1994:352).

However, as much as agreement did exist as to the empirical observation's validity regarding this absence of war between democracies, there was, at the time, and there still is now, less agreement regarding its cause. Of course there are those skeptics who bring forth alternative explanatory variables unrelated to democracy. Such skeptics ascribe the absence of war to explanations like economic development, Cold War mechanisms, Small N of democracies, and lack of shared borders between the few democracies that do exist. But, such critics offered no interest for Maoz and Russett in their 1993 article. For them, and for many others—as Levy states very forcefully—this debate was over. Maoz and Russett accepted their thesis as almost self-evident: "There is something in the internal makeup of democratic states that prevents them from fighting one another *despite the fact that they are not less conflict-prone than nondemocracies"* (1993:624). In other words, it is their democraticness, and no other variable, that prevents states from fighting each other.[6] The second point this quotation highlights is that democratic peace is dyadic and valid only within democracy dyads. The task Maoz and Russett took upon themselves in the article was to decide which of the two explanations—the normative or the structural—is the strongest, which one provided the correct and valid theory of democratic peace.

The normative theory of democratic peace is based on two assumptions. First, "States, to the extent possible, externalize the norms of behavior that are developed within and characterize their domestic political processes and institutions." Second, "The anarchic nature of international politics implies that a clash between democratic and nondemocratic norms is dominated by the latter, rather than by the former" (1993:625). These assumptions jointly construct an explanation based on the fundamental role of political norms, which they call "democratic norms"—norms that state: "Political conflicts in democracies are resolved through compromise rather than through elimination of opponents. This norm allows for an atmosphere of 'live and let live' that results in a fundamental sense of stability at the personal, communal, and national level" (1993:625). The critical point is that these norms are public knowledge and create an image that is transmitted internationally between democracies (1993:625), and help to settle their conflicts peacefully by resorting to compromise rather than arms. Put differently, the democratic norms of compromise transcend the international borders of democracies and cause their relations to be peaceful—hence the term "democratic peace."

The structural theory of democratic peace is also based on two assumptions. First, "International challenges require political leaders to mobilize domestic support to their policies. Such support must be mobilized from those groups that provide the leadership the kind of legitimacy that is required for international action" (1993:626). Second, "Shortcuts to political mobilization of relevant political support can be accomplished only in situations that can be appropriately described as emergencies" (1993:626). Together, these two assumptions construct an explanation that stresses the crucial role played by the democratic institutions of checks and balances between the different branches of democratic government, and no less important, between the executive branch and the electorate to which it is accountable. All these place hurdles before a government's ability to muster legitimacy for unnecessary international adventurism. Additionally, the democratic structure slows down decision-making and policy implementation, and allows more time to settle conflicts peacefully. Thus,

> due to the complexity of the democratic process and the requirement of securing a broad base of support for risky policies, democratic leaders are reluctant to wage wars, except in cases wherein war seems a necessity or when the war aims are seen as justifying the mobilization costs. The time required for a democratic state to prepare for war is far longer than for nondemocracies. Thus, in a conflict between democracies, by the time the two states are militarily ready for war, diplomats have the opportunity to find a nonmilitary solution to the conflict. (1993:626)

Although the normative and structural models are presented as different, Maoz and Russett readily admit that they are not mutually exclusive, and that they only emphasize "different facets of democratic politics that are presumably responsible for the democratic-peace phenomenon" (1993:626). The question is then, why bother with what seems like an artificial exercise of pinning down an elusive variable? Of fishing out what naturally exists in concert? This is not the kind of effort found in Kant, or Doyle. They took quite the opposite approach. They seemed to weave together different threads into a more holistic understanding of the operative mechanisms of democracy (or more accurately, republicanism in Kant, and liberalism in Doyle) to achieve peaceful relations. Theirs was a philosophical approach, whereas Maoz and Russett seem driven by a scientific quest for a parsimonious explanation, to identify that single variable that offers the strongest causal relations between different phenomena. This scientific compulsion drives them to discover that magic ingredient in democracy that produces peace, even when that factor does not, and cannot, exclude other things in democracy. Can democratic norms really explain peace, or is it the democratic structure that can explain it? Kant and Doyle, who represent the more philosophical kind of inquiry, would probably find this quest for a parsimonious explanation not too attractive. Probably they would have settled with what Maoz and Russett admit, but struggle against, "Note that our stability measure is not fully distinct from structures. It can also be an institutional constraint in the limited sense than an unstable democracy is subject to overthrow, releasing the institutional constraints on leaders" (1993:630).

Add to that the operationalization of distinguishing the two models—"Obviously, it is extremely difficult to distinguish between these models in terms of contradictory predictions. Normative and structural explanations are often not well differentiated conceptually, thus enhancing the difficulties of testing them as alternative hypotheses" (1993:626). We are left staggered by the enormous effort to distinguish the two models. Even more so, we are puzzled by the conclusiveness with which Maoz and Russett decide between them. For Maoz and Russett, although the structural model provides some explanatory power, the normative model carries the day and is hailed as the valid theoretical explanation for the democratic peace.

> The relationship of the structural model to conflict occurrence is not nearly as robust as the normative results. Institutional constraints do prevent escalation to war, but they do not prevent states from entering into lower-level disputes-engaging in the kind of lower-level bargaining behavior that conveys toughness and commitment . . . Normative restraints, on the other hand, help to prevent even the emergence of conflicts. Insofar as democracies only rarely engage in such conflicts, normative restraints seem to deserve the greater credit. (1993:634–35)

This certainty is especially mystifying once we note two other problems in their research program. The first is that although they try to quantify and measure all of the data, they admit having to apply their judgment to the most problematic—and critical—cases.

> Toward the extremes, these judgments are not problematic, but around zero the regime characteristics are not clearly defined. Either democratic and authoritarian features may cancel each other out if a state scores fairly high on both, or the power concentration score may be so low that even if the regime is predominantly democratic or authoritarian the characteristics cannot effectively express themselves. This situation is common in highly unstable political systems or in systems undergoing rapid change. Though more recent than these codings, conditions in the Soviet Union in 1990–92 offer a good example. (1993:628)

A second problem that springs from their research program is that due to the significant problems of measuring norms, they use mainly structural criteria to measure the degree of democratic-ness of different states: "the level of authority of a political system as a combination of (1) competitiveness of political participation, (2) regulation of participation, (3) competitiveness of executive recruitment, (4) openness of executive recruitment, and (5) constraints on the chief executive" (1993:628). These are definitely structural criteria. And to measure democratic norms, they use the highly problematic proxy measures of deaths from political violence and extent of domestic conflict (1993:630). These proxy measurements are based on the plausible assumption that democratic norms prevent violence and death. But, plausible as this may be, it is precisely what they ought to have established and proved. As it stands, the article tells us that Maoz and Russett fell into the common trap of assuming what must be proven. Which leaves us with a striking discrepancy. On the one hand, Maoz and Russett declare they have scientifically and quantitatively examine the two models—the normative and the structural—but in fact, the measurement they actually employ are structural, and these structural measurements too are based on personal judgment. Taking these problems together, it is highly surprising to find these researchers so convinced of the superiority of the normative model, and it is important to challenge the basis for their assurance. Their conclusiveness is certainly not based on positivist proofs. On the contrary, positivist methodology has become so enknotted that there is only one way out—a priori normative assumptions. The theoretical conclusiveness enjoyed by Maoz and Russett stems from no more than their liberal moral convictions and commitment to the normative, participatory, and deliberative understanding of democracy. We also find support for this in other writings by Russett where he shows a clear and strong commitment to the normative and participatory understanding of democracy (see, for example, Alker Jr. and Russett 1965; Hartley and Russett 1992; Maoz and Russett 1992b; Russett 1993a; Russett, O'Neil, and Sutterlin 1996).

Another issue raised by the article concerns the mutually constitutive relations between the two fundamental theoretical/political concepts of democracy and war/peace. The superiority of the normative explanation is owed to the fact that democratic norms actually limit the very possibility of conflict, whereas structural restraints merely prevent the escalation of conflict into war.

> The relationship of the structural model to conflict occurrence is not nearly as robust as the normative results. Institutional constraints do

prevent escalation to war, but they do not prevent states from entering into lower-level disputes-engaging in the kind of lower-level bargaining behavior that conveys toughness and commitment . . . Normative restraints, on the other hand, help to prevent even the emergence of conflicts. Insofar as democracies only rarely engage in such conflicts, normative restraints seem to deserve the greater credit. (1993:634–35)

It is clear from this quotation that a structural understanding of democracy is grounded in an understanding of peace as simply the absence of war, whereas the normative understanding of democracy offers a more positive reading of peace—as the absence of conflict—as a sort of rudimentary security community at least. This reading is further substantiated if we read Russett's article in Adler and Barnet's edited book on *Security Communities* (1988). Here, Russett clearly integrates the two theoretical agendas into a single theory in which democratic peace clearly relates to the construction of a community, a security community based on a strong "we feeling." Indeed, the concepts of democracy and peace do not exist in isolation, but rather are seen to endow each other with meaning.

A final important point with regard to Maoz and Russett's article is that they conclude their article with a normative assertion, "But if enough states become stably democratic—as may be happening in the 1990s—then the possibility emerges of reconstructing the norms and rules of the international system to reflect those of democracies. A system created by autocracies may be recreated by a critical mass of democratic states" (1993:637). This is a normative conclusion that to some extent goes against Maoz and Russett positivist commitment, which assumes and prescribes a sharp distinction between the research and what is being researched, as well as between fact and value. To blur these two fundamental distinctions undermines positivist aspirations toward objective science. From their concluding remarks, one can detect that Maoz and Russett's factual analysis is in fact entangled with normative goals. If not my previous musing, this should provide sufficient support for the normative agenda that does drive democratic peace scholars.

A second article exemplifying normative theory is William Dixon's article "Democracy and the Peaceful Settlement of International Conflict," which was published a year later, in 1994, again by the *American Political Science Review*. This article is also infected by the same bewilderments reflected in Maoz and Russett's work. In this article, Dixon also examines the two explanations for democratic peace, opting for the normative model, which he believes explains why democracies lend themselves to peaceful settlements. Dixon starts and ends his article similarly to Maoz and Russett's opening and conclusion. He begins the article by linking the theory to Kant and stressing its dyadic formulation.

> We now know, as Kant could only speculate, that over the last two centuries democratic states have rarely engaged one another in violent military conflict and, by some criteria, virtually never in a full-scale war. Yet we also know that democracies are no less prone to foreign conflict and war than states organized under alternative arrangements. Unfortunately, there is considerably less consensus about why democracies behave this way. (1994:14)

He then goes on to emphasize that there is broad agreement over the fact of democratic peace, yet no agreement about its explanation, "There is little doubt about the existence of the democratic peace; on this, the historical record has been manifestly clear. What is not yet settled is *why* democratic states behave in this curious way" (1994:15). Like Maoz and Russett, he goes about deciding between the two models, even though as he himself admits, "norms and institutions go hand in hand and any effort to untangle their causal implications faces serious obstacles" (1994:15). To confront this challenge, Dixon says we must begin "with a clear conception of democracy" (1994:15). And the essential feature of democracy, the characteristic that defines it conclusively, is for Dixon the norm of bounded competition (1994:15). Moreover, in an act that links him to the normative and participatory understanding of democracy, Dixon assigns fairly extensive roles to the citizens of democracies, "Competitive processes may take a wide variety of forms and involve many types of actors, including the political elites who legislate and execute policy at all levels and the citizens who organize and express their interests through a bewildering array of associative arrangements" (1994:15).

All this points to Dixon's endorsement of the normative understanding of democracy. And when Dixon tries to measure the indicators of democracy, the picture becomes clearer still. While he supposedly examines the normative model and embraces a normative conceptualization of democracy, he actually brings as corroboration those same structural indicators endorsed by Maoz and Russett. He explicitly identifies them as institutional indicators "Because the notion of democracy underlying this scale emphasizes political institutions, I follow Gurr, Jaggers, and Moore . . . in referring to it as *institutionalized democracy*" (1994:21). Structural indicators are the easiest markers, and maybe even the only operationalizable method to measure democracy and identify a parsimonious explanation (1994:23). But then you wonder if this involves looking for a coin under a street lamp when you know you lost it somewhere else, somewhere dark and unlit by street lamps? Dixon does not engage himself in such questioning. He sets himself the awkward task of proving the superiority of the normative model by examining structural criteria. It is the same problem identified in Maoz and Russett, and I offer the same answer as I offered earlier. We can understand this puzzle if we understand Dixon's moral and ideological convictions, and his commitments and allegiance to the normative and participatory understanding of democracy—convictions and commitments that are also evident from the political roles he assigns democracies' citizens.

In Dixon's case as well, we find the mutually constitutive relationship between democracy and war/peace. For Dixon, the added value of his article lies in establishing that democracies not only cause peace but assure accommodation and what he calls "peaceful settlement."

> In brief, I argue that democratic states locked in disputes are better equipped than others with the means for diffusing conflict situations at an early stage before they have an opportunity to escalate to military violence. This explanatory logic is consistent with the published findings on democracy and war and also entails an empirical proposition, namely, that disputes between democracies, more than other types of disputes, lend themselves to a form of accommodation I term *peaceful settlements*. (1994:14)

The democratic norms of bounded competition and the participatory role of the democratic citizen are externalized between democracies to guarantee this sort of mutual accommodation and reconciliation, which already exists in their own domestic political arena. This accommodation is far stronger and more robust than the mere absence of war.

> Each party to a purely democratic dispute is secure in the knowledge that its opponent is also normatively proscribed from violent and coer-

cive means for reconciling divergent values and interests, at least in the domestic political arena. These norms are externalized to foreign affairs only if the practices underlying them are sufficiently robust to foster mutual expectations of congruent behavior beyond borders. (1994:17)

Like Maoz and Russett, Dixon's article ends on a similar note of normative hope and expectation: "In the meantime, however, this study has given us further reason to hope for an expanding zone of democratic peace not altogether unlike the one Kant envisioned some two centuries ago" (1994:30). This concluding remark raises the same post-positivist puzzlement regarding Dixon's objective positivism as noted earlier for the role of normative goals in the positivist research program.

The question now is: can we find the same results in the structural explanations of the democratic peace? Initially, I described the structural explanations as focusing on the structural dimensions of democracy, arguing that the division of power, checks and balances, and leadership accountability to the public makes the decision-making process complex and slow, and allows decision makers in democratic states to settle their conflicts peacefully. However this definition was very rudimentary, even simplistic. Structural theory has developed into a very sophisticated body of literature, analyzing how the structure of democracy generates mechanisms that reduce the chances of war between democracies. In the following pages, I focus on two exemplary articles that demonstrate the theoretical sophistication of this theory, but demonstrate, once again, that theory is indeed a theoretical construction, a form of political thought that endows its theoretical/political concepts with meanings borrowed from normative reasoning. The first article is James Fearon's "Domestic Political Audiences and the Escalation of International Disputes" (1994), another in the *American Political Science Review*'s remarkable series of outpouring on the democratic peace. The second is "An Institutional Explanation of the Democratic Peace" (1999), by Bruce Bueno de Mesquita, James Morrow, Randolph Siverson, and Alastair Smith, published once again in the *American Political Science Review*.

Fearon's article incorporates the concept of audience cost into the democratic peace literature. This theoretical step helps him to integrate the democratic peace thesis with the theoretical framework of the security dilemma. Using formal modeling, Fearon explores the impact of audience cost on the dynamics of crisis escalation and de-escalation. As with game theory and formal modeling, Fearon makes several very strong assumptions that crisis is a dynamic process that builds up in stages, over time. At each stage the parties signal their intentions and their determination. The result is a "war of nerves." Troop deployment and public threats cause crises to become public events in which domestic audiences observe and assess their leadership's performance" (1994:577). Leaders on both sides attempt to assess their rival's intentions, capabilities, and determination, and decide whether to take the crisis to the next step, or to de-escalate. Fearon additionally assumes that different political structures generate different sensitivity to audience cost. Although Fearon never formally defines audience cost, generally speaking, it is considered the price a leader will pay to keep the leadership. In a democracy, the audience cost is higher, and according to Fearon, a leader who chooses to de-escalate a crisis will find it harder to keep his or her post. Thus, audience cost is a crucial—maybe even the most crucial—consideration for leaders when deciding whether to escalate or de-escalate a crisis. Moreover, the public in both countries also knows the audience cost as it is communicated publicly between the parties to the crisis. It is a sort of public knowledge, and thus influences each leader's assessment of the other side's determination, "audience costs make escalation in a crisis an informative although noisy signal of a state's true intentions" (1994:577).

The result of this theoretical apparatus is that it is public knowledge that democracies means business in their crisis management. No sane democratic leader would choose escalation if he or she has reason to believe they will have to chicken out. If a democratic leader opts to escalate a crisis, the reasonable conclusion is that he or she means business, and will be willing to go all the way. As in any formal modeling, Fearon's assumptions are very strong, even crude, which he readily admits, especially with regard to democratic leaders being more sensitive to audience costs. Fearon acknowledges that "the price of losing power is often greater for a dictator than for an elected leader" (1994:582). This, of course, complicates matters a little, though he insists all the same that, "The idea that democratic leaders on average have an easier time generating audience costs is advanced here as a plausible working hypothesis that has interesting theoretical and empirical implications" (1994:582). Thus, "stronger domestic audiences may make democracies better able to signal intentions and credibly to commit to courses of action in foreign policy than nondemocracies, features that might help ameliorate "the security dilemma" between democratic states" (1994:578). However, since sensitivity to audience cost is the model's main basic assumption, admitting this weakness shakes the reliability of the model.

Fearon shows an entirely structural understanding of democracy. His is a political structure with such a high audience cost that any leader with the universal desire to keep his or her post will take this factor into consideration. Fearon introduces the idea that actual audience cost has a strong conventional aspect, and that its form and the way it is experienced "depends on shared perceptions and expectations in a society" (1994:581). But this is essentially it with regard to norms and values. All that is theoretically important is the leader's sensitivity to audience costs, and that, basically, is Fearon's only insight on the essence of democracy. Democracy is indeed the kind of regime that due to its structural features generates high sensitivity to audience costs. Here, the key concept is accountability, which is conceptualized as the scrutiny of leaders by their citizens ("the audience")—and nothing more.

Fearon's understanding of the chances of democracies going to war is similarly thin. He does not completely rule out the possibility of war. Rather, he couches his belief in the reduced possibility of war between democracies in very modest and cautious phrasing, "If democracies are better able to communicate their intentions and to make international commitments, then the security dilemma may be somewhat moderated between them" (1994:587). Fearon voices his reflections on the paradigmatic affinities of his theoretical findings in a similar vein: "I have shown how the presence of a politically significant domestic audience can improve a democratic leader's ability to commit to a course of action and to signal privately known preferences and intentions in a clear, credible fashion. These are advantages that could help in the game of realpolitik and might also make democracies better able to cope with the security dilemma" (1994:587). It is not the realm of Kant that dominates here, but rather a restrained Hobbes. Realism rules, though in a regulated format; one that accepts the possibility for a rational solution to the allegedly insolvable problem of the security dilemma, though, of course, only between democracies.

The same themes were further developed five years later, again in the *American Political Science Review*, in an article authored by Bruce Bueno de Mesquita, James Morrow, Randolph Siverson, and Alastair Smith. Bueno de Mesquita et al. are not satisfied with explaining the phenomenon of democratic peace alone, and they tie it into eight patterns, which they claim are related to it through the independent variable, democracy.

> Associated with this so-called democratic peace are seven additional empirical regularities related to war proneness and democracy, all based on empirical observations. (1) Democracies are not at all immune from fighting wars with nondemocracies . . . (2) Democracies tend to win a disproportionate share of the wars they fight . . . (3) When disputes do emerge, democratic dyads choose more peaceful processes of dispute settlement than do other pairings of states . . . (4) Democracies are more likely to initiate wars against autocracies than are autocracies against democracies . . . (5) In wars they initiate, democracies pay fewer costs in terms of human life and fight shorter wars than nondemocratic states . . . (6) Transitional democracies appear more likely to fight than stable regimes . . . (7) Larger democracies seem more constrained to avoid war than do smaller democracies. (1999:791)

They argue that a sound theory of democratic peace will need to explain all, or at least, as many as possible of these regularities.

The behavioralist perspective of Bueno de Mesquita et al. treats norms and values as nothing more than behavioral incentives, where the only universal incentive they acknowledge is the desire to achieve and retain office. This is the nexus around which their structural analysis is centered. Like Fearon's article and other game modeling, they advance simplistic assumptions that are too simplistic, even according to them. This is especially true with regard to their main assumptions that the primary goal of all leaders is to retain their seat. Similar to Fearon, Bueno de Mesquita et al. make a brief comment that, "being ousted is more often fatal for autocrats than democrats. Our assumption, however, is that the primary goal of all leaders is to keep their job. Given this, the principal, component in every leader's objective function is reselection" (1999:797). Disregarding any questions as to the verity of this assumption, questions to which they themselves refer, they proceed with their sophisticated theoretical construction. Instead of talking about audience cost, they talk about selectorates and winning coalitions. The former refers to all those with a right to participate in choosing a government; the latter is a subset of the selectorate, whose support is necessary to form and keep the government (1999:793). According to this cynical reading of politics, incumbents do all in their power (and legitimate power is not considered a limitation to executive power) to keep their job. They will tap into scarce national resources in whatever way will efficiently allow them to buy support from the winning coalition. The incumbent must therefore decide whether to use the national resources as a public good to be distributed among all members of the selectorate, or as a private good allocated just to the winning coalition. The decision will not be based on norms and values, only on the tactical utility. However, the problem in a democracy is that the selectorate is large, and so is the winning coalition. Therefore, because of the considerable size of the winning coalition, allocating them private goods would not do, as each member of the winning coalition would be left with only a small quantity of these goods (1999:797). Thus driven by necessity, the incumbent will opt for the public good allocation tactic. And that means he or she will be concerned with policy failure, especially with regard to winning and losing wars: "One consequence is that democratic leaders, being just as eager to retain office as their authoritarian counterparts, must be especially concerned about policy failure. To reduce the risk of policy failure and subsequent deposition, they make a larger effort to succeed in disputes. This means that they are willing to spend more resources on war effort and only engage in fights they anticipate winning" (1999:794). Take note, the conceptualization of accountability employed by Bueno de Mesquita et al. is a very restricted and structured one, constrained by the incumbents' calculations of the efficiency of tactics available for buying the job. All is permissible in this view of democracy, and the only difference between democracy and autocracy is the size of the winning coalition as a proportion of the selectorate. As they are keen to emphasize, "Our model explains these diverse phenomena without attributing superior motives or greater civic mindedness to one kind of leader over another. The explanation is driven purely by self-interested leaders who seek to retain office and face alternative institutional arrangements" (1999:805). It is very much an elitist Schumpeterian perception, in which democracy is no more than a competition between members of the elite over governance. According to this view, the public's only role is to participate in elections every few years and decide which contestant wins.

The next theoretical move in the model is that due to their inability to buy their seats with private good and their consequential need to succeed in their policies, especially their wars, democratic incumbents do not attack if they do not anticipate victory, and they also try harder to win the wars they do fight (1999:799). Hence, "Because autocrats do not try as hard in war, they make attractive targets for democracies" (1999:799), and democracies will tend not to attack each other. But as this is the reason and not some sort of normative commitment or democratic communal bonding, the peace between democracies is indeed merely the probabilistic and temporal absence of war. There is no guarantee for peace, far from it.

> Our theory does not state that a war between democracies is impossible. Rather, we show that the conditions under which a democrat will attack another democrat are more restrictive than the conditions under which a democrat will attack an autocrat . . . Autocrats always are the more attractive targets, but when two democratic leaders have unsuccessful domestic policies, war between democracies is most likely. (1999:804)

Thus, the way one conceptualizes democracy helps to fashion the way he or she conceptualizes war, and vice versa. These concepts endow each other with meaning in both the normative and structural explanations of the democratic peace.

Conclusions

This chapter examined a number of exemplary articles on the democratic peace and demonstrated how they act as a form of political thought, theoretical construction: configurations of decontested concepts that endow each other with meaning. As such theories are founded on and derived from normative commitments and ideological convictions so that the political concepts they advance are morally and ideologically laden. That being said, it is important to stress that theories are not ideologies. They are different from ideologies as a result of the epistemic and methodological guidelines (or requisites) that constrain and shape the process through which theories act to normatively decontest concepts. We see this most clearly in the way the various theories conceptualize democracy. The normative theories of democratic peace, exemplified here by Zeev Maoz and Bruce Russett and by William Dixon, which are based on the normative understanding of democracy, show a commitment to a more participatory and deliberative conceptualization of democracy. On the other hand, James Fearon and Bruce Bueno de Mesquita, James Morrow, Randolph Siverson, and Alastair Smith have a structural understanding of democracy, and demonstrate a commitment to a much narrower conceptualization of democracy—one that is limited to an apparent balance of threats between the incumbents and their winning coalitions (Bueno de Mesquita et al.) or their audiences (Fearon). This understanding is far more elitist and structural in essence, following theories of Schumpeter, Walter Lippmann, and the like. This chapter also demonstrated how the conceptualization of democracy helps to fashion the theoreticians' understanding of war and the possibility of its eruption. Using a normative understanding of democracy, war is seen as a very remote possibility, if possible at all. For the structuralists, on the other hand, even though the democratic structure considerably reduces the chances of war between dyads of democratic states, it is by no means absent from their repertoire of behavior. Democratic states are always expected to resort to war, even against other democracies if their interests dictate so.

The commitments to different understandings of democracy can also be examined by focusing on specific explanatory variables and mechanisms in the two theories. Let us examine, for example, the explanatory reasoning in the variable of the public's ability in a democracy to translate its preferences into policies, and in our case into peaceful resolution of conflict between democracies. Arguably, this is an important mechanism in pacifying the dyadic relations between democracies. Structural theoreticians interpret this process of translating preferences into policies as incentives facing the elites, or better still, as checks on the policies available to ruling elites. Hence, Bueno de Mesquita et al. argued that the survival of political leaders with large winning coalitions (e.g., in democracies) is dependent on successful policies. This means that democratic leaders will make greater efforts than non-democratic leaders, so that more often than not, will win against non-democrats, and not fight other democrats. It should be noted that in this explanation, the public's preferences are translated into leaders' incentives via structural considerations. As analyzed earlier, this is a very restricted and structural comprehension of accountability. Similarly, Fearon conceptualizes the same elites' incentives using the term audience costs, and thus employs a comparable structural logic.

Conversely, the normative explanation of the democratic peace operationalizes the same translation process, only by focusing on its normative foundation—in other words, its transparent and bounded nature. As evident from both Maoz and Russett, and Dixon, the important elements in democracy in terms of the translation of preferences to policies are both the bounded nature of the competition involved in deciding what policies will be chosen and executed, as well as the process' transparency, both of which are democratic norms. Furthermore, this transparency is not limited within the democratic polity itself, but is freely communicated between democratic polities. The translation of the public preferences to policies therefore causes pacification among democracies and is based on the democratic norms of the bounded and transparent nature of the political conflict. It is embedded in a more comprehensive understanding of democracy—one which conceptualizes norms and values as inseparable from the democratic regime and its fundamental foundation.

In sum, the first section of the chapter argued and demonstrated how the different understandings of democracy—the structural and the normative—are founded on and derived from different normative and ideological convictions. The structural understanding is an offshoot of a more conservative worldview, whereas the normative understanding is an offshoot of a more progressive liberal worldview. We can therefore see how the different theories of democratic peace form triptychs of political theories and ideological worldviews (see also Ish-Shalom, 2006a); one triptych of structural democratic peace theories/structural understanding of democracy/conservative worldviews vis-à-vis a second triptych of normative democratic peace theories/normative understanding of democracies/liberal worldviews. These two triptychs powerfully demonstrate and support the argument defended here that social science theories, democratic peace included, are a form of political thought that offers their readers a comprehensive understanding of their world—one that is much more comprehensive than mere explanations. This comprehensive reading is ready to be taken away from academe and be transformed from theoretical constructions into public conventions and then into political convictions. The next chapter deals with this migration.

3

DEMOCRATIC PEACE AS A PUBLIC CONVENTION

The multiplicity of configurations and the multiplicity of options within each configuration support the claim that theory indeed is a theoretical construction, or a mode of political thought in Freeden's sense. Theories offer not just explanations for complex phenomena, but also an inclusive understanding of the phenomena. They do this by defining the political concepts and thus decontesting them. This is a point worth stressing: theories do offer explanations—that being their manifest function, after all—but on a prior and deeper level, they define political concepts for *us* and in so doing, equip *us* with a road map to navigate the world.

But this is just the first stage of the hermeneutical mechanism: it is the stage where meanings are attached to the political concepts, though still confined to the academy. That is why I emphasized "us" in the above paragraph: "us" in the sense of "we theoreticians" who are engaged in the academic discourse of writing and reading scholarly, theoretical essays. To have a real political impact, however, theories must migrate from remote theoretical discourse to the public sphere; they need to become public conventions—namely, general background knowledge about the world that is taken for granted and shapes the commonsensical codes of thinking and behavior. As such, they can frame the public common sense, or at least the common sense of key segments of the public, and mainly policymakers and foreign-policy pundits. This is what indeed happened to the democratic peace thesis, and is the subject of this chapter: the initial stages of the thesis' migration from academia to the public sphere.

This chapter examines the political context which facilitates this migration by providing incentives for office-seeking politicians to mobilize academic theses and theories. The main focus of the chapter is Bill Clinton's embracement of the democratic peace thesis in his 1992 presidential campaign, and his consequent success in recruiting the neoconservatives to his side. Here, I also analyze Clinton's positions on democracy, democratization, and the democratic peace as a policy blueprint. Some attention will be given to the liberal milieu of Clinton's era, and I briefly touch on the support for the thesis from across the Atlantic, especially from Tony Blair. These political forces all effectively joined hands with the neoconservatives to establish the democratic peace thesis (along with its various theories) as a public convention. However, significant differences are evident between the different actors' understanding of the democratic peace thesis, democracy, and democratization. These differences can help us to understand the differences between the Clinton and Bush administrations in terms of policy.

The Political Context

Although the empirical observation that democracies do not fight one another was treated skeptically at first, it came to be more and more accepted, until it achieved its present, almost indisputable standing. This was followed by the gradual acknowledgment of the thesis that democracies do not fight each other because they are democracies. It should be stressed that although the academic standing of the thesis is not as strong as the empirical observation, by now it is a widely established, almost consensual assertion. Moreover, the thesis came to be almost universally accepted by many outside of academe—as almost a "natural law"—the only one known to exist in international relations (Gleditsch 1992; Levy 1989). In other words, it was transformed from a theoretical discourse to a public discourse, and converted from a mere theoretical construction into a public convention. Put differently, it eventually came to be taken for granted and to shape the commonsensical codes of thinking and behavior.

Two main factors contributed to the spread of the democratic peace idea within the American public and American political spheres. The first is America's collective identity and self-image as a well-established republic and leader of the democratic world in its quest for peace. The second, and probably most important of the two factors was the end of the Cold War. With its constant tension between the superpowers, the Cold War seemed to threaten a third world war—inducing anxiety, and facilitating the acceptance of realist theories of international relations. Therefore, when the Cold War ended, a sense of euphoria followed, along with a public mood much more susceptible to optimistic liberal theories of international relations. One outgrowth of this optimism was Francis Fukuyama's *End of History* (1989, 1992). Another was the tendency to accept the democratic peace thesis. A combination of ideal and material factors produced a public atmosphere conducive to the transformation of the democratic peace theories' theoretical constructions into public convention. The rare combination of a new, relatively peaceful world order, and a compelling theory that fits the collective identity and self-image of the sole remaining superpower, resulted in a public convention that democracies do not fight each other, which was accepted by policymakers and foreign-policy pundits.

The transformation of the democratic peace into a public convention followed an all-but-one-way route from academe to the public arena. It involved both purely intellectual debate and political incentives of internal power alignment and realignment. The academic discourse is relatively familiar, and was described and analyzed in the previous chapter. However, it is worth focusing on the political incentives that came into play—in other words, the sociopolitical processes that helped the theoretical constructions of democratic peace to become public conventions.

In the late 1980s and early 1990s, the end of the Cold War led to confusion and identity crisis among the neoconservatives, for whom the main—almost sole—rationale for existence was fierce anticommunism. In their search for a new rationale, some prominent neoconservative thinkers, first Joshua Muravchik and Carl Gershman, and later Charles Krauthammer and others (Gershman 1990; on endorsing the new agenda of promoting democracy, see also Ehrman 1995:184; Halper and Clarke 2004:76), adopted the relatively new thesis of democratic peace and realigned themselves around it, calling for a revival of the Wilsonian commitment to democratizing foreign countries. As Muravchik proposed in 1991, "the more democratic the world, the more peaceful it is likely to be. *Various researchers have shown that war between democracies has almost never occurred in the modern world*" (Muravchik 1991:8; emphasis added). These thinkers argued that the democratic peace thesis shows that there is no real gap between morality and interest in foreign policy—that it is high time to abandon the support of local dictators in the name of stability, and that promoting democratization abroad will actually expand the zone of peace.

This ideological identity crisis played a crucial role in the 1992 presidential campaign. As supreme commander of the swift victory in Operation

Desert Storm, President George H. W. Bush enjoyed high ratings on foreign policy issues. Hence, challenger Bill Clinton opted to focus his campaign on the economy, as is well remembered by his memorable slogan, "It's the economy, stupid." But he did not turn his back on foreign policy completely, and a recurrent theme in his addresses and writing was the need to promote democracy abroad. Thus, for example, during his election campaign, in one of his public addresses at the Los Angeles World Affairs Council on August 13, 1992, he declared, "Our strategic interests and moral values both are rooted in this goal. As we help democracy expand, we make ourselves and our allies safer. Democracies rarely go to war with each other or traffic in terrorism" (1996:270). Seeking to forge a power base within the Democratic Party and gain as much of the electorate's support as possible, and aided by his prominent role in the centrist Democratic Leadership Council, Clinton turned to the neoconservatives who were disappointed by Bush, mainly because they saw him as pragmatist and realist on foreign policy, and his failure to push the military victory in Iraq to what they saw as its desired end: the toppling of Saddam Hussein.

We must recall that at that time, the neoconservative migration from the Democratic to the Republican Party was not yet complete. They tended to fluctuate between the two parties, seeking support for their absolutist position and aggressive policies. Though President Ronald Reagan eventually failed them—mostly in his second term[1]—he was for them a champion that lead the free world against the communist menace with a policy of aggressive containment and support for democratization abroad. His personality and rhetoric magnetized them, and when they understood that President Bush's stand on foreign policy and democratization would weaken Reagan's legacy, they severed their support for the Republican Party. It was this question of supporting democracy abroad that provided a point of convergence between the contender Clinton and the neoconservatives. Where they found President Bush lacking, Clinton provided new hope. What they offered him he took, and during the campaign he presented himself as an ardent supporter of spreading democracy.

Furthermore, the Republicans did not totally abandon the rhetorical arena. At about the same time Clinton first used the theory, James Baker, Bush's secretary of state, also started employing the term "democratic peace" and citing its main theoretical themes, linking it very tightly with the free market economy. The Cold War was ending, and the prospects for peaceful international relations seemed rosier. In that historical moment, Baker's main interests were forging stable relations with the then-democratizing Russia, and establishing warm relations with the newly freed states of central and Eastern Europe. For that purpose, along with the political expediency that Clinton was also attempting to utilize, the democratic peace came in very useful. Thus on April 9, 1992, Baker asserted before the Senate Foreign Relations Committee:

> With our hopes for the 21st century firmly in mind, I come here today to advance our work toward one overriding goal: to overcome history's rivalry and to build instead a democratic peace with the peoples of Russia and Eurasia, and enduring peace that can help unite the world well into the next century. (1992a)

Baker, who Tony Smith (2007:74) defined as Bush's primary emissary of supporting democracy abroad, made similar declarations over the following months. One of the most noteworthy was on the occasion of the Christian A. Herter Memorial award ceremony on June 29, 1992. He called his address "From Cold War to Democratic Peace," and in it he gave his understanding of the democratic peace.

> A democratic peace is a real and enduring peace: a peace rooted in a shared commitment to democratic government; a peace nurtured by the prosperity that only the free market can provide.
> It is a peace based on the same values upon which our own great nation is founded: responsible representative government, respect for human rights, the rule of law, and private property.
> The peace we hope to build with Russia and the other new and independent states is the peace that we enjoy today with Western Europe and Japan—a peace that has let us flourish as no other nations in history, attaining unprecedented peace and prosperity. It's a peace that makes even the idea of war between the United States and its allies the stuff of fantasy. (1992c; see also Baker 1992b. See also his retrospective reflections in Baker 1995:654)

It can be seen that Baker's understanding of the democratic peace is entwined together with what he understands as the phenomenon's potential strategic and economic benefits for the United States in the international arena. The theory is not left in its abstract and universal nature, but is politically and rhetorically concretized around American interests. In this way, democratization—rationalized in terms of democratic peace thesis—became a campaign issue. Two political camps fought over who would become its champion, and the political stakes were quite high—the support of the powerful neoconservatives and other policy elites. In this tug of war, two victories were observed: one was Clinton, and the other was for the public standing of the theory; namely, democratic peace as a public convention. Two came through defeated: Bush, and (as we came to understand much later) the academic and theoretical integrity of the democratic peace, which continued to be eroded in the political sphere following the migration of the thesis into it. Neoconservatives perceived Bush and Baker's efforts as too little, too late, and they defected from the Republican Party into the Clinton camp. In Gramscian terminology, an historical block was formed between neoconservatives and Clinton and the Democratic Party, which was instrumental in the migration and transformation of the theoretical constructions of democratic peace into public conventions.

However, it is worth stressing that neoconservatism is not a monolithic creed, and not all neoconservatives endorsed the democratic peace thesis. Nor did they, as a group, embrace Clinton the Democrat. As Stefan Halper and Jonathan Clarke rightly argue, with the end of the Cold War—and especially during the second half of the 1990s—an ideological gap, drawn mainly along generational lines, divided the neoconservatives (Halper and Clarke 2004:98–103). The older cohorts among the neoconservatives—most notably Irving Kristol and Nathan Glazer—aligned themselves with the realist cause, thus abandoning the Cold War rhetoric of anti-totalitarianism and pro-democratization. The younger cohorts, including Muravchik, Gershman, Krauthammer, and William Kristol, aligned themselves with the interventionist cause of promoting democracy as a means of stabilizing regions plagued by authoritarianism and war.[2] Therefore, many of the young cohorts opted for the short-lived cooperation with Clinton during the 1992 presidential campaign. As Muravchik's public endorsement of Clinton shows, it was the issue of promoting human rights and democracy abroad that became the point of convergence between Clinton and the neoconservatives: "The hope for any such order [New World Order] rests on the continued advance of democracy, because democracies behave more responsibly and peacefully" (1992:2).[3]

But the political cooperation was indeed short lived, and President Clinton soon disappointed neoconservatives. It did not take long before they started blaming him for pragmatism and realism, and for failing to endorse a strong commitment by the United States to promote democracy abroad (Ehrman 1995:186–87; Halper and Clarke 2004:76–81). It was Muravchik who led this sobering process; for example, in his "Lament of a Clinton Supporter," in which he portrayed Clinton as too liberal domestically, not firm enough on security and military issues, and too timid with regard to promoting democracy (Muravchik 1993).[4] Especially painful for neoconservatives was Clinton's willingness to compromise with authoritarian states such as China and Saudi Arabia. He was not insistent enough in pressuring such authoritarian states to democratize, giving up his campaign commitment to spreading democracy abroad for the sake of stability and economic interests (see, for example, Kaplan 1997, 1999; Kagan 1996; Tell 1996; Perle 2000).[5] Thus, for example, he was willing to strike a deal with China to endorse its membership of the World Trade Organization (WTO). Furthermore, he did not even condition acceptance to the WTO with improving China's record on human rights. Indeed, it should be noted that in his first term Clinton was quite pragmatic and hesitant on foreign policy, especially after the October 1993 debacle in Somalia (Smith 2007:74). His rhetoric of promoting democracy was forceful, full of principles and ideals, but the reality was less heroic. Richard Haass characterized it aptly writing that "the Clinton era was marked by a preference for symbolism over substance" (Haass 2000). It is not surprising then that globally speaking, not much was achieved, particularly when judged against the great expectations, high aspirations, and lofty criteria set by neoconservatives. Even Clinton's interventions in Haiti and the Balkans were pursued hesitantly, belatedly, and only following the harsh criticism in the United States against his inaction (Smith 2007:74–75). This was surely not the determined leadership neoconservatives sought in the American president.

The picture was somewhat different in his second term, when Clinton had no reelection concerns to consider. During those four years, when he was freer to pursue a more idealistic and principled foreign policy, he mainly seemed to consider history and the historical records of his presidency. It was during those four years that his legacy as an interventionist and a promoter of democracy was fostered, albeit rather exaggeratedly. And it was mostly Clinton's second term that frames our memory of him. Notable examples of interventionism are his (failed) attempts to resolve the Israeli-

Palestinian conflict; the more successful Good Friday Agreement of April 10, 1998, in Northern Ireland; and the 1999 NATO bombing of Yugoslavia, code-named "Operation Allied Force."

With regard to rhetoric, for the purposes of tracing the migration of the democratic peace thesis into the public and political spheres, it seems that rhetoric plays an important role in this transmigration, which is almost as important as the actual policies themselves. As the act of persuasion, rhetoric helps to frame the common sense and the public discourse. Rhetoric facilitates the migration, and a forceful enough rhetoric can, in fact, foster it, becoming a crucial component in transforming a theoretical construction into a public convention. As chapter 1 discussed (and the empirical chapters show), the political discourse assumes rhetorical control of the academic discourse and transforms the thesis into public conventions and political convictions.

Clinton's Conceptualizations of Democracy, Democratization, and Democratic Peace

During both his terms, Clinton indeed led a forceful discursive and rhetorical campaign to justify the strategic merit of promoting democracy abroad. This campaign included references to the democratic peace. Public address by public address he consolidated the public stature of the thesis, helping it achieve the status of public convention. At times he was as forceful as his successor, George W. Bush. For example, in his address to the National Assembly of South Korea on July 10, 1993, he avowed "Democracies not only are more likely to meet the needs and respect the rights of their people, they also make better neighbors. They do not wage war on each other, practice terrorism, generate refugees or traffic in drugs and outlaw weapons" (1993a). He similarly affirmed in his State of the Union Address on January 25, 1994, that "Democracies don't attack each other, they make better trading partners and partners in diplomacy. That is why we have supported, you and I, the democratic reformers in Russia and in the other states of the former Soviet bloc" (1994a). Those statements are forceful, but more so they are absolutist and communicated in the political avowal vernacular, defined in the introduction to this book as forceful declarations rhetorically uttered in slogan-like fashion to confirm and convey political stands.

Yet, more often than not, Clinton showed a greater understanding than George Bush of the probabilistic nature of the thesis. He was more cautious in stating the proposition of the democratic peace. We find that he utilizes a host of alternative wordings to indicate the probabilistic nature of the thesis. Thus he argues, "Democracies rarely wage war on one another" (1993b), and "We know democracies are less likely to wage war, to violate human rights, to break treaties" (1994b), or more forcefully yet still acknowledging a tendency rather than an absolutist law, "And we know that democracies are far less likely to tolerate that sort of thing than dictatorships are" (1994d). This probabilistic prudence keeps his discourse closer to theoretical construction than to political conviction; closer, that is, than what we will find in either the case of the Israeli right or the case of American neoconservatives.

Like Bush and the neoconservatives, Clinton also cites history as the ultimate source for affirming the democratic peace, "History shows that nations where rights are respected and governments are freely chosen are more likely to be partners in peace and prosperity" (1996). Still more interestingly from our perspective, even when Clinton affirms the probabilistic nature of the thesis he does not refrain from concretizing the historical and abstract lessons, and he points out the American interest in advancing the democratic peace, "History teaches us that democracies are less likely to go to war, less likely to traffic in terrorism and more likely to stand against the forces of hatred and destruction; more likely to become good partners in diplomacy and trade. So promoting democracy and defending human rights is good for the world and good for America" (1995). It seems that with Clinton we have a mixed record of the uses of discursive genres. At times he does use the political avowal vernacular, but as a rule he is discursively softer and much more cautious. Through Clinton's endorsement, the democratic peace thesis was on its way to becoming a public convention, although it was not yet established as the dogmatic political conviction it would later become.

Even when employing the forceful political avowal vernacular, Clinton never went so far as to support gunpoint democratization. Thus, even though he favored policies that promoted democracy, his preferred tools of democratization were in no way similar to President Bush. Moreover, it was not only his more pragmatic and prudent attitude to world politics that prevented him from adopting a policy of coercive democratization (although that is surely part of the explanation), it was also his conceptualization of democracy and derived conceptualization of democratization that prevented him from championing its imposition by force. Clinton regarded democracy as a highly complex political and social phenomenon that required political patience. In Pakistan, in March 2000, he remarked,

> I know democracy isn't easy; it's certainly not perfect. The authors of my own country's constitution knew that as well. They said that the mission of the United States would always be, and I quote, "to form a more perfect union." In other words, they knew we would never fully realize our ideals, but that we could keep moving closer to them. That means the question for free people is always how to keep moving forward. (2000b)

Democracy, we learn from Clinton, is a process. And later in that same year, in England, he added,

> democracy is not just about elections, even when they seem to go on forever. Democracy is also about what happens after the election. It's about the capacity to run clean government and root out corruption, to open the budget process, to show people an honest accounting of where their resources are being spent, and to give potential investors an honest accounting of what the risks and rewards might be. (2000c)

Furthermore, democracy is "about dialogue" (2000a); it is, in theoretical parlance, a deliberative project of bringing the citizenry into the public sphere as an influential agent of policy-making. As analyzed in the previous chapter, this conceptualization of democracy is organized in terms of culture, norms, and values. Democracy is seen as a substantive set of values and rights, and, overall, this understanding is very much a progressive conceptualization of democracy. It is very different from conservative and neoconservative theorization of democracy as a structural, formal, and elitist project.

It would come as no surprise then to find that Clinton's State of the Union Address on January 25, 1994, included the following sober observation, "Our support of reform must combine patience for the enormity of the task and vigilance for our fundamental interest and values" (1994a). Advancing the cause of democracy is thus both moral and pragmatic, and in any case, it is an enormous task that requires patience. Clinton's sensitivity to the substantive morality and normativity of democracy was accompanied by its own conceptualization and operationalization of democratization—

one that does not lend itself easily to gunpoint democratization. On the contrary, Clinton emphasized democratization that would focus on instilling democratic norms and values in the target civil society. He thus advocated channels of communication with it. In the context of China, Clinton stressed "This program will include increased broadcasts for Radio Free Asia and the Voice of America, increased support for nongovernmental organizations working on human rights in China, and the development with American business leaders of a voluntary set of principles for business activity in China" (1994c). He also insisted that the more important organs of democratization should not and could not be state organs. The state might facilitate those processes, but mostly in an indirect manner and by supporting nongovernmental organizations, "We must support the nongovernmental organizations that seek to strengthen Asia's building blocks of civic society, such as open elections, trade unions, and a free press" (1993a). Clinton understands that a direct and blatant involvement in domestic politics and processes could lead to the discretization and delegitimation of democracy and democratization. The target society may see them as simply a form of masked foreign imperialism. Clinton understood well that to avoid this kind of atmosphere, it is better to work through nongovernmental organization and domestic agents of democratization that can better handle the dissemination of democratic norms and values to a civil society. Democratization, seen this way, is about constructing a democratic culture and community, rather than building a democratic structure.

The Liberal Milieu

Clinton's rhetorical enthusiasm and speaking capabilities affected the public stature of the democratic peace thesis in a very real way. In a gradual, yet continuous process, democratic peace made its way into the heart of the foreign policy discourse in the United States. And just as neoconservatives advised and backed President George W. Bush in the 2000s, so intellectuals and ideologues from the American left shared similar ideas to those of President Clinton. They thus lent intellectual and public support to his agenda, and to democratic peace as a public convention. Liberal pundits and thinkers like Paul Berman and Michael Mandelbaum toyed with the democratic peace thesis in different ways.[6] At the beginning of his book Terror and Liberalism (2003), Berman, whose reasoning was very similar to Natan

Sharansky's, asserted that "Maniacal dictatorships do not prosper in times of peace and plenty, when the citizens have sufficient tranquility to go out in the sunlight and look around; but war and hysteria keep everyone down in the basement" (2003:5). It is therefore no surprise that this policy-oriented statement appears toward the end of this book: "In the anti-nihilist system, freedom for others means safety for ourselves. Let us be for the freedom of others" (2003:210). In Mandelbaum's case, his popular book *The Ideas That Conquered the World* (2002), devotes a whole chapter full of praise to the theory of democratic peace (2002:chapter 8; see also Mandelbaum 2001:32).

The same holds true for the think tanks: Just as the neoconservatives organized themselves in think tanks that helped them to publicize and institutionalize their views, so did the American liberals. The Progressive Policy Institute (PPI), which was affiliated with the Democratic Party (being the think tank of the Democratic Leadership Council), and aimed at vitalizing the Third Way as a public philosophy, also embraced the requisite-less version of the democratic peace. As early as July 1991, Larry Diamond, a renowned scholar of democracy and democratization and a frequent contributor to PPI publications, wrote "The experience of this century bears important lessons. Democratic countries do not go to war with one another. Democracies do not sponsor terrorism against one another. They do not build weapons of mass destruction to use on or threaten one another" (2000). This is almost the exact phrasing we would expect to find in neoconservative writing. The same themes can be found in the writings of Will Marshall, PPI president since its foundation in 1989, who wrote in January 2000, "By the same token, 20th-century history shows that democratic governments, constrained by public opinion, competing domestic interests, and accountable political institutions, are less likely to start wars and more inclined to cooperate with other countries and adhere to international agreements and norms" (2000). He titled his foreign policy strategy, "Democratic Realism," bringing into mind Krauthammer's own proposal.[7]

It is no surprise to find that on October 30, 2003, five months into the Iraq War, the PPI published a policy paper entitled, "Progressive Internationalism: A Democratic National Security Strategy." The paper reaffirms the Bush strategy of promoting democracy for the sake of American security while criticizing him for squandering it tactically.

> Democrats believe that America should use its unparalleled power to defend our country and to shape a world in which the values of liberal

democracy increasingly hold sway. History amply demonstrates that true peace and security depend not only on relations between states but also between state and society. Rulers who abuse their own people are more likely to threaten other countries, to support and spawn terrorism, to violate treaties, and otherwise flout norms of civilized conduct. British Prime Minister Tony Blair put it succinctly in his July 2003 address to Congress: "The spread of freedom is the best security for the free. It is our last line of defense and our first line of attack." (Progressive Policy Institute 2003)

Evident in the PPI's paper is the same phenomenon of absolutizing and totalizing theory into something that is more political than academic. The American left was an active agent in facilitating the migration of the thesis from academia to the public and political spheres, and some of the liberal intellectuals utilized the political avowal vernacular. The responsibility does not lie solely with the right, but—as claimed by Tony Smith in 2007[8]—with ideologues of every political coloration. Though, as is clear from analyzing Clinton's discourse, each political perspective has its own understanding of democracy, democratization, and the nature of democratic peace.

As the Iraq War began to be publicly conceived as a failure, and the policy of democratization discredited, the PPI pundits and scholars were driven to emphasize the differences, rather than the similarities, between their own position and the Bush Doctrine. They stressed that although democratization was the culmination of the Third Way as a foreign policy, the instruments for its actualization were far removed from the gunpoint democratization enacted by Bush and his neoconservative advisors. They were quick to emphasize such themes as civil society and soft power (see, for example, Eberly 2008; Marshall 2006). These were the tools and the theoretical frameworks that were supposed to facilitate democratization abroad, thus securing both interests and values of the United States.

The PPI 2003 policy paper quotation also indicates that President Clinton was not the only world leader at the time who furthered the migration of the democratic peace into the public sphere. Both inside his administration and across the Atlantic, similar views were held and acted upon. On January 13, 1993, Warren Christopher, Clinton's first secretary of state, declared in his confirmation hearing that:

> Promoting democracy does not imply a crusade to remake the world in our image. Rather, support for democracy and human rights abroad can and should be a central strategic tenet in improving our own security. Democratic movements and governments are not only more likely to protect human and minority rights, they are also more likely to resolve ethnic, religious, and territorial disputes in a peaceful manner and to be reliable partners in diplomacy, trade, arms accord, and global environmental protection. (1998:28)

On March 22, 1993, Christopher declared before the Chicago Council on Foreign Relations, that "By helping promote democracy, we do more than honor our deepest values. We are also making a strategic investment in our nation's security. History has shown that a world of more democracies is a safer world. It is a world that will devote more to human development and less to human destruction. And it is a world that will promote what all people have in common rather than what tears them apart." Madeleine Albright, Clinton's second secretary of state and an International Relations scholar by training, also fell in with him on this issue and was quick to begin her term advocating that America should stand by democracy for security and peace. On January 8, 1997, as Secretary-Designate, she stated before the Senate Foreign Relations Committee that "we will continue to promote and advocate democracy because we know that democracy is a parent to peace, and that the American constitution remains the most revolutionary and inspiring source of change in the world."

Anthony Lake, Clinton's national security advisor between 1993 and 1997, asserted similarly in his well-known address "From Containment to Enlargement," which he delivered at Johns Hopkins University on September 21, 1993, "The addition of new democracies makes us more secure because democracies tend not to wage war on each other or sponsor terrorism. They are more trustworthy in diplomacy and do a better job of respecting the human rights of their people" (1993). The policy implication for Lake was that "*The successor to a doctrine of containment must be a strategy of enlargement—enlargement of the world's free community of market democracies*" (1993; emphasis in the original. See also Brands 2008:106; Linklater 2000:987; Light 2001:85; Lane 1994:46). The theory of democratic peace informed Lake's understanding of foreign policy, causing him to approve democratization for strategic purposes and to advocate policies for promoting democracy abroad. And as we saw, Lake was not alone in this: these were the beliefs commonly held by the Clinton administration, and they were the ideas that the administration acted upon, at least to some extent.

Prime Minister Tony Blair held the same view across the Atlantic, in Britain. Mark Schafer and Stephen Walker have traced down and demonstrated how Blair internalized the democratic peace theory into his operational code. They convincingly argue that Blair internalized the strategic dictates of the theory in a similar way to Clinton. Accordingly, he displays a cooperative belief system towards democracies as does Clinton, and much less cooperative belief system toward non-democracies.[9] It is not surprising then, to find Blair using the political avowal vernacular and forcefully declaring his endorsement of the democratic peace in slogan-like fashion. This happened on July 17, 2003, four months into the Iraq War. On the occasion of being awarded the Congressional Gold Medal, Blair addressed a joint session of the U.S. Congress, and avowed, "The spread of freedom is the best security for the free. It is our last line of defense and our first line of attack. And just as the terrorist seeks to divide humanity in hate, so we have to unify it around an idea. And that idea is liberty." Surely, the strategy of achieving peace by democratization was then still in its heyday. Blair, who had internalized the strategic dictates of the democratic peace, also advocated this policy, and he was a partner in establishing the democratic peace as a public convention and political conviction, and contributing to its sorry ramification: the Iraq War.

Similar processes of theory's migration took place all across Europe as is evident from Chris Patten, former European Commissioner for External Affairs. In November 30, 1999, Patten told the Human Rights Discussion Forum plenary session that "the EU was formed partly to protect liberal values, so it is hardly surprising that we should think it appropriate to speak out. But it is also sensible for strategic reasons. Free societies tend not to fight one another or to be bad neighbors" (1999). And these views were carried into the December 12, 2003, European Security Strategy, as set out in the document entitled, "A Secure Europe in a Better World." In this strategy document, we find that "The best protection for our security is a world of well-governed democratic States. EU policies are aimed at bringing this about." Like the EU, the 1999 "Charter for European Security" of the Organization for Security and Cooperation in Europe (OSCE) expressed similar ideas linking democracy and security, "Peace and security in our region is best guaranteed by the willingness and ability of each participating State to uphold democracy, the rule of law and respect for human rights" (Organization for Security and Cooperation in Europe 1999; see also Light 2001:85). Democracy as a cure for international violence was not an exclusive American belief (and certainly Bush had no proprietary claim to it). It swept the democratized world in a process that was initiated in the early 1990s, and culminated in the early 2000s, with 2003 the dramatic, crucial, and even tragic climax to which everything came.

Conclusions

As the thesis migrated from academia to the public sphere, it became politicized, simplified, and widely publicized. Twelve years after Muravchik introduced it into the public sphere by citing "various researchers" (Muravchik 1991:8), his fellow neoconservatives, Lawrence Kaplan and William Kristol, proclaimed democratic peace to be "a truth of international politics" (Kaplan and Kristol 2003:104). A disputable academic thesis came to be conceived as an uncontested certainty, a policy blueprint to be strategically implemented. As this chapter demonstrated, political considerations and calculations facilitated the instrumentalization of the thesis. By employing political avowal vernacular, certain politicians and high-ranking officials—some of them sincerely convinced of the validity and soundness of the thesis—paved the way to its complete politicization. Clinton's (successful) presidential aspirations meshed with the neoconservatives' attempts at self-revitalization, and with other political forces, and set in motion the thesis' translation into something public; namely, public convention (later to be trivialized and dogmatized into political conviction). This political alignment, or in Gramscian terms, "historical block," cohered with a suitable historical context of the euphoria following the end of the Cold War, and an American collective identity and self-image as a well-founded republic, and the leader of the democratic world in its quest for peace. This coherence produced a set of sociopolitical conditions that facilitated the migration process of the thesis, and its dissemination within certain sectors in the public—mainly, the policy elites who accepted it as a public convention—that is, general background knowledge about the world that is taken for granted and shapes the commonsensical codes of thinking and behavior.

In other words, with the help of ideologues and politicians seeking office the academic democratic peace thesis was publicized, and went through a migration from academe to the public sphere, along with the conversion from mere theoretical constructions into powerful public conventions. The stage was now ripe for the third phase—the transformation into political convictions.

4

WORD-LORDS
The Israeli Right's Mobilization of the Rhetorical Capital of Democratic Peace

On June 24, 2002, President Bush brought out a new plan for peace between Israel and the Palestinians. That plan, which became known as the "Roadmap," was based on a two-state solution and presented two novelties: (1) for the first time, the United States committed itself publicly and officially to an independent Palestinian sovereignty, and (2) for the first time, the United States also conditioned Israeli concessions on Palestinian democratization. This chapter explores the role of the democratic peace thesis in bringing about these novelties: it examines how the thesis was mobilized politically by Israeli politicians to advance their ideological aims by influencing American policies, and how and why the politicians found the thesis useful. This chapter is then a study of the rhetorical capital of social science theories—or more accurately, of the political mobilization of the rhetorical capital of theories. Rhetorical capital, as was theoretically explored earlier, is defined as the aggregate persuasive resources inherent in entities. This concept applies to various entities—both material, such as commemorative monuments, and abstract and ideal entities, such as theories. This chapter focuses on the rhetorical capital inherent in social science theories, and more specifically, in the democratic peace thesis.

This chapter has two complementary missions in mind. The first is to identify which general and specific features of the democratic peace thesis comprise its rhetorical capital. We will be asking the question: what constitutes the rhetorical capital of theories? In other words, what features of theories make them vulnerable to political and rhetorical abuse? These features consist of the general features that most theories share; namely, the structural duality of accessibility and incomprehensibility overlaid with the prestige of objectivity, and features specific to particular theories. The rhetorical capital of the democratic peace theories has four specific features.

The first is the status of the democratic peace thesis among policy elites as a public convention; that is, as a law-like phenomenon governing the realm of world politics. The second is the existence of two distinct families of theories—one structural, the other normative—that try to explain the phenomenon, and that each deliver a different political message. The third relates to the policy implications of subscribing to the democratic peace thesis' conclusions; namely, a political commitment to the democratization of nondemocratic states in the interests of national security. And the fourth is the prestigious heritage of the thesis, which many ascribe to Immanuel Kant.

This chapter's second task is to empirically examine the rhetorical mobilization of the democratic peace thesis' rhetorical capital by two influential Israeli politicians: Benjamin Netanyahu and Natan Sharansky. These politicians have, each in his way, both subordinated the thesis expediently and rhetorically to their own ideological purposes. Moreover, both politicians have also used a political avowal vernacular; namely, forceful declarations rhetorically uttered in slogan-like fashion to confirm and convey political stands. Whereas Netanyahu mobilized the thesis for what might be termed a "politics of postponement," Sharansky used it as a "politics of avoidance." While Netanyahu sought to delay the resumption of negotiations with the Palestinians, Sharansky wished to avoid it completely. Ultimately, their mobilization of the democratic peace thesis helped to lay the groundwork for President Bush's Roadmap.

The Democratic Peace Thesis' Rhetorical Capital

Five features of the democratic peace thesis comprise its rhetorical capital: (1) The feature common to rhetorical capital of theories in general; namely, the structural duality of accessibility and incomprehensibility overlaid with the prestige of objectivity; (2) the second is the status of the democratic peace thesis within policy elites as a public convention; that is, a law-like phenomenon governing the realm of world politics; (3) the third is the existence of two distinct families of theories, which both try to explain the phenomenon while delivering a different political message; (4) the fourth relates to the implications of accepting the conclusion of the democratic peace thesis—that democratization creates a zone of peace—namely, that accepting the conclusions could lead to a political commitment urging the democratization of nondemocratic states for the sake of national security; and (5) the long and prestigious heritage of the thesis, being ascribed rightly or wrongly to Immanuel Kant.

The persuasive resources of the democratic peace thesis stem from these properties and provide its rhetorical capital, which makes the thesis and its theories a useful tool for political persuasion, especially when forcefully evoked in a political avowal vernacular. And as this current chapter shows, the democratic peace thesis has indeed been mustered politically and forcefully by Netanyahu and Sharansky as a means of promoting their political agendas

Here, I start by analyzing the specific features of the democratic peace that comprise its rhetorical capital. As we saw before, an ever-burgeoning theoretical and empirical literature has established the soundness of the observation that democracies never—or, in the qualified and academically held version, rarely—go to war with each other. This observation has been hypothesized into a thesis that claims that democracies never (or hardly ever) go to war with each other for no other reason than the fact that they are democracies. Despite harsh criticism of both the observation and the thesis, both have been generally accepted in academic spheres, and furthermore, have migrated to the public sphere, where they are accepted as a public convention by politicians, ideologues, and pundits from a wide political spectrum, as a valid, law-like regularity that governs relations among states. The assertion that democracies have not, and will not, fight each other, can be found in the thinking of conservatives and neoconservatives such as Francis Fukuyama (1999), Charles Krauthammer (2001, 2004b), and William Kristol (Kaplan and Kristol 2003:104), and of liberals such as Paul Berman (2003) and Michael Mandelbaum (2002). More significantly, this thinking can be found in both the words and deeds of Presidents Bill Clinton and George W. Bush, indicating the width and depth of penetration of the democratic peace thesis into the common sense of American elites.[1] The notion that democracies do not fight each other became the bedrock of the American perspective on world politics, and was established as a widespread American public convention, and as is shown in this chapter, it also became a widespread political conviction. This feature—the policy elites' acceptance of the thesis as public convention and political conviction—provides a major source of its rhetorical capital, even more than the broad theoretical agreement on its validity.

Notwithstanding the broad theoretical agreement on the validity of the thesis, disagreement over the causal mechanism that links democracy and the absence of war has produced, as chapter 2 showed, two competing explanatory families of theories. The first explains the democratic peace phenomenon by focusing on the structural dimensions of democracy, while the second highlights the normative dimensions of democratic societies. Especially when they are broadly acknowledged as public conventions, which is what happened, these theories carry real-world implications. Once it is accepted that democracies do not fight each other, the policy implication should be to support democratization abroad. Allegedly, each state that becomes a democracy is no longer a security threat to other democracies. To increase the number of democracies means to enlarge the zone of peace. Thus, the stakes in the validity of the democratic peace thesis are not only theoretical, and the theories are far from the ordinary abstract material that is usually the exclusive province of theoreticians. The theories raise real-world issues that appeal to policymakers, and this appeal is another source of their rhetorical capital: in the case of democratic peace, the theoreticians speak the policymakers' language. It is one of those times when truth (science) speaks to power (politics). But this common language and interests allow able rhetors to mobilize theories to their political needs and although truth may inform power, power can, and does, distort truth for expediency's sake.

However, the implications of democratization are not as straightforward as they seem if we consider the nature of democratization, its agents, and the means for achieving it. Advocates of the structural theories of democratic peace tend to stress the structural features of democracy and regard democratization as a relatively simple process, which involves building a democratic structure of checks and balances, periodic elections, and so forth. Seen from this angle, democratization can be initiated and maintained by external agents, and even be achieved in a relatively short time. In contrast, adherents of the normative theories of democratic peace tend to emphasize the normative and cultural features of democracy, and see democratization as a complex process of constructing and consolidating democratic norms. To be both efficient and legitimate, it is believed that democratization must be achieved by internal agents, as it involves the slow extensive process of socialization, education, and the spread of norms.

Note, too, that the differences in the conceptualizations and operationalizations of the processes of democratization are neither arbitrary, nor based on methodological and theoretical foundations alone. The comparison of the different theories of the democratic peace in chapter 2 highlighted the ideological and moral reasoning underlying their differences. The structural theories follow the logic of conservative ideology and offer an elitist prescription for governing polities democratically. The conservative skepticism regarding human rationality leads to the structural, minimalist, and elitist conceptualization of democracy that characterizes these theories. The normative theories, on the other hand, are based on liberal ideological reasoning, and provide a participatory prescription for governing polities democratically. The liberal trust in human rationality guides the conceptualization of democracy in the normative, maximalist, and participatory terms that characterizes these normative theories. Those normative and ideological differences substantially account for the differences between the adherents of the two families of theories in conceptualizing and operationalizing the democratization process.

Differences in the definitions, conceptualization, operationalization, and expectations of democratization open up a political space that can also be mobilized by able rhetors to deliver various political messages. In other words, the general acceptance of the democratic peace thesis supplemented by the different theoretical meanings is another feature and source of rhetorical capital that can be mobilized politically. Here, we can see the relational nature of the theory's features, which network together to form its rhetorical capital (see relevant section in chapter 1). Definitions and concepts are internal-to-the-theory features. Yet they (the internal-to-the-theory features of the normative and structural theories of democratic peace alike) network (or, more accurately, are networked by rhetors) with the equivalent definitions and concepts of the other theory (or, in other words, with the other theory's internal features), and by opening a political space amenable to delivering different political messages, augment the thesis' rhetorical capital. Finally, the internal-to-the-theories features are networked yet again with the general acceptance of the thesis, and constitute a powerful asset of persuasion: the resource of rhetorical capital. Shortly, we see how politicians rhetorically interact and network the theories with other cultural and political beliefs (external structures) to further serve their political agendas. The most powerful cultural and political external-to-the-theory structure is the idea of "us" against "them." In the hands of politicians employing political avowal vernacular, the rhetorical capital of the democratic peace thesis can support and justify this belief, while exploiting and reframing it as a "democratic us" against an "autocratic them."

This thesis naturally gains in prestige when it is ascribed, as it is so often, to Immanuel Kant, that towering philosopher of the Western world, and godfather of reason and morality.[2] The relations of the democratic peace thesis to Kant's "Perpetual Peace" are not straightforward as many of the thesis' adherents have suggested. Kant put his faith in republicanism, and was quite abhorred by democracy. Notwithstanding contemporary attempts to negate, or at least placate, this difference,[3] the historical fact is that Kant's was a republican, not a democratic, peace. And yet, due to the fact that the democratic peace thesis is more often than not presented as the direct theoretical offshoot of Kant's "Perpetual Peace" in our times, it gains ready acceptability. Being the offspring of Kant makes it a heavyweight resource of persuasion, and contributes significantly to the democratic peace thesis' rhetorical capital.

Let us now examine the general features of the rhetorical capital of theories—the structural duality of accessibility and incomprehensibility overlaid with the prestige of objectivity. Theories offer explanations (usually causal explanations) for regularities. The basic requirement and expectation of a theory is to explain phenomena. This function—of relating explanans to explanandum—is central to a theory's structure. Other auxiliary, structural, and procedural features surround this center. First among these features is the principle of objectivity, which, according to positivistic and conventional wisdom, governs theorizing. Theories are supposedly developed for the pursuit of scientific knowledge, and as such, are oblivious to political partisanship and moral and ideological persuasion. The function of explanation and the prestige of objectivity affect the attractiveness of theories in politics because policymakers seek causal mechanisms to help them devise effective policies. By offering causal mechanisms credited with objectivity, rather than tainted by partisanship and ideology, theories represent the perfect apparatus for meeting this need.[4] The features and sources of the rhetorical capital of theories rely on their accessibility to the public. Without accessibility, theories remain obscure and remote in their ivory tower, despite their real-world implications and attractiveness to policymakers. And since theorizing is conducted in a democratic public sphere, and since theories circulate rather freely, they are indeed highly accessible to the public. The accessibility of theories assists their migration to the public sphere and is a major source of rhetorical capital.

Still, there are some technicalities and subtleties of theorizing that are incomprehensible to the public at large, and do not travel well from academe to the public sphere. In particular, there are the four requisites of theorizing which were examined in detail in chapter 1, which do not fare well in the public sphere, and are lost in migration. First, in the academic world, theories are subject to ongoing evaluation, critical review, and possible refutation (though bounded by the three factors discussed in chapter 1); that is how it works in the skeptical culture of academia. But once a theory escapes from this skeptically driven, cautious, self-reflective, critical climate, it can grow to be accepted as an absolute and unchallengeable truth. Second, in theorizing and in evaluating theories, conditionality is applied that specifies the restrictions of their applicability. Most theories are explicit about the conditions of their validity. For example, many democratic peace theoreticians insist that peaceful democratic relations are dyadic, and only valid within pairs of democracies. Another important conditionality of the democratic peace thesis is that it is only valid between consolidated democracies. Transition to democracy is dangerously disposed to destabilization, and democratization could lead to both domestic and international violence. These conditionalities disappear in the political sphere when theoretical assertions become totalistic claims—for example, that democracies are peaceful overall, and that democratization is the surest method to secure peace. Third, theory is probabilistic in essence, indicative of strong tendencies. When this requisite is ignored, theory can be perceived as a law-like assertion of absolute universal patterns. Fourth, theoreticians are bound by logic. The dictates of logic stipulate what we can validly infer from a theory, and what we cannot. For example, we cannot infer from the theoretical assertion that democracies never (or rarely) fight each other that an authoritarian regime is belligerent, or that other dyads (such as a democracy and a nondemocracy, or a nondemocracy and another nondemocracy) are necessarily war-prone. These dictates of logic do not necessarily operate in the public sphere, and may be subsumed by popular sentiment and political standards.

We should bear in mind that the incomprehensibility of theory, including the democratic peace theories, is not in itself an asset of persuasion. It only becomes an asset of persuasion when a theory becomes accessible—or, to put it differently, it becomes an asset as a result of theory's structural duality of incomprehensibility and accessibility. Because of its incomprehensibility to the wider public, politicians can mobilize theory's rhetorical capital; that is, exploit its circulation and renown for their political advantage.[5] So, in effect, theory's accessibility is, in and of itself, a resource of rhetorical capital, while incomprehensibility becomes such a resource due to theory's accessibility, making theory vulnerable to rhetorical misuse and abuse.

Discarding these four requisites of theorizing results in a simplistic and totalistic yes-no reading of theories—in a public and political representation and misrepresentation, rather than theory itself, in public conventions and political convictions, rather than theoretical constructions—that is, highly amenable to manipulation by able rhetors and political mobilization. This aspect of rhetorical capital, the crude reading of theories, is evident in cases of political mobilization of the democratic peace thesis' rhetorical capital.

The Political Mobilization of the Democratic Peace' Rhetorical Capital by the Israeli Right

This section analyzes the political mobilization of the democratic peace thesis' rhetorical capital by Binyamin Netanyahu and Natan Sharansky in the service of their respective political and ideological purposes. In Netanyahu's case, this was a "politics of postponement," and in Sharansky's case it was a "politics of avoidance."

Benjamin Netanyahu and the Politics of Postponement

Benjamin Netanyahu—the Israeli prime minister in 2013, who also served from 1996 to 1999—is an able politician locked in a web of conflicting interests and political commitments. Those conflicts are also evident in his contradictory public declarations, when at times he approves a demilitarized Palestinian state, and at times rejects even this compromise option. It is therefore quite difficult, with any accuracy, to assess his real attitude on compromise with the Palestinians. It seems, however, that he has unhappily accepted that some sort of territorial compromise with the Palestinians is required. His aspiration, though, is for the terms of this compromise to be decided less by bilateral negotiation than through facts on the ground (i.e., more settlements), and by persuading the United States to agree to and legitimize the settlements in order to pressure the international community and the Palestinians to accept a bargain that does not include Israel's withdrawal to its 1967 borders. To achieve this, Netanyahu has adopted tactics of postponement in conjunction with a massive public relations campaign aimed at both the Israeli and American publics.

Benjamin Netanyahu has enjoyed a meteoric political career; in 1996, age forty-seven, he was elected Israel's youngest-ever prime minister. His political career was launched in 1982, when Moshe Arens, then ambassador to the United States, chose him as his second-in-command, as the Deputy Chief of Mission in Washington, D.C. Two years later, he became Israel's ambassador to the United Nations. Upon returning to Israel in 1988, he was elected a Likud Member of Knesset, and was appointed deputy foreign minister to Arens. In these positions, he won the hearts and souls of the Likud supporters, and was elected as Likud leader in 1993, heading the opposition during the Oslo negotiations of 1993–95. In 1996, he was elected prime minister, defeating Shimon Peres, the acting prime minister since Yitzhak Rabin's assassination on November 4, 1995. The elections took place in the wake of a bloody terror campaign, which helped Netanyahu electorally, given his image as a fierce fighter against terrorism. During Netanyahu's administration, Israel adopted a much tougher stance on fulfilling the Oslo accords, insisting on reciprocity, and when violations by the Palestinian side were identified, refused to move forward with the process. Netanyahu did not, however, abandon the Oslo process, and he did negotiate several interim agreements, including a partial withdrawal from the town of Hebron on January 1997. This policy zigzagging led to the deterioration and final collapse of his coalition in 1999, when he lost the elections in a landslide victory to Labor candidate Ehud Barak. Netanyahu then left politics, but only briefly, and when Likud returned to power and formed another government in 2001 under Ariel Sharon, Netanyahu returned to positions as Israel's foreign minister and, later, as finance minister. During the entire time, he never lost hope of regaining the premiership, which indeed he did on March 31, 2009.

Netanyahu is one of Israel's most eloquent spokespersons, and in his efforts to present Israel's case, he has mobilized the rhetorical capital of the democratic peace (see also Cohen 1994:223; Maoz 1998:8). One of his first articulations of the idea that Middle East peace must be based on democratization was in his 1993 book *A Place among the Nations*. It was written with the help of Dr. Yoram Hazony, a political philosopher by training, who is affiliated with neoconservative think tanks, and acts as consultant to Netanyahu. Later, Hazony established the most successful Israeli conservative think tank, the Shalem Center, which provides intellectual backing to the Israeli Right.[6]

In *A Place among the Nations*, Netanyahu draws from Kant's "Perpetual Peace," and distinguishes between two types of peace. The first is between nondemocratic states, or between a democracy and a nondemocratic state, and is based on deterrence and the balance of power. It is "peace through strength" (1993:250), temporal, reflecting interests, and not to be relied on. In other words, this is peace as seen by the realist tradition. Netanyahu and Hazony also follow Kant in envisaging a second type of peace; namely, peace between democracies. And this is the Kantian perpetual peace, or in more contemporary terms, stable peace. The Netanyahu-Hazony argument is that this is the peace we must aspire to for the Middle East, and it involves promoting democratization. Until such time as the Middle East is democratic and makes stable peace possible, Israel must rely on military might and settle for "peace through strength." According to Netanyahu and Hazony, this applies to Israel's bilateral relations with various Arab states—though not with the Palestinians, who should accept Israeli sovereignty over all of Greater Israel, including the territories taken in the 1967 War, and settle for a limited autonomy in those territories and a civic status in Jordan, which Netanyahu and Hazony view as the legitimate Palestinian state.

Some interesting points can be inferred from the Netanyahu-Hazony thesis, as presented in their book. First, there is a type of peace that is feasible with a nondemocratic state. It is not a stable peace, but there are not many who question Israel's military might and its ability to rely on such "peace through strength." Moreover, according to their analysis, this type of peace does exist, and has been maintained with Egypt (and also later with Jordan). Second, at least in 1993, when the book was written, Netanyahu's ideological commitment to a Greater Israel was very apparent. This was not a commitment to the pursuit of democratic peace as a means to resolving the Israeli-Palestinian conflict, nor was it a plan for Palestinian sovereignty.

A third point concerns the reasons Netanyahu and Hazony give for this vision of democratic peace. Why does Netanyahu think democracies are "immersed in a physical, psychological, and political state of peace"? Netanyahu and Hazony consider two popular arguments in the democratic peace literature: the structural argument and the normative argument. In a structural argumentation, they assert that "democracies require the consent of the governed to go to war, and that is not easy to secure" (1993:240). But they also claim, using more normative argumentation, that "the whole idea of politics in democratic states is the *nonviolent* resolution of conflict" (1993:240). This normative view of democratic peace, however, evaporates in light of the historical examples they cite, in which democratic regimes turned authoritarian and immediately resorted to force in their international conflicts; for example, Argentina in the Falklands/Malvinas case, Greece in Cyprus, and Nicaragua's aggressive regional behavior. According to Netanyahu and Hazony, when these states re-democratized, they resolved their conflicts in peaceful ways. Yet, quick transitions from democracy to authoritarianism and back leave the regime in a state of flux. The democracy being formed is an institutional type of democracy, not consolidated normative-cultural democracy. In other words, the norms and culture of democracy do not crystallize instantly; rather democratization is the product of long and difficult cultural and social processes. Thus, citing historical examples of instant democratization such as Argentina, Greece, and Nicaragua creates the impression that the democracy Netanyahu means is a structural one, and that his model for democratic peace is structural.

It was with this set of ideas that Netanyahu later constructed his vision of democratization as a key to peaceful coexistence in the Middle East, including in his term as prime minister between 1996 and 1999. He took an active role in the Israeli persuasion campaign regarding the Israeli-Palestinian conflict. Using his oratorical talents, Netanyahu used a series of public addressees to try to convince the American public and decision makers that no advance in the peace process was feasible until the Palestinian Authority (PA) democratized. In his role as persuader, Netanyahu can be considered a political entrepreneur of the idea of democratic peace; a promoter of its status as a political conviction guiding policies and strategies.

One of Netanyahu's best-known speeches took place on July 10, 1996, shortly after his first inauguration, when he addressed a joint session of the U.S. Congress. In it, Netanyahu referred to the normative understanding of democracy, arguing that an unwavering commitment to democracy by both the United States and Israel is what binds the two countries together. He went on to praise democracy, saying: "It is to be able to disagree, to express our disagreements, and sometimes to agree after disagreements. It means an inherent shift away from aggression towards the recognition of the mutual right to differ." In this address, Netanyahu introduces three novel ideas not present in A Place among the Nations. First, that democratic peace may also be valid regarding the Palestinians. This implies that he has abandoned his Greater Israel vision, accepting, as indeed he declared in his election campaign, the principles of the Oslo accords. But Netanyahu conditioned his acceptance of the Oslo agreement on three requirements: security, reciprocity, and democracy. Second, Netanyahu affirmed what he had written in his book, that a second type of peace exists: the deterrence-based peace with nondemocratic states. However, he did not see this as an option with the Palestinians; for them he demanded a third condition—democracy. In other words, what Netanyahu was willing to accept with the much stronger Syria—peace through strength—he was unwilling to accept with the impoverished and weak Palestinians.

Third, without referring explicitly to the democratic peace thesis, Netanyahu treated democratic peace as a well-established fact. "I am not revealing a secret to the Members of this Chamber when I say that modern democracies do not initiate aggression. This has been the central lesson of the 20th century. States that respect the human rights of their citizens are not likely to provoke hostile action against their neighbors." Netanyahu does not claim to be citing an eighteenth-century philosopher, but a modern, documented fact, supposedly proven by the social sciences.[7] He also assumes nonbelligerence of democracies to be common knowledge for Americans—in other words, an American public convention of world affairs—"I am not revealing a secret. . . ." Having stated this common knowledge, he uses the political avowal vernacular to decontest the political concepts of democratic peace in an altered form. First, he reinforces what he maintains is an observed fact about democracies: "modern democracies do not initiate aggression." Second, he claims that it is states that are the subject of these observations. True as it is, the political consequences of this declaration are that before democratizing the Palestinians, we need to enable them to establish a state. But to do that, we need to end the Israeli civil and military presence in the Palestinian territories. This implication, however, is absent from Netanyahu's analysis; it contravenes his political agenda. What this marks is the political misuse of the democratic peace as a public convention; Netanyahu ideologically and rhetorically decontests its political concepts according to the political needs of his own agenda, distorting some of the theory's claims, and ignoring others.

Another tenet of Netanyahu's address was already found in his book (1993:249–50); namely, the collective identity of democracies and the need to strengthen Israel on the basis of this common identity. Thus, "the proper course for the democratic world, led by the United States, is to strengthen the only democracy in the Middle East, Israel." He emphasized this even more in speeches after September 11, 2001, when global terrorism became the main topic on the U.S. international agenda. Netanyahu was no longer prime minister by then, but rather foreign minister in Sharon's government, and it is evident that he seeks as much political benefit as possible from the new situation. In this new context, Netanyahu advances the requisite-less version of democratic peace even further, discarding the conditionalities and probabilities of the theoretical constructions. Democracy is no longer just less aggressive—it does not practice terrorism—and hence, democratization is the ultimate solution to terror. This is the main theme of Netanyahu's address to the U.S. Senate on October 4, 2002: "The open debate and plurality of ideas that buttress all genuine democracies and the respect for human rights and the sanctity of life that are the shared values of all free societies are a permanent antidote to the poison that the sponsors of terror seek to inject into the minds of their recruits" (2002a).[8] Here, we can identify the close relationship between ideas and reality in forming public conventions—historical block of ideal and material described by Gramsci. The new realities of world politics, particularly the war against global terrorism, added to the attractiveness of democratic peace, and led to the re-decontestation of the concepts involved. Democratic peace no longer concerned just bilateral relations between states, but also the more abstract entity of global terrorism. Moreover, Netanyahu also uses political avowal vernacular to stress that terror is sponsored by states or "terrorist regimes," and that democracy is the desired solution.[9]

This is yet another opportunity for Netanyahu to build up a feeling of collective identity shared by democracies due to the common enemy they ostensibly face: "I have come before you today to ask you to continue to courageously and honorably carry that torch [of freedom] by standing by an outpost of freedom that is resisting an unprecedented terrorist assault. I ask you to stand by Israel's side in its fight against Arafat's tyranny of terror, and thereby help defeat an evil that threatens all of mankind." If Israel is part of the free world of democracies, then Arafat is part of global terror—the enemy. He and the Palestinians are stripped of their concrete claims, and of the specificity of their territorial demands. It all meshes together in Netanyahu's use of the concepts: "democracy" as identity, which implicitly means "democratic culture," and "terror" as the aggressive totalitarian "other," to be defeated by introducing democracy.

These same themes were the hallmark of another address Netanyahu gave as foreign minister on May 5, 2002—about six weeks before Bush's declaration of his Roadmap plan for the Middle East—at the Ashbrook Center for Public Affairs at Ashland University in Ohio (2002c). While repeating most of the earlier-mentioned themes, this time he returns to Kant as the source of his inspiration. But after describing the two types of peace argued by Kant, Netanyahu indicates that Kant's arguments are unsuitable for the twenty-first century with its new threat—terror. One of Kant's two types of peace—peace with nondemocratic states—would leave those states' totalitarianism intact, and terror would continue to flourish. "The totalitarian mindset is the root cause of terrorism.... If we leave this last region of the world [the Arab and Islamic world] undemocratized, unventilated by the winds of freedom, we are toying with our common survival. Not with Israel's survival, but the survival of our civilization." Netanyahu contends that the United States' role is to provide leadership to the free world, and compliments President Bush for doing so. Here again we witness the re-decontestation of political concepts: democratic peace has been transformed into an antidote not only against war among states, but also against terrorism, and en route is used to demarcate a democratic "we" from a nondemocratic "they." This political and rhetorical maneuvering is based on a cultural definition of democracy, but it only offers a structural cure for the plague of terrorism.

Although we can view Netanyahu's alternation between the structural and normative explanations of the democratic peace in his addresses and writings as internal inconsistencies, it is better to consider them part of a well-crafted public relations effort. Netanyahu should not be evaluated as a theoretician committed to coherence, but rather as a politician committed to political goals. It is as a politician that Netanyahu makes maximal use of the different aspects of the democratic peace thesis, using each to obtain a different political advantage. Accordingly, it is better to understand these inconsistencies as different subtexts that Netanyahu subtly tries to transmit to his readers and listeners. When using the normative theories of democracy and democratic peace, Netanyahu stresses commonality of identity: the democratic "we" against the autocratic (terrorist) "they." The potential political gain of this identity subtext is the strengthening of United States-Israeli ties, and further weakening the shaky United States-Palestinian relations. But when Netanyahu shifts to a structural reading of democracy and democratic peace, the message he sends is different. By stressing the structural theories, he tacitly suggests that it is not that difficult to democratize and to be democratized. If democracy means certain political structures, then what is required is no more than a structural reform of the political institutions, rather than a long and arduous process of socialization and norm dissemination. Indeed, the Israeli reservations to the Roadmap, as presented in a fourteen-point document on May 25, 2003, insist more on structural reforms of the Palestinian Authority than on democratization of Palestinian society (Israel Government 2003). This subtext of structural definition and explanation harbors two interlinked messages. The first is that striving for democratization is the best strategy for obtaining peace: on the one hand, it secures stable peace; on the other hand, it is quick, easy, and demands few resources. Hence, the best peace strategy is to insist that the Palestinian Authority democratize. This means, of course, suspending the peace process until they do so, which would afford Israel more time to change things on the ground; namely, build more settlements. But there is a second message as well. If all that is needed to democratize and secure peace is a few, rather easy structural reforms, and the Palestinians do not achieve this, then it means they do not really want peace or democracy. If they do not really want democracy, it further underscores the identity claim of "we" against "they." Of course, no doubt intentionally, this concept ignores several issues. The first is the implications of the normative definition of democracy—a definition Netanyahu himself uses when it is advantageous for his purposes. Actually, democratization is no easy process to achieve, as it involves not only political institutions, but also society and individuals. It is a process that might lose its legitimacy in the target state, if foreign powers were perceived to have imposed it. Furthermore, the tacit subtext suggesting that democratization is the best strategy for achieving peace also veils other strategies for promoting peace; namely, those that address mutual hatred, poverty, refugees, Jerusalem, and above all, the occupation and the spread of Jewish settlement.

This subsuming of other peace strategies is also linked to the implicit blame of the Palestinians for failing to achieve democracy. Democratization is not only a long and difficult process; it is also burdened by the Israeli military presence in the Palestinian territories. As Anatol Lieven rightly asked, how can we expect the Palestinians to democratize under military occupation, continuous curfews, and unresolved borders? (Lieven 2002) The proponents of peace by democratization do not ask this question; instead, they seek to gain politically by veiling it and blaming the Palestinians.

Evident in Netanyahu's rhetorical use of the democratic peace thesis is what I term the structural duality of the accessibility and incomprehensibility of theories. Netanyahu relies on the accessibility of theory, on their being generally known and broadly acknowledged among policy elites as valid and objective—in other words, as beyond partisan disputes. At the same time, Netanyahu does away with the subtleties and technicalities of theorizing in ways that are politically and rhetorically advantageous to him. He ignores the probabilistic nature of the theoretical claim, treating it instead as a law-like regularity. More significantly, he ignores the laws of inference. Even if it is true that democratizing the Palestinian Authority would bring about a stable peace, one cannot logically infer that stable peace is a nonpossibility with a nondemocratic Palestinian Authority. There is, after all, stable peace both with Egypt and Jordan. Furthermore, Netanyahu overlooks the terms of conditionality. In his formulations, democracies do not merely avoid war with other democratic states, they are overwhelmingly peaceful in nature and, moreover, they also provide an antidote against terrorism. Netanyahu also overlooks the inherent risk of destabilization in the transition to democracy. Thus, in his hands, the democratic peace thesis ceases to be probabilistic, debatable, and limited, instead becoming a magical, surefire remedy for every kind of political violence. Netanyahu's mobilization of the democratic peace thesis is thus logically flawed, but politically sound. It is not democratic peace as a theoretical construction, but democratic peace as a public convention (en route to being a political conviction), and the genre he uses is not the discursive genre of theoretical explanatory vernacular, but the discursive genre of political avowal vernacular.

Netanyahu's many public addresses over the past few years reveal him as an adept political entrepreneur in exploiting the democratic peace phenomenon.[10] At the time, Netanyahu's political and rhetorical uses, misuses and abuses of the democratic peace thesis successfully fostered an American public atmosphere that was supportive of Israel and conducive to Bush's Roadmap of June 2002, bringing about yet another delay in resuming negotiations with the Palestinians following the second intifada. This politics of postponement allowed the development of new Israeli settlements in the occupied territories, which the Israeli government regarded as facts on the ground that would carry weight in future final status negotiations. This successful politics of postponement is also evident in President Bush's letter to Prime Minister Sharon of April 14, 2004, in which he affirms Israel's claim that the final resolution must consider the map of Israel's settlements (Israel Ministry of Foreign Affairs 2004). Overwhelming majorities endorsed this letter both in the House of Representatives as Resolution 460 on June 23, 2004, and in the Senate as Resolution 393 a day later.

Natan Sharansky and the Politics of Avoidance

Another Israeli politician who utilized the democratic peace thesis rhetorically as a public convention was Natan Sharansky. Sharansky gained fame as a dissident in the former Soviet Union, a close associate of Nobel Peace laureate Andrei Sakharov,[11] and as a man who challenged the Soviet Union for its policy of banning Jewish emigration to Israel. He was a political prisoner for nine years until his release in 1986 as part of an East-West prisoner exchange. Upon his release he was awarded the U.S. Congressional Gold Medal, emigrated to Israel, and in 1995 turned to politics, forming the Russian immigrant party Yisrael B'Aliyah.[12] Although mainly focused on Russian immigrant problems, the party took a right-wing position on security matters. Under Sharansky's leadership, Yisrael B'Aliyah joined coalition governments with the leftist Labor and rightist Likud parties. Sharansky served in several ministerial positions: industry and trade, interior, housing and construction, Jerusalem and the Diaspora, and was appointed deputy prime minister. Following the Likud's landslide victory in 2003, Yisrael B'Aliyah, having lost much of its electoral strength over the years, merged with Likud. Upon his appointment to the cabinet he was assigned the post of Minister without Portfolio, responsible for Jerusalem and Diaspora affairs. However, after his opposition to the disengagement plan from Gaza, Sharansky resigned from the cabinet. In November 2006, he resigned from the Knesset and was appointed chairman of the Adelson Institute for Strategic Studies at the rightist think tank Shalem Center. In June 2009, he was elected Chairman of the Jewish Agency for Israel.

Throughout Sharansky's political career, while propounding Palestinian Authority democratization as a precondition for peace, he was a vocal opponent of every peace initiative. We can reasonably infer from Sharansky's consistent hawkish stands that he used the democratic peace thesis to utterly avoid resuming negotiations with the Palestinians, and the concomitant Israeli territorial concessions. Sharansky, in other words, practices a politics of avoidance.

Since entering Israeli politics as a right-wing leader of the Russian immigrant community, Sharansky has argued against the Oslo accords. His criticism was harsh, and at times personal. In a 2003 op-ed article, he condemned what he termed the "gang of Oslo blazers," or "Beilin's gang" (Sharansky 2003). Usually, though, his criticism was aimed at what he saw as the flawed logic of the Oslo accords: "Take a dictator from Tunis, bring him to the West Bank and Gaza, give him control over 98 percent of all Palestinians, offer him territory, legitimacy, money, an army, and economical tools—and, as a result, he will be so interested in playing the role of a leader of his people that he will become our partner. That was the idea" (2002b). This criticism in itself is not necessarily linked to the democratic peace thesis. Its origins, as he himself declares, lie in his personal distrust of authoritarian regimes stemming from his experiences in the former Soviet Union. Nevertheless, his criticism is tied to the democratic peace thesis in two ways. The first is the logic Sharansky uses to support his personal convictions. The second is his use of the rhetorical capital of the democratic peace thesis to deflect some of the American criticism of the Israeli occupation and convince the Americans to adopt a different Middle East strategy.

Sharansky himself says that he draws the logic of his argument from the teachings of Andrei Sakharov.

> Long ago, Andrei Sakharov taught me that a society that does not respect the rights of its own citizens will never respect the rights of its neighbors. The reasons for this are simple. Democratic leaders are dependent for their rule on the will of a free people and as such have a vested interest in promoting the peace and prosperity that all free societies desire. In doing so, the nations they govern naturally assume a nonbelligerent

posture toward their neighbors, particularly when those neighbors are also democratic states pursuing the same objectives. (2000b)

This gives rise to the axiom that "democracies do not go to war with one another" (2000b). In other words,

> in a democracy, the leader has to be concerned about the well-being of his people. For him, war is always the last resort, because people want to avoid war at all costs. A dictator, however, does not depend on his people; the people depend on him. His primary goal, and greatest headache, is how to keep the people under control. To do so, he always needs an enemy, against whom he can constantly mobilize his people. The enemy can be an external one, an internal one, or if the dictator, like Stalin, is particularly adept, both external and internal concurrently. (Sharansky 2002b; see also Sharansky 2001)

Sharansky makes a point of saying that he considers Sakharov his mentor. Notably, Sakharov's writing contains much that resembles Kant's ideas on peace. Sakharov deals with the need for governments to be accountable to their citizens, and to govern according to their needs and wishes. Sakharov, however, offers an additional prodemocracy argument regarding the importance of total freedom of information and exchange of views.[13] Sakharov's reasoning mainly resembles the structural explanations of democratic peace focusing on the need for regime accountability. This accountability ensures that the public plays a role in the political equation of checks and balances, operating as another branch alongside the executive, legislative, and judicial branches. Thus the public is part of the democratic structure, which slows down decision-making and contributes to de-escalating dyadic crises and stabilizing relations between states. Herein also lies the affinity of Sharansky's views with democratic peace argumentation. Sharansky's criticism of the Oslo accords stems not just from personal anger against despotism, whether Stalinist or Arafatian in form. Instead, it reflects a deep conviction that despotism brings war, while democracy prevents it.

Sharansky proposed an alternative to the Oslo accords. In a *Jerusalem Post* article published in May 2002, he set out a peace program, which he called "a seven-point plan of action towards a permanent peace settlement" (2002a). The points proposed:

1. An International Coordinating Body to establish a Palestinian Administrative Authority (PAA).
2. For the PAA to be responsible for the day-to-day administration of Palestinian affairs.
3. Israel to be responsible for security.
4. The PAA and the International Coordinating Body to be responsible for developing a democratic way of life.
5. The immediate dismantlement of the refugee camps and the Arab countries and United Nations to finance the resettlement of the refugees.
6. An international economic fund to be established for the creation and finance of industry and infrastructure development.
7. After a three-year transition period under the administration of the PAA and the International Coordinating Body, free and open elections would be held in the areas administered by the PAA, after which negotiations for a permanent peace would begin.

Significant in this plan is the democratization of the Palestinian polity as a precondition for permanent peace. Other issues are also addressed, such as the implied need to dismantle the existing Palestinian Authority, the internationalization of the conflict, and the postponement of final negotiations. But points 4 and 7, which make democratization a precondition for negotiating the final settlement, are its core.[14] Although point 4 implies the need for democratic education, point 7 makes it clear that elections and accountability are the ultimate criteria for democratization. These conceptions of structural democratization on the one hand, coupled with a minimal, structural definition of democracy on the other, mutually reinforce one another. Thus Sharansky consistently links democratic peace, the definition of democracy, and the type of democratization that can solve the Israeli-Palestinian conflict.

Sharansky presented this plan in many forums, including to Prime Minister Sharon, and in many public addresses in American universities. For example, in September 2003, he gave a one-week, whistle-stop lecture tour of thirteen American universities, including Boston University, Columbia University, New York University, and the University of Maryland. The series was sponsored by Beit Hillel, a Jewish student organization. Introduced as the former Soviet dissident, and facing audiences that were not all supportive, Sharansky presented his views on the necessary linkage between democracy and peace. As he asserted at Boston University on September 16, 2003, "I believe that peace is possible, and I believe a two-state solution is possible . . . but only when Israel no longer is the only democracy in the Middle East" (Craig 2003).

Sharansky's most successful talk was at the AEI (American Enterprise Initiative) World Forum in Beaver Creek, Colorado, on June 20, 2002. He was invited to the conference by Richard Perle, one of the leading neoconservative advisers to the Bush administration. Although at the beginning of Sharansky's anti-Oslo campaign he was often ridiculed and was swimming against the current, this was no longer the case in 2002. Several developments contributed to this change: the outbreak of the second intifada and the collapse of the peace process, which many perceived as the fulfillment of Sharansky's forecasts; the 2000 elections and the formation of a new right-wing government headed by Sharon; the outbreak of a new wave of world terror, purportedly directed by Osama Bin Laden and epitomized by September 11, 2001; and the rise to power of neoconservatives in the U.S. administration. The neoconservatives were looking for new strategies to combat terror, and were amenable to the ideas that Sharansky, the famous Soviet dissident, and one of the great warriors against the Soviet Union's evil empire, was voicing.[15] They were especially amenable to his ideas as many of them themselves envisaged the democratic peace as a public convention; namely, as is its requisiteless version (this is the subject of the next chapter). Sharansky and the neoconservatives were, so to speak, brothers in ideational arms. The AEI World Forum was attended by close associates of the neoconservatives, including Vice President Dick Cheney and Deputy Defense Secretary Paul Wolfowitz. Sharansky, who was one of the keynote speakers, tellingly called his lecture "Democracy for Peace" (2002b).

Sharansky, as usual, mentioned his intellectual debt to Sakharov, his criticism of the Oslo accords, and the need for democracy to guarantee peace. He emphasized four main points: democracy as the cure for terror, the shared identity of the democratic nations, the collective identity of all terror, and the feasibility of introducing the democratic ideal to the Arab and Islamic world. Sharansky began with the declaration, "We are in the midst of the first world war of the twenty-first century, waged between the world of terror and the world of democracy." Addressing mainly the Reagan-era veterans in his audience, Sharansky praised Reagan's tough stance on the

Soviet Union and made the familiar claim that terrorism had taken over from communism as a global menace.[16] Sharansky then referred to Stalin as the prototype of the dictator who mobilizes his people against purported external and internal enemies. From Stalin he moved to Arafat, claiming that Arafat had rejected Barak's offers because as a dictator he needed Israel as an enemy to mobilize his people. From Arafat he moved on to praise the war in Afghanistan in the name of democratization. Thus, in one oratorical sweep, he meshed together America's past and current threats, its self-perceived mission in the world, and Israel's current threats. He invoked, in other words, the eternal struggle between the democratic "we" and the despotic "they."

Here, we can detect a brief alternation in the definition and conceptualization of democracy; a tactical move similar to that of Netanyahu. Sharansky tried—quite successfully—to establish a feeling of common democratic identity between Israel and the United States. To this end, he briefly offers a cultural-normative definition of democracy, before returning to his familiar structural conception. He asserts that just as "we" won the Cold War, "we" will also win this new world war, because "we" are democratic. In his own words, "What a powerful weapon, democracy! What a drug for the people! Give it to them, and it will be the best guarantee of security." Sharansky maintains that people cannot resist the freedom of democracy: the freedom to express beliefs without fear of reprisal. Democracy is irresistible universally, even to the Islamic and Arab world, as long as it is defined minimally by structural criteria.[17] Thus, to defeat terrorism and promote Middle East peace, we need to promote democracy. Toward the end of his speech, Sharansky briefly summarized his seven-point plan for a lasting Israeli-Palestinian peace. He uses the same rhetorical tactics as Netanyahu, relying both on the accessibility and incomprehensibility of the democratic peace thesis, expediently relating the thesis to the popular belief of "us" against "them," and finally strategically reframing it as "democratic us" against an "autocratic them," and generally dispensing with such subtleties and technicalities of theorizing as cautiousness, probability, and conditionality. This was Sharansky at his best—with his political avowal vernacular flowing, as he painted a requisiteless picture of democratic peace using forceful declarations in slogan-like fashion.

Sharansky gave this address less than a week before Bush's Rose Garden speech in which he announced the launch of his Roadmap. Several commentators believe that Sharansky's meetings with Cheney and Wolfowitz considerably influenced the final version of the Roadmap speech (Ephron and Lipper 2002; Milbank 2002; Rosenblum 2002). Indeed, as Dana Milbank points out, we find many similarities between Sharansky and Bush's ideas on several issues, such as the need for a new Palestinian leadership, a three-year transitional period, an international coordinating body to supervise and support Palestinian institution building, and of course, the need for a free and open Palestinian society as a guarantee of peace and security for Israel (Milbank 2002).

Sharansky's use of the rhetorical capital of the democratic peace thesis therefore seems to have hit its mark. His public addresses and private meetings apparently established democratization as the hallmark of the Roadmap. Later Bush's plan was also adopted by the Quartet—the international mediating body—and a more detailed and operative plan was drafted in April 2003. The impact of Sharansky's ideas on Bush's policy was dramatic indeed. And it was still further heightened following the publication of Sharansky's book *The Case for Democracy* in 2004 (Sharansky with Dermer 2004). The book appeared at a politically intense juncture, when the war in Iraq was the focus of controversy during the American presidential election campaign. Sharansky's lucid and popular formulations, along with his personal prestige as a freedom fighter and dissident for democracy, boosted Bush's rhetoric. Sharansky's influence is very clear in Bush's second inaugural address. Both President Bush and Secretary of State Condoleezza Rice, boasted of reading the book, which they praised, thereby further endorsing Sharansky's ideas in the United States (see Milbank 2004; Murphy 2005).

But, I would argue there is reason to suspect Sharansky's sincerity in his use of the democratic peace thesis. There may be a doubt that he was wholeheartedly committed to a two-state solution, and he seems to exploits the rhetorical capital of the democratic peace and the status of democratic peace as a public convention in American commonsense thinking. Essentially, he practices a politics of avoidance. Sharansky tabled the idea of democratizing the Palestinian Authority as a way of diverting American attention from other, much more critical issues to resolving the Israeli-Palestinian conflict, such as the settlements, refugees, and Jerusalem.

The moment he entered Israeli politics, Sharansky showed a hawkish stance, and with it a vision of a Greater Israel. Even as a member of Ehud Barak's government, which supposedly was committed to advancing the peace process, he put up fierce internal opposition.[18] And as a coalition member of Likud governments he proved a vocal opponent of every political initiative, including Sharon's June 2004 proposal for unilateral withdrawal. One way to understand Sharansky's opposition and rejection of the Israeli government proposals is to assume he believed that Israel's political initiatives would strengthen the Arafat dictatorship and were doomed to failure, and to generate ever more violence. But, it would be wrong to ascribe this view to Sharansky because the logic he uses reveals a fundamental commitment to a Greater Israel. We see this from the fact that Sharansky rarely discussed the full extent of his ideology, or his vision of the map of a future democratic Palestinian state. In one of his articles, which appeared in the Israeli daily *Haaretz*, we do, however, find a real glimpse of what his true views are. The article, "The Temple Mount is More Important than Peace," published on October 16, 2003, deals with Jerusalem and the most sacred site of all, the Temple Mount (Sharansky 2003).[19] Sharansky argues that the Jewish people's religious, historical, and national ties to the Temple Mount constitute the roots of the Zionist movement; they are the raison d'être of Zionism, of the Jewish's people's return to Israel. As such, the Temple Mount is essential to Jewish national existence in Israel, and hence is even more important than peace. Ceding the Temple Mount, Sharansky asserts, would mean the end of Zionism and the state of Israel. Although the article relates just to the Temple Mount, its arguments can be extrapolated to the occupied territories as a whole. The religious and historical significance of the West Bank, a region referred to in Israel by its biblical name: Judea and Samaria, is also very strong. These are the same landscapes that biblical figures once trod, and whomever believes in the existential religious, historical, and national importance of the Temple Mount, presumably shares the same beliefs concerning Judea and Samaria.

But Sharansky's commitment to a Greater Israel is evident, however, not only based on his support for Israeli sovereignty over the Temple Mount. He was also one of the supporters of the Israeli settlements, and worked on their behalf in his different ministerial positions. The Israeli state comptroller provided evidence of his efforts in his May 2004 report, which identifies Sharansky, in his position as minister of housing and construction, as responsible for the massive transfer of funds to settlements and to unauthorized settlements ("outposts") in the Palestinian heartland—in apparent abuse of his ministerial powers (Israel State Comptroller 2004:345–74, esp.

365–67). In other words, Sharansky exploited his position as minister to finance and strengthen Israel's hold on the territories—or, to frame it in different terminology—he bolstered the Israeli occupation.

Assisting settlement development is at odds with the argument that the road to peace lies through democratization. It is one thing to say that Israel should not participate in the peace process unless the Palestinians are fully democratized; it is another thing to work against that process. Yet that is exactly what happens when Israel builds more settlements. As noted earlier, Lieven argues that one cannot expect the Palestinians to aim for a free and open society when there is military occupation, ongoing curfews, and a lack of recognized borders (Lieven 2002). Democratization is not a real possibility when Palestinians see more and more land of their ostensible future state confiscated from them. The vision of this state's viability being ruined by the loss of territorial contiguity is counterproductive to working toward a future democratic form of government. If Sharansky was truly interested in seeking a two-democratic-states solution, he would not have helped build ever more obstacles in its path.

When we examine Sharansky's words and deeds more closely it thus becomes clear that he used the democratic peace argument to successfully deflect the United States from the conflict's more troublesome issues, such as settlements, refugees, and Jerusalem. Thus, he succeeded in averting negotiations and helping to strengthen the Greater Israel project. Sharansky did not just use the democratic peace thesis; he abused it in a manipulative, political manner to serve his ideological agenda. Relying on its status as a public convention he transformed it into a political conviction of the impracticability and danger of conceding territories to the authoritarian Palestinian Authority, and of advancing the peace process if the Palestinian Authority failed to democratize.

Conclusions

This chapter traced the rhetorical uses by Israeli rightist politicians of the democratic peace thesis. One contribution of the chapter is empirical: its examination of the role of the Israeli right's rhetoric in the road to the Roadmap and the hidden political agendas informing these rhetorical efforts. While Benjamin Netanyahu mobilizes democratic peace in a "politics of postponements," Natan Sharansky mobilizes it in a "politics of avoidance." The former tries to postpone negotiations with the Palestinians in order to establish more "facts on the ground"; that is, more settlements to help Israel secure a bigger chunk of the occupied territories following peace negotiations. The latter tries to avoid negotiations entirely for the sake of a "Greater Israel." Their respective efforts have indeed proved successful: President Bush's Roadmap and its insistence on Palestinian Authority democratization as a precondition to progress in the negotiations; the consequent exchange of letters with Prime Minister Sharon, in which President Bush committed the United States to acknowledging "new realities on the ground" (as Israel continued to build new settlements and enlarge existing ones); and the U.S. Congress resolutions affirming Bush's commitments, testify to this rhetorical success. Still, one must be cautious in asserting these claims too strongly. Rhetoric hardly ever operates alone in shaping policies. Rhetoric helps to foster certain readings of reality that facilitate certain policies while hindering others. In other words, while not determining reality, rhetoric works within the terms of reality to help advance certain agendas.

However, this chapter's main aims have not been empirical, but theoretical. Its primary aim has been to use the theoretical concept of "rhetorical capital," which it defines as the aggregate persuasive resources inherent in entities. The concept of rhetorical capital is valuable in that it not only allows researchers to study the rhetor's skills, but to evaluate the assets available to him or her: which features facilitate the rhetor's use of theories (or any other material or ideal entity) to his or her rhetorical advantages. This chapter's second aim was to present the applicability of the concept of rhetorical capital to the study of theories and the relation between theory and reality. As explained in chapter 1 and demonstrated in this chapter, I side with some of the claims made by rhetoric of science scholars, but part way with their more substantial assertions regarding relativism and the irrationalism of science. Theoreticians, I concur, use rhetoric, whether to raise research grants, convince their colleagues in the soundness of their findings and merits of their theories, or bolster their personal prestige. A good example of rhetoric in the hands of theoreticians is their titling the absence of war "democratic peace." What was historically recorded negatively, as no-war, in theory has been positively dubbed peace. And as "no-war" and "peace" are not identical, and as the former is less alluring than the latter, this titling is indeed a work of rhetoric performed by theoreticians. However, titling is marginal to the work of science (be that natural science, social science, or the humanities). As such, it is applicable with my general thrust that the claim of scholars of the rhetoric of science is too sweeping. Later, this move also helps me to establish a normative theory of the theoreticians' responsibilities to society; a normative theory that by its nature takes morality seriously, and rejects the relativism espoused by the literature of the rhetoric of science.

Accordingly, while endorsing some of the claims of the literature of the rhetoric of science, I prefer to focus the study of rhetoric away from the theoreticians, and to study the rhetorical uses, misuses, and abuses of theories by politicians instead. The concept "rhetorical capital" is most useful in this. This chapter identified several resources of the rhetorical capital of theories. The first are general and shared by most theories: they relate to the structural duality of accessibility and incomprehensibility overlaid with the prestige of objectivity. The other four are specific to theories of the democratic peace and are: the status of the democratic peace thesis among policy elites as public convention—that is, as a law-like phenomenon governing the realm of world politics; the existence of two distinct families of theories trying to explain the phenomenon, each helpful in delivering a different political message; the immediate implications of subscribing to the conclusions of the democratic peace thesis—namely, the ensuing political commitment urging the democratization of non-democratic states for the sake of national security: and fourthly, the long and prestigious heritage of the thesis, being ascribed rightly or wrongly to Immanuel Kant. All these resources have indeed been mobilized rhetorically by both Netanyahu and Sharansky, who employed political avowal vernacular to achieve their political agendas.

5

THE CIVILIZATION OF CLASHES
The Neoconservative Reading of Democratic Peace

A specter is haunting American neoconservatism—the specter of promoting democracy. It exorcises whatever prudence conservatism might otherwise espouse; it drives neoconservatives' grand strategy to experimentalism that otherwise they would condemn as "social engineering." This chapter explores the part played by the democratic peace thesis in bringing this about, and examines another case in which the theory of democratic peace underpinned a political conviction—the political conviction that framed the American neoconservative grand strategy of promoting democracy by force.

The specter—or urge—to democratize runs counter to several philosophical and political tenets that supposedly hold conservatives back from foreign adventurism. These restraining tenets are varied and are manifested differently and take various forms: (1) Contemporary conservatism, which contrary to the more traditional nineteenth-century conservatism, is aligned with the justification and defense of an almost unrestrained individual liberty. Conservatism is associated nowadays with the political philosophy of libertarianism with its inherent distrust of strong central government and its appeal for low taxation and weak government that do not and cannot invest scarce public resources in outbound adventurism; (2) Conservatism, following Edmund Burke, considers the concept of universal rights as an abstract conceptualization that fails to account for the historicity and particularities of actual societies and cultures. It takes a skeptical view of intervention in matters of foreign societies and cultures—even for humanitarian reasons, as vividly advocated in 1979 by Jeane Kirkpatrick; (3) The conservative scorn for policies that interfere with the historicity of actual societies, especially when they place excessive trust in the faculty of rationality and seek to redistribute private and public resources. Consequently, welfare policies are tagged as "social engineering," and are feared as leading to social destabilization. This scorn is also evident in global affairs and limits the incentive to reform other societies; (4) Prudence, especially in matters of foreign affairs, which conservatives hold in high esteem as a political virtue, and, (5) Modern conservatism preaches market economy and profit-driven policies that might serve as checks for costly outbound adventurism.

Historically, none of these restraints has prevented conservative leaders and societies from waging unnecessary and expensive wars. Nor have they prevented conservative-led nations from mounting imperialist and colonialist expansionist projects. Conflicting conservative tenets such as paternalism and visions of national grandeur, together with a host of spatial historical reasons and political dynamism, are always at work and indeed, at times, encourage outbound adventurism. However, the contemporary creed of American neoconservatism seems unparalleled in its resolve to experiment in outward "social engineering." In their unprecedentedly aggressive grand strategy of gunpoint democratization, contemporary neoconservative ideologists eschew whatever conservative restraints there are, and the highly controversial Bush Doctrine is evidence of that.

Prior scholarly explanations of the Bush Doctrine and the strategic thinking of neoconservatism emphasized power seeking in light of the September 11, 2001, terror attacks and the attendant threats of global terrorism, rogue states, and weapons of mass destruction (WMD) (Hymans 2004; Kellner 2004; Rosen 2003; Miller 2006–2007); the philosophy of Leo Strauss (Drolet 2011; Drury 1997; Norton 2004); visions of national exceptionalism and imperial aspirations (Cox 2003; Ikenberry 2002; Ferguson 2003; Jervis 2003; Snyder 2003); ideological and religious articles of faith (Boyle 2004; Mazarr 2003; Monten 2005); and the drive to control the oil market (Nell and Semmler 2003; Pelletiere 2004; Research Unit for Political Economy 2003a, 2003b). Notwithstanding these explanations, I wish to highlight the contribution of the democratic peace thesis' public conventions to the Bush Doctrine. It was, after all, a prominent neoconservative, Joshua Muravchick, who started the balling rolling of transforming the theoretical constructions of democratic peace into public conventions. It should now be no surprise to learn that these same public conventions played such a crucial role in neoconservative strategic thinking. Through the neoconservatives' efforts the public conventions of democratic peace thesis were transformed once again into powerful political convictions that were conducive to the formulation of the Bush Doctrine, and useful to the political campaign to explain and legitimate it.

This chapter tracks the process of translating the public conventions into political convictions. It shows that in the specific case of the neoconservatives the political representations and misrepresentations of the structural theories of the democratic peace were responsible for generating the neoconservative grand strategy. These are the theories that try to explain the absence (or near absence) of war between democracies by pointing to the structural attributes of democracies, such as checks and balances, division of powers, and periodical elections. I argue that the political representations and misrepresentations of those theories played multiple and crucial roles in shaping and in marketing the neoconservative agenda of promoting democracy abroad. The democratic peace as public conventions helped the neoconservatives overcome their post–Cold War identity crisis and the demise of their old archenemy—communism. The strategic program of promoting democracy revived neoconservatism, endowing it with new coherence and purpose.

A decade after the Cold War ended, the neoconservatives faced yet another identity crisis when confronted with the apparent incompatibility between two major conservative theoretical frameworks: the pessimism and relativism of Samuel Huntington's *Clash of Civilizations*, and the optimism and universalism of Francis Fukuyama's *End of History*. The structural theories of democratic peace offered the neoconservatives a middle ground between the two, together with a both cautiously optimistic and mildly relativist political platform. The political platform consists of three major premises: (1) expanding democracy will enlarge the zone of peace and overcome the threats of civilizational wars, global terrorism, and rogue states; (2) democracy should be understood structurally, rather than culturally and morally, and (3) the structures of democracy can also be built in civilizations whose cultures and moralities are incompatible with those of the democratic West. These three premises explain the neoconservative preoccupation with promoting democracy abroad, particularly in the Middle East, by force if necessary. In other words, the public conventions of the structural theories of democratic peace resolved some of the neoconservatives' major difficulties, and generated the grand strategy of forceful democracy promotion.[1]

Moreover, by insisting on the scientific validity of the claim that democracies do not fight each other, the neoconservatives successfully marketed their agenda to the American public and the Bush administration, proclaiming the proved strategic merits of exporting democracy. This, it should be stressed from the start, was an act of political entrepreneurship. It was an act of transforming relatively weak public conventions into much stronger political convictions that were capable of driving—and indeed did drive—political action. It should also be obvious by now that although the neoconservatives insisted on the scientific validity of their claim, that claim was unfounded. What they embraced and preached was not the scientifically based theoretical construction, but rather a simplified version; namely, the public convention. Yet, it is this insistence on the scientific validity of public conventions that has worked very well in politicizing public conventions and transforming them into the more highly politicized and powerful political convictions. This was one of the sources of influence of the Bush Doctrine and its preoccupation with promoting democracy.

This chapter has five sections. The first outlines the major reasons for the neoconservatives' endorsement of the structural theories of democratic peace. The second explores the democratic peace thesis and its various theories to explain why the neoconservatives choose the structural theories, rather than the normative ones. The third section demonstrates the strategic outcomes of adopting the public and political representations of those theories, and maintains that this was what transformed neoconservatism into what I metaphorically term the "civilization of clashes"[2]—an ideology of endless military crusades aimed at spreading democracy. The fourth section analyzes the efforts by realist theoreticians Stephen Walt and John Mearsheimer to revitalize realism as a public convention and political conviction, and to foster a viable political opposition to the Bush Doctrine. The final section offers a conceptual critique of the neoconservative grand strategy, identifying two acute internal incoherencies. It also points to a political harm caused by the neoconservative embrace of the political conviction of democratic peace; namely, the rigidity and dogmatization of American foreign policy.

Reasons for Endorsing the Structural Theories of Democratic Peace

Five factors contributed to the neoconservatives' adoption of the structural theories of democratic peace:

1. The end of the Cold War
2. Their affiliation with Israeli politicians such as Benjamin Netanyahu and Natan Sharansky, who, in the latter half of the 1990s, made use

of the democratic peace thesis in attempting to delegitimize the Oslo accords
3. The longstanding neoconservative agenda of toppling Saddam Hussein
4. The terror attacks of September 11, 2001
5. The intellectual perplexity resulting from the conflicting theoretical frameworks of two major conservative works: Fukuyama's *The End of History*, and Huntington's *The Clash of Civilizations?*[3]

In the late 1980s and early 1990s, American foreign policy—after what was seen as its greatest success, the collapse of the Soviet Union and the end of the Cold War—experienced a phase of bafflement. The loss of America's archrival destroyed the purpose and coherence of a well-institutionalized foreign policy. What was bafflement for some verged on existential crisis for others, primarily the neoconservatives for whom their main—almost sole—raison d'être was fierce anticommunism.

This crisis manifested itself in various ways. In 1989–1990, one of the flagship neoconservative journals, the *National Interest*, published a series of articles, mostly authored by conservatives and neoconservatives, on America's purpose after the Cold War. Irving Kristol, one of the godfathers of neoconservatism, wrote:

> It is very difficult for a great power—a world power—to articulate a foreign policy in the absence of an enemy worthy of the name. It is, after all, one's enemies that help define one's "national interest," in whatever form that definition might take. Without such enemies, one flounders amidst a plentitude of rather trivial, or at least marginal, options. That, it seems to me, is the condition of the United States today, as we enter the post–Cold War era. (1990:16)[4]

In their search for a new rationale, some prominent neoconservative thinkers like Joshua Muravchik and Carl Gershman, and later also Charles Krauthammer, William Kristol, and others, adopted the relatively new theories of democratic peace, calling for a revived Wilsonian commitment to democracy promotion. As Muravchik wrote in his 1991 book *Exporting Democracy*: "the more democratic the world, the more peaceful it is likely to be. *Various researchers have shown that war between democracies has almost never occurred in the modern world"* (1990:8, emphasis added; see also Gershman 1990:86; on the endorsing of the new agenda of democracy promotion, see also Ehrman 1995:184; Halper and Clarke 2004:76). According to these thinkers, the democratic peace thesis showed there was no real gap between morality and interest in foreign policy—that it was high time to stop supporting local dictators in the name of stability, and that promoting democracy would broaden the zone of peace. Moreover, as Michael Williams pointed out, it was also the neoconservative vision of American exceptionalism that supplied the rationale for the idea of promoting democracy (Williams 2005:318–19). By linking the American present to its past, and especially to the founding era of the American republic, the neoconservatives could offer some continuity and coherence at the time of the identity crisis that succeeded the Cold War.

As chapter 4 showed, following the 1993 Oslo accords, two prominent Israeli rightist politicians mobilized the democratic peace thesis to delegitimize the agreements. Netanyahu and Sharansky criticized Oslo on the ground that peace with the Palestinians would be impossible until they had democratized. The neoconservatives lauded Netanyahu and Sharansky's positions (see, for example, Krauthammer 2002; Stoll 2002). Praise for Sharansky grew with the publication of his 2004 book *The Case for Democracy*, which, as discussed, had a significant impact on President Bush (see Puddington 2004; Wurmser 2004). This led to a revival of the neoconservatives' interest in the democratic peace thesis, particularly its application to the Middle East, and specifically to the Palestinian Authority. The result was a neoconservative demand, adopted by President Bush in his Roadmap announcement of June 24, 2002, that the Palestinians needed to democratize prior to any Israeli concessions.

Toppling Saddam Hussein had long been on the neoconservative agenda, at least since the first Gulf War and—as they saw it—its untimely ending. Or as William Kristol and Robert Kagan said, "The United States, which had mustered the world's most awesome military force to expel Saddam Hussein from Kuwait, failed to see that mission through to its proper conclusion: the removal of Saddam from power in Baghdad" (Kristol and Kagan 2000:6).[5] Initially, though, their demand for regime change in Iraq meant changing the leader, and not necessarily the regime itself. But when the prospects for another war in Iraq increased during the early 2000s, the neoconservatives called for a regime change that went far beyond personal cosmetics: they now championed the democratization of Iraq. For example, Gary Schmitt, executive director of the neoconservative think tank Project for the New American Century, declared: "A decade ago, the first Bush administration decided that leaving Saddam Hussein in power was acceptable. Now, a new Bush administration insists not only that Saddam's regime must go, but that, in its place, a decent, tolerant and representative government need arise" (Schmitt 2002:11).

Functional mobilization of the democratic peace thesis for the sake of strategic goals is not alien to neoconservatives. In a 1986 article, Robert W. Tucker, the notable scholar identified with neoconservatism, looked for a middle ground between excess foreign intervention for the sake of democratization, and too-little intervention. He advised that the United States could promote democracy most effectively by offering an exemplary democratic role model. He also suggested that to convince Americans to assume this role, democratization "must be effectively equated with security, and security must be given, in the first place, a conventional meaning" (Tucker 1986:72). What Tucker means is that moral argumentation is insufficient for mobilizing the American public to support policies of promoting democracy abroad, and that democratization should somehow be linked with security in order to be persuasive. To express this in the terms employed in this book, an argument with more rhetorical capital is needed, and that kind of rhetorically successful argumentation is supplied by the security rationale. This is especially so following the Vietnam War, whose shadows, according to neoconservatives and loathed by them, loom darkly over the American public, producing the "Vietnam Syndrome"; namely, anxiety at the prospect of a military expedition (Gelernter 2004). In his 1986 article, Tucker neither mobilized nor mentioned the democratic peace thesis. Indeed, 1986 was much too early for that as the thesis was relatively new and had yet to start its migration from academia to the public and political spheres; in fact, at that time, it still remained secluded in academia as a theoretical construction. However, in later articles, Tucker indeed used the democratic peace thesis to argue the need to promote democracy abroad. In 1993, two years after Muravchik's initial endorsement of the thesis, Tucker claimed—using what seems like the functional reasoning he called for in 1986—that promoting democracy enhances the security of the United States, since democracies do not fight each other (see, for example, Tucker 1992–1993:36). Other neoconservatives followed suit, endorsing the democratic peace thesis by advocating policies of democracy promotion.

On a different front, the neoconservatives adopted Netanyahu and Sharansky's creed: democracy is the antidote to terror. This notion does not stem directly from the democratic peace thesis,[6] and is rather an extension, and to some degree, a distortion of it, propelled by ideological reading and political needs. It is not necessarily a legitimate inference of the theory as a theoretical construction, yet it is a plausible reading of the theory's political representation. The line between representation and misrepresentation is very fine, and can be easily crossed as in this case. Concluding that democracies do not engage in terror based on the dyadic theoretical assertion that democracies never—or rarely—fight each other is not even a bad theoretical inference: it is a political misuse; a political misrepresentation deliberately designed to fit a political agenda. Searching for persuasive arguments to overthrow Saddam, the neoconservatives used the political misrepresentation of the democratic peace thesis to proclaim that occupying and democratizing Iraq was vital for stabilizing the Middle East and defeating global terrorism. After the war ended, and other arguments for it, especially the WMD rationale, were discredited, they only redoubled their use of the democratic reasoning (see, for example, columns by Krauthammer ([2003a, 2003b]); see also Miller 2006–2007:21). Put differently, once the war ended, a supplementary political value was added to the democratic peace thesis—that of ex post facto rationalization and legitimization.

To some extent, the effects of the September 11, 2001, terror attacks on U.S. soil resembled the end of the Cold War: both were viewed as a sea change that warranted new paradigms of strategic thinking. As Lawrence Kaplan and William Kristol argued, "We thought it [the Cold War] would always be with us. And when we found during the 1990s that it no longer was, we took a holiday from history, presuming that we could rely on commerce and globalization to achieve peace and stability. But the complacent assumptions of the post–Cold War era were destroyed on September 11. That day brought us to a new era, for which we need a new roadmap" (Kaplan and Kristol 2003:vii; see also Kristol 2004). Reuel Marc Gerecht, a former CIA specialist and prolific neoconservative writer, clarified the essence of this road map: "That the spread of democracy in the Muslim Middle East remains the only cure for the sacred terror of 9/11" (Gerecht 2004a:27; see also Gerecht 2004b).

Neoconservatives also used this occasion as an excuse for bashing the Saudi dynasty (another old bugbear of theirs), and severing the tight relations between the United States and Saudi Arabia. The neoconservatives were critical of United States-Saudi relations, maintaining that American considerations of strategic stability had led to tolerance of an authoritarian regime that was no more than a hornet's nest and breeding ground for terrorists. Henceforth, the argument went, the United States needed to pressure the Saudis to reform their regime and move toward democracy, thus eliminating the reasons for terror and terror itself (Schwartz 2001; Pipes 2002–2003; Alexiev 2003; Hanson 2002).

The search for a new paradigm of international politics was prompted by yet another source of perplexity: a debate among conservative intellectuals. Two famous works symbolize the endpoints of the conservative spectrum of international relations. At one pole we find the universalism and optimism of Francis Fukuyama's *The End of History and the Last Man*; at the other, the relativism and pessimism of Samuel Huntington's *The Clash of Civilizations and the Remaking of World Order*. Whereas Fukuyama claims the victory of Western/U.S. capitalism and liberal democracy, Huntington foresees the decline of the West/United States, and the rise of China with its civilization. Whereas Fukuyama believes in universal truth and morality, according to Huntington, the systems of truth and morality of the contrasting civilizations are incompatible.

These two works not only represent the endpoints of conservative thinking, but also the beginning and end of an era. Fukuyama's book (and the article that preceded it) stemmed from the end of the Cold War and resultant sense of euphoria. Huntington's book (and preceding article), while published before September 11, 2001, reflected the awakening from this euphoria. According to Huntington, Fukuyama was not only too optimistic to argue that perfection was near;[7] what was happening instead was a deterioration in international relations. It was no Kantian eternal peace that awaited humanity, but rather a reversion to a Hobbesian state of affairs that would be worse this time due to the involvement of basic human attachments of identities and civilizations, making the wars even deadlier than before. Indeed, the lighthearted 1990s ended before they had really begun when the Balkans erupted in yet another round of their eternal conflicts.[8]

It is hard to reconcile these two modes of thought. It is even harder to come up with a strategy that would counter the pessimism and sense of determinism in *The Clash of Civilizations* (although there is also a sense of determinism in Fukuyama's works). The price of no reconciliation, however, might be too high in terms of neoconservative self-identity and internal cohesiveness. Huntington and Fukuyama are both leading thinkers of the American right,[9] and their arguments resonated strongly. Indeed, both books made the *New York Times* best-seller list—a rarity for academic works.

Moreover, each of their theses fitted in well with certain conservative and neoconservative premises. Fukuyama's position was palatable to the conservative belief in the teleological nature of history that actualizes an historical scheme devised by some higher rationality. It also reinforces the belief in the supremacy of the free market. Huntington's thesis jibes with the conservative conviction that individuals are circumscribed by their communities, and that these communities evolve historically and gradually—that is, as civilizations; it also resonates with Burke's philosophy of historical rights and, even more so, with the Fichtean conflictual version of Herder's historiography. Huntington's thesis is also amenable to the neoconservative view of international politics as a Manichean battle between the democratic world and the world of terror. And, as Andrei Tsygankov showed in 2003, these theses also share yet another common conservative tenet—ethnocentrism. Hence, neoconservatives are torn between the two thinkers and their conflicting theses.

As we see from much of their writing, the neoconservatives indeed accept Huntington's arguments. They deem the values and norms of other civilizations incompatible with their own, including their democratic norms. This is especially true regarding the Islamic or Arabic civilizations. William Kristol, for example, gives a Straussian reading of President Bush. He quotes Bush—"Anyone in the world, including the Arab world, who works and sacrifices for freedom has a loyal friend in the United States"—and then adds: "Why 'including the Arab world'? Because that world—or better, perhaps, the Middle East or the Islamic world—is the heart of the problem" (2003:9). Kristol asserts that this is the true meaning of President Bush's declaration, despite Bush's need to conceal it for political reasons. He thus uses a Straussian methodology to rescue Bush's true, esoteric meaning—to which Kristol himself subscribes—regarding the cultural and normative incompatibility between the West and the Islamic world.

Cultural incompatibility is also a theme in Muravchik's writings. As he asserted in *Commentary*: "[the Middle East] region [is] characterized by paranoia, apocalypticism, tyranny, and violence, a region where differences are settled by the sword" (Muravchik 2002a:29; see also Muravchik 2002b;

Muravchik 2004). In a similar spirit, Stanley Kurtz—another prolific neoconservative writer—asserted in the *Weekly Standard*, "Islamic society may still adapt itself to democracy and capitalism. Yet at this point, to ignore the incompatibility between Islam and modernity is willful blindness" (Kurtz 2002:38). This cultural clash is a common motif in neoconservative writings (see, for example, Podhoretz 2002a; Karsh 2003:23; Kurtz 2002).

But while accepting this aspect of Huntington, the neoconservatives refused to surrender to his pessimism and vision of the "decline of the West/ United States,"[10] and continued to heed Fukuyama's optimism about the expected—if not determined—victory of the West led by America. This was clearest when neoconservatives compared the two works. For example, in his 1997 *Commentary* review of Huntington's book, Richard Pipes claims it was written in response to Fukuyama's argument (1997:62). He then asserts that whereas Huntington is right in stressing the role of civilizations in world politics (1997:63–64), his pessimism is misplaced because the West is not in decline (1997:64). Pipes's concluding remarks are especially enlightening: "I suspect that the truth lies somewhere between Fukuyama and Huntington: the two books complement each other. Fukuyama seems to be correct in predicting the ultimate triumph of westernization, but he is oblivious of the immense difficulties which the west will have to overcome—difficulties which Huntington spells out in a very persuasive manner" (1997:65).

Five and a half years later, in September 2002, Pipes's more theoretical perspective took a political and strategic turn in an article by former *Commentary* editor Norman Podhoretz. Podhoretz praises President Bush's strategic shift after September 11 2001, defining it as a shift from realism to idealism—namely, Bush's new endorsement of democracy promotion. Analyzing the series of addresses in which Bush reacted to the terror attacks and presented a new U.S. strategy, Podhoretz writes:

> Then, in a fascinating leap into the great theoretical debate of the post-Cold-War era (though without identifying the main participants), Bush came down squarely on the side of Francis Fukuyama against Samuel Huntington. . . . Having endorsed Fukuyama's much-misunderstood view of "the end of history," Bush now brushed off Huntington's rival theory of a "clash of civilizations." . . . All this was fully consistent with the two previous speeches Bush had made on September 20 and January 29. But—a very big but—it was not consistent with the realities on

the ground on the Middle East. In the Islamic world, and particularly the Arab countries (including such of our "friends" as Saudi Arabia and Egypt), mothers and fathers were *celebrating* Palestinian children (including their own) who blew themselves up as a way of killing as many Israeli Jews as possible. (2002b:24)

Podhoretz further argues that Bush recognized that these tendencies stemmed from a hatred of the freedoms practiced in the United States (2002b:24). Here, using the same Straussian methods as Kristol, Podhoretz argued that despite maintaining publicly that there is no real clash of civilizations, Bush knows fully that it indeed exists, although his political constraints prevent him from speaking his mind. This interpretational maneuver places Bush in a kind of middle ground between Fukuyama and Huntington—the same place where, as I claim, the neoconservatives stand as they try to reconcile the two points of view.

The Democratic Peace Thesis

Yet, however necessary for self-identity and internal cohesiveness, the question remains: how it is possible to hold such a middle ground between conflicting viewpoints? One way to reconcile Huntington's relativism and pessimism with Fukuyama's universalism and optimism is via the political representations of the democratic peace thesis, and more specifically, of its structural theories. Having analyzed the thesis and its various theories in chapter 2, I now wish to offer a brief description of the various democratic peace theories, including the structural ones. Thus I will be able to explain later how these theories—or more accurately their political representations—helped to untangle the neoconservatives' intellectual perplexities.

As was described and analyzed in chapter 2, the theoretical literature of the democratic peace falls into two competing families of theories, or two paradigms. The first explains the democratic peace phenomenon by focusing on the structural dimensions of democracy. The second highlights the cultural-normative dimensions of democratic societies. What is of interest here is the link between the structural democratic peace theories and the more conservative understanding of democracy that defines it in structural terms of checks and balances, as opposed to cultural terms of democratic political culture; in procedural terms of elections, rather than in normative terms of democratic values, and as an elite project (i.e., of the elected elite) of leading the people, rather than a polity run by its deliberating citizens. The minimalist structural definition of democracy is embedded in a conservative skepticism with regard to human faculties. According to this view, it is not rationality that drives human action, but a mix of perennial desires, instincts, and communal traditions. This mix is extrarational, and drives the human quest for power. There are two major consequences to this. First, because everyone seeks power, there is a constant danger of destabilization in social and political organizations. The second outcome is the converse—the constant danger of dictatorial concentration of power in the hands of those who succeed in grasping it. The conservative solution to these two dangers is a minimal, structural democracy. On the one hand, by regular elections, democracy guarantees that no power will last forever, and no dictatorial concentration of power can be achieved. Likewise, by confining political participation to elections, it precludes political and social destabilization.

Related, more practical issues arise concerning democratization, such as, what qualifies as democratization, and what sort of democratization is effective? The alternative paradigms of democracy; namely, the structural and normative, not only exist in the abstract; both can also lead to a discrete policy. Once one accepts that democracies do not fight each other, the policy implication should be to support democratization abroad. Allegedly, each state that becomes a democracy is no longer a security threat to other democracies. To enlarge the circle of democracies is to enlarge the zone of peace.[11]

But how can other countries and societies be democratized? Broadly speaking, democratization policies can be divided into two types derived directly from the definitions of democracy. If democracy means a structure with elections, division of power, and checks and balances, democratization means *building this structure*; that is, emphasizing the formal, the procedural, and the structural. It also means investing effort in the state apparatus, in the "old" or institutional politics. If, however, democracy refers to a culture and morality of the sort that create a civic community, then democratization means *constructing that community*. It means the socialization and dissemination of democratic values so as to foster a democratic society and culture, mainly by facilitating domestic agents of political and social transformation in the target country. It means investing efforts on the social and individual levels, trying to construct a civil society of informed, involved, and participating citizens.

Understood thus, the structural theories of democratic peace and their ensuing policies of structural democracy promotion might seem neatly compatible with the conservative concept of democracy. If so, these theories can be well accommodated into the neoconservative understanding of world politics. They could thus resolve the intellectual perplexity by offering a way to reconcile relativism and universalism—Fukuyama's optimism and Huntington's warnings of decline. The democratic peace thesis implies that democratization, if somehow possible, might save us from the dangers of war, including civilizational war. As Krauthammer asserts, "To extend the peace by spreading democracy and free institutions. This is an unassailable goal and probably the most enduring method of promoting peace.... The zone of democracy is almost invariably a zone of peace" (2001). And if democratization is *structural*, rather than *normative*, then these enlarged zones can even extend to other civilizations.

Yet, we should remember that because of their very nature as academic theories, structural theories of democratic peace have several features that do not and cannot fare well with conservative ideology—or any ideology, for that matter. Those features arise from the requisite of theorization and are independent of a theory's content, its theoretical bottom line, and even its normative premises. As we saw earlier, there are actually numerous affinities between structural theories of democratic peace and conservative and neoconservative ideologies, mainly relating to their shared conceptualization of democracy. Nevertheless, structural theories follow the four requisites of sound theorization: (1) cautiousness and sense of criticism, (2) terms of conditionality, (3) probabilistic nature, and (4) laws of logic that govern the process of analytic inference. These four fundaments distinguish theories from ideologies and supposedly guard theory from collapsing into ideology. The neoconservatives, as we see shortly, sidestepped these requirements in order—to paraphrase President Woodrow Wilson—to make theory safe for ideology. They removed the safeguards, which shield theory from ideology. And en route, they transformed theoretical constructions into public conventions, and then into political convictions. In the process, the structural theories of the democratic peace were simplified, politicized, and equipped as ideological apparatuses, ready to be mobilized for the political ends of rationalizing failed policies and legitimating immoral strategies.

To conclude this section, now, I would like to present two points on the positions of Fukuyama and Huntington—the two great adversaries themselves—regarding the structural theories of the democratic peace and the policies of democratization they produce. The first point relates to the hesitancy with which Fukuyama greeted democracy promotion, and the hostility with which Huntington welcomed it. With conservative considerations in mind, these two thinkers criticized efforts toward democratization, and urged their readers and audiences to consider the inherent flaws of such a process. They perceived it as inconsistent with conservative ideology overall. Fukuyama points out its resemblance to "social engineering," to the compromise of conservative prudence, and to its reliance on the gradual historical evolution of societies (Fukuyama 2004). Huntington focused his criticism on two considerations: (1) the fallacy that the United States can impose its values on different civilizations, and (2) the clash with conservative prudence in international relations (and also the virtues of the balance of power), which prevents global dictatorship and fosters the desired prudence in politicians (Huntington 2005). These conservative concerns are developed in detail in this chapter's conclusion. Suffice it to note at this stage that the neoconservative reconciliation between the two theoretical positions was naturally a compromise between two opposing frameworks, which conceded aspects of each, together with some essential conservative philosophical postulations and political commitments. What neoconservatives saw as an ideological and politically necessitated compromise, both Fukuyama and Huntington saw as the dangerous omission of essential conservative creeds; in fact, both thinkers resented the compromise, emphasizing what they each believed was more essential than compromise.

The other point worth stressing is how the perception of the democratic peace thesis changed in Fukuyama's theoretical framework. Thus, while Huntington continued to reject it, Fukuyama accommodated himself to it. And though he continued opposing the policies of democratization, he embraces the democratic peace thesis. In a gradual process exemplifying the spread of the thesis in conservative circles, Fukuyama reshaped his thesis from its original form, which never mentioned the democratic peace thesis (Fukuyama 1989), to a half page allusion to it in his book (Fukuyama 1992:262–63), and finally, in a newer article, to revisiting his thesis entirely, which he totally reshapes as a mere offshoot of the democratic peace thesis (Fukuyama 1999).

Strategic Outputs and Policy Outcomes

Endorsing the political representations of the structural theories of the democratic peace, the neoconservatives preached democracy promotion for the sake of national security. This was true of Krauthammer's "democratic realism" (Krauthammer 2004b), and also the more global version favored by William Kristol, who, with Lawrence Kaplan, argued that, "The strategic value of democracy is reflected in a truth of international politics: Democracies rarely, if ever, wage war against one another" (Kaplan and Kristol 2003:104; see also Puddington 2004:74; Wolfson 2004; Kupchan 2004:35; Boot 2003; Lane 2000:29; Kaplan 1998:29; Kaplan 1999; Lindberg 2004; Lindberg 2007; Odom 1995:43). What we see in Kaplan and Kristol's statement is a simplification and politicization of the theoretical constructions of the democratic peace thesis and their metamorphosis into public conventions. In their conceptualization we have a totalized and absolute "truth," one that is not subject to doubt or probability, but a "truth" of international politics waiting to be explored and employed in the service of America's vital interests, and harnessed to a policy of democratization for the sake of U.S. security and stability.

Thus, neoconservatives view democratization as a tool to enhance U.S. security and structural democratization as the only viable option. As Krauthammer wrote, "until this administration conceived a radical war plan, executed it brilliantly, liberated the country and created from scratch the *structures* of democracy" (Krauthammer 2004c; emphasis added). Neoconservatives assume that structural democratization can be grafted onto any civilization, any set of norms and values. This is based on the belief that democracy embodies the only truly universal human aspiration—the aspiration for freedom, and that freedom can only be guaranteed through the structure of democracy, which limits state involvement in people's lives (Krauthammer 2005; see also Dobriansky 2004:41). Both conservatives and neoconservatives assume that this universal aspiration for freedom is the sole normative foundation of democracy and that the other foundations—separation of powers, checks and balances, and periodic elections—are structural. And, as can also be learned from officials in the Bush administration such as Under Secretary of State for Global Affairs, Paula Dobriansky, and Deputy Assistant to the President and Director of Strategic Studies Peter Wehner, this structure can be transplanted to any civilization without affecting or damaging that civilization's cultural foundation (Dobriansky 2004:41; see also an op-ed by Peter Wehner 2006).

As noted earlier, this structural definition of democracy jibes well with the neoconservative view of human nature and politics—a view grounded in the traditional pessimism of conservatism. It also encourages the adoption of structural, rather than normative, political representations of the theories of democratic peace. Thus, neoconservatives are able to reconcile pessimism and optimism, relativism and universalism, and produce cautious optimism and mild relativism, while arming themselves against the despair of a deterministic process that supposedly dooms the United States to decline.

Another point, however, is the aggressiveness of the ensuing policies. So far we have dealt with democratization as a security related goal. However, endorsing the structural theories of democratic peace also influences the means of achieving democratization as it entails the use of the military. If democratizing other countries and drawing them into the zone of peace is a vital U.S. interest, then this interest has to be attained even against intense resistance.

The neoconservatives' conservative understanding of democracy as mainly a structure- and elite-driven set of responsible political behaviors, and their acceptance of Huntington's civilizational relativism, affects their view of democratization, which they only perceive as viable in its elitist, institutional, and structural form. Thus, all they see is regime change: reform of an existing structure into a structure with periodic elections and some sort of checks and balances. And that structure can be built along a general set of guidelines that are applied from above and outside. Hence, it is reasonable to expect the success of democratization at gunpoint (see Boot 2003:29–30; Donnelly and Kristol 2004). It should not even take much effort. After all, occupation of a country motivated by democratization unleashes the universal aspiration for freedom among its citizens, who seize the opportunity to imprison their former oppressors and realize their yearnings. They will cooperate with the occupation in building a democratic structure while the occupying army establishes the right conditions for such reforms. This army may delegate greater responsibility to local elites, or import an elite from outside (such futile efforts are personalized in the tragicomic experience of Ahmed Chalaby). Thus, the occupying army can graft democratic structure onto a nation which, though readily welcoming it (or doing so with the help of a tamed elite), maintains what cannot be changed: its civilizational identity, norms, and culture.

If, however, democratization is conceived as a lengthy, intrasocietal process of learning and socialization, norm dissemination and consolidation—as understood by the normative paradigm of democracy and the normative theories of democratic peace—then imposing democratization from the outside is illegitimate and futile. This cultural and normative conceptualization of democratization was one explanation for Europe's harsh criticism of America's strong-arm efforts to achieve the rapid democratization of the Middle East.[12]

Much changed in the world following the terror attacks on America of September 11, 2001. One of the first leaders to experience a sea change was the incumbent president of the United States, George W. Bush. George W. Bush's bid for the presidency against Al Gore portrayed him as a neo-isolationist who wished to reduce American involvement and commitment in world affairs to bare basics. He displayed an almost outright disdain for international involvement, and his ignorance of world affairs and world leaders became a political trademark that Americans enjoyed joking about, but also seemed to find refreshing and positive after President Clinton's active second administration.

Bush the isolationist, who went into hiding during the aftermath of the uncertainties on that tragic day of September 11, 2001, reemerged as a new president with new concerns and a new understanding of U.S. security problems. He sought a new agenda and new strategy that would enable him to confront the reconceived threat of terrorism—and this he found in the lessons preached by the neoconservatives, and which they were trying to promote. The latter were well positioned to exploit the administration's confusion and to convince President Bush of their ideas. They used political representations of the democratic peace thesis to convince the president, along with the American public, that democratization was the key to American security. They repeatedly stressed the academic support for the thesis, thus rhetorically invoking scientific objectivity to urge an ideological agenda.

It was not long before democratization became the new creed—the backbone of the "global war on terror." Less than a year later, the U.S. military occupied Afghanistan and ousted the authoritarian Taliban regime at the head of an international campaign seeking regime change and democratization in Afghanistan. Elections were indeed held, but it is highly debatable that democracy was brought to Afghanistan, or is even on its way. Then, in Iraq, there was a second successful military campaign, to oust dictator Saddam Hussein, dismantle the alleged weapons of mass destruction, and lead a regime change toward democracy. However, weapons of mass destruction were never found in Iraq, and although elections were held, the country now seems headed toward chaos and civil war, rather than stability and democracy.

To be sure, good marketing and a neoconservative persuasion were not the sole reasons for the wars in Afghanistan and Iraq. Neither were they the sole source of influence on President Bush and the formation of his doctrine, as is evident from his many speeches on these topics. Those speeches contain typical neoconservative themes such as the unity of values and interests, the global appeal of freedom, and the power of freedom and democracy to bring peace. As Bush declared on November 16, 2005, in Kyoto, "Free Nations are peaceful nations, free nations do not threaten their neighbors, and free nations offer their citizens a hopeful vision for the future. By advancing the cause of liberty throughout this region [Asia-Pacific Region], we will contribute to the prosperity of all—and deliver the peace and stability that can only come with freedom" (2005c). At the same time, certain beliefs and views in Bush's speeches transcend neoconservative convictions, framing democracy in broader terms than the purely structural and elitist conceptualization. Bush discusses, for example, such themes as broad political participation, democratic reform from within, respect for human and minority rights, and a culture of reconciliation (2002, 2004, 2005a, 2005b, 2005d, 2006a).

However, the democratic peace thesis with its reputation for objectivity (as presented by the neoconservatives), President Bush's self-proclaimed democratic commitment, and the country's sense of confusion, rage, and urgency, combined to help democracy promotion become the backbone of the new Bush Doctrine. What began as a theoretical construction, completed its metamorphosis into a political conviction—defined as specific knowledge engendering a strong, opinionated view that necessitates political action. The neoconservatives who embraced the thesis stripped it of the requisite of sound theorization and presented President Bush and the American public with a supposedly theory-based guide on how best to pursue vital interests. Accordingly, democracy promotion—along with unilateralism and preemption (executed actually as prevention)—became the new creed. This was especially true regarding the Middle East, and is evident not only from the Afghanistan and Iraq wars, but also from the Roadmap with its insistence on structural democratic reforms in the Palestinian Authority; the Greater Middle East and North Africa project of building a democratic alliance, and the United States National Security Strategy of September 17, 2002, which institutionalized democracy promotion as the main strategy for fighting global terrorism in order "to create a balance of power that favors human freedom" (White House 2002:foreword). No wonder William Kristol could boast along with Tom Donnelly in a *Weekly Standard* editorial that: "U.S. forces will be active and present in the region, in the service of furthering a decent alternative to the violent, corrupt, and anti-American status-quo. Afghanistan and Iraq are the beginning, not the end, of what National Security Advisor Condoleezza Rice described as a 'generational commitment'" (2004:7). Also evident in their boast is the use of the discourse, defined earlier as political avowal vernacular; namely, forceful declarations uttered rhetorically in slogan-like fashion to confirm and convey political stands.

In sum, we have seen that neoconservatives' efforts to reconcile Fukuyama's *End of History* and Huntington's *Clash of Civilizations* led them to endorse the structural theories of democratic peace and transform them into public conventions, and then into political convictions that were conducive to ushering a new grand strategy of forceful democratization. This has turned neoconservatism into what I metaphorically term the "civilization of clashes." A good marketing strategy had succeeded, and their creed came to be reflected in the Bush Doctrine, and in a lengthy military crusade originally designed as a democratizing project.

Walt, Mearsheimer and the Attempt to Resurrect Realism

The war did not go unopposed, and criticism kept on mounting as the initial military success in Iraq became a prolonged quagmire of occupation and the insurgency an unacknowledged civil war. It mounted as the death toll kept rising among the American military services and the Iraqi soldiers, officials, and citizens. Two of the most persistent and vocal opponents of the war even before its launch were the prominent neorealist theoreticians John Mearsheimer and Stephen Walt. They were active participants in the public debate that preceded the war, and remained so throughout. Under the umbrella of the "Coalition for a Realistic Foreign Policy," and in a series of articles and op-eds (Mearsheimer and Walt 2002a, 2002b, 2003a, 2003b), the two joined hands in opposing the war.[13]

The realists were not the only the IR theoreticians who opposed the war, yet they had one very important asset that helped them to become the backbone of the academic opposition. That asset was the established tradition of the realist theoretical constructions, which, once, at the height of the Cold War, had enjoyed the status of a public convention and political commitment. Mearsheimer and Walt attempted to restore that status and rekindle the discredited public representations of realist theory to political life.

As we saw in chapter 3, the end of the Cold War marked a sea change. In the terms that have been used here, the Cold War was a combination of objective, material, and structural conditions (material factors), and subjective or intersubjective processes of analyzing, understanding, and evaluating those conditions (ideal factors). The Cold War was a combination of global conflict, with a mortal hatred and distrust of communism, and an overwhelming and utter fear of total nuclear annihilation. Exacerbating this explosive mix was the American public's self-perception as targeted by the Soviet menace. This, in combination with a picture of global belligerence, generated an atmosphere conducive to the pessimism of realism that theorized a state of everlasting conflict. Added to this was the fact that Henry Kissinger, wearing the two hats of theoretician (albeit, a historically oriented theoretician) and practitioner, was the political entrepreneur responsible for the widespread acceptance of realism as an international relations truth. Thus, Kissinger served as a crucial agent at this time, who released realism from the realm of theoretical construction and translated it into public conventions and political convictions.

Just as the political convictions arising from the democratic peace thesis helped in shaping the Bush Doctrine, so the political convictions of realism helped shape Nixon's policies regarding the Soviet Union and China. President Richard Nixon, with Kissinger at his side sharing the management of U.S. foreign relations, surprisingly relented on the United States position on China. A semi-tripolar global structure thus emerged in which the United States and the Soviet Union were the superpowers, and China was acknowledged as a significant power for the first time. This tripolar structure allowed Kissinger to conduct the kind of diplomacy he believed in, based on the model of the golden era of nineteenth-century European diplomacy. This era was the subject of Kissinger's doctoral dissertation, which he later published as his first book (Kissinger 1957). It focused on Metternich and Castlereagh's conduct of the famous Concert of Europe. According to Kissinger, Europe's multipolarity allowed the European diplomats to maneuver flexibly in and out of alliances in order to maintain the balance of power and safeguard international stability. According to Kissinger's realist theoretical framework, as well as that of Hans Morgenthau, Europe's enduring stability during the long nineteenth century was the result of a balance of power that could be managed flexibly. Kissinger sought this kind of flexibility in his diplomatic maneuvering vis-à-vis the Soviet Union, and when orchestrating the clandestine preparations for Nixon's surprising visit to China in February 1972. Having established diplomatic relations with China, Nixon and Kissinger assumed themselves involved in a tripolar global structure, and were sufficiently assured to allow greater flexibility in their relations with the Soviet Union; hence the launch of détente. As this short account illustrates, the public and political representations of the realist theoretical constructions framed the strategic thinking of President Nixon and the commonsensical thinking of the American public. For a time, the theoretical accounts of the Balance of Power mechanism formed American public conventions and political convictions, thus helping to shape American policy en route to détente.

I will not review the full history of the Cold War here. However, Kissinger's prestige and influence lasted up to the late 1970s, and with his departure, realism as a public convention and political conviction suffered a serious blow. Yet, it was not until the very end of the Cold War that realism's public and political representations lost their grasp on the commonsensical thinking of the American public. The end of the Cold War enabled the significant structural change needed to conclude the political life of the realist school. The new structure that emerged was conducive to the more optimistic liberal theories of IR, and indeed in the early 1990s people began the serious search for an alternative. Thus started the political life cycle of the democratic peace theories, which the neoconservatives then embraced.

What Walt and Mearsheimer sought was to rekindle the political life cycle of realism that democratic peace theories seemed to have replaced. After all, it was not that long ago that the public convention of the American public and the political conviction of the American policy elite were based on realism. They therefore sought to activate the one-time established tradition of realism in their opposition to the Bush Doctrine and its most disastrous expression: the war in Iraq. It is interesting how cleverly Mearsheimer and Walt fashioned their campaign. They knew to avoid burdening the public with too much theoretical jargon and subtleties. In the terminology used here, they were aware that they needed to bypass the requisite of sound theorization, and to replace the theoretical explanatory vernacular with the political avowal vernacular. Mearsheimer and Walt not only acted as public intellectuals, they assumed the function of political entrepreneurs in crafting political representations from theoretical constructions. They wished to offer the American public a simplified version of realism that was light and easy to digest. To achieve this, they were willing to disregard the bread and butter of their profession and toss out the requisite of sound theorization, which were in fact the requisites whose methodical application in their theoretical work had gained them academic prominence. The most obvious act of simplification involved brushing aside internal theoretical disputes between offensive and defensive realism, and offering the American public and policy elites a coherent theoretical framework and broad theoretical consensus.

Mearsheimer and Walt espouse different realist theories; they belong to rival subschools of realism. Walt is one of the leading proponents of defensive realism, and Mearsheimer is the leading proponent of offensive realism. According to defensive realism, survival calculations in an anarchic system can lead states to moderate their behavior and perhaps even to cooperate (Miller 1995; Glaser 1996; Walt 1987). Offensive realism argues that calculations of survival in an anarchic system inevitably lead to aggression and expansionism (Mearsheimer 1994–1995; Mearsheimer 2001). Both subschools recommend different strategies for coping with the hazards of international politics—strategies spanning an entire spectrum from cautious balance of power to more aggressive balancing acts. Though, they do share some common ground: neither school will go so far as to embrace a policy of democratization for fear of its destabilizing consequences. So although in their academic life they disagree, as political entrepreneurs, Mearsheimer and Walt brush aside the theoretical nuances that lead to disagreement and emphasize the commonalities. Their joint articles propound such ideas as containment and deterrence as opposed to the preventive war of the Bush Doctrine. Moreover, their public papers advocate the importance of international consensus and cooperation in contrast to the neoconservative unilateral impulse. Still, we should bear in mind that neither international consensus nor cooperation are integral features of realist theories. On the contrary, realism usually treats these concepts with disdain, dismissing them as liberal illusions. We can infer that the theoreticians' embrace of these concepts is not theoretical but political, and that they wish to offer a policy guideline that is at once at odds with the Bush Doctrine, and also more palatable to a weary public, which would rather share its burdens of combating global terrorism with the international community. Mearsheimer and Walt bow to these expediencies, and with the help of the political avowal vernacular, present a coherent, simplified, and acceptable version of realism with the potential to become a public convention and political conviction.

In the short run, they failed. The Iraq War started, and initially it enjoyed a high degree of public approval. The more relevant question concerns the longer run and what happens if the war in Iraq turns into a Vietnam-like disaster. Would realism reemerge as the stance of the American public? Though not in the prediction business, the following analysis can indicate the conditions that might favor Mearsheimer and Walt's political program, and those which may not. It will consider the objective, material, and structural conditions that support and oppose Mearsheimer and Walt's political program, and the subjective and intersubjective processes involved in analyzing, understanding, and evaluating them. Favorable to realism is the conflictual structure the world has turned to following the relative calm of the 1990s. The 1990s was ideal soil for liberal theories of IR and their focus on cooperation and multilateralism. However, in the 2000s, with interest in security high, the public may return to a belief in the relevance of realism, which some think is better equipped theoretically to handle the issues of security. On the intersubjective level, America grew tired of the Bush administration and its policies. This was one of the reasons Democrat Barack Obama was elected president in 2008. Moreover, the public conventions and political convictions based on the democratic peace thesis are being discredited (see, for example, Etzioni 2007; Smith 2007). People may therefore start questioning once more and, searching for an alternative, realism could beckon as a secure and well-trodden path for addressing security problems.

Whereas at first glance the unfavorable conditions for realism are not as obvious as the favorable ones, they may be too challenging for Mearsheimer and Walt to handle. While the current global picture is indeed conflictual, the conflict is the type that realism does not cover properly. Realism focuses on relationships between sovereign states. According to realism, states are the main actors in international relations, and in order to analyze international relations parsimoniously, we should focus solely on states' behavior. One effect of this line of focus is to discount other types of actors, especially transnational social movements. However, the current conflict does involve such an actor—namely, Al-Qaeda—which is difficult to analyze and understand within the realist theoretical framework. The difficulties Mearsheimer and Walt faced were heightened when the Bush administration and neoconservative pundits succeeded in framing the Iraq War as a war on terror. Thus, despite being a war against a sovereign state, and although the realists have tried to frame the conflict in statist terms, the current intersubjective understanding of the conflict in fact works against them as it combines international structure and how it is understood in a way that is unfavorable to the realist political endeavor. And Mearsheimer and Walt's project has a lot to fight against.

Eventually, even though the public conventions and political convictions based on the theoretical constructions of the democratic peace thesis may suffer a blow and be discredited, there is no guarantee they will be replaced by conventions and convictions based on realist theoretical constructions.

Conclusions

A lot may be said against President Bush's creed of democratization. His policies can be accused of being imperialistic, paternalistic, destabilizing crusades, of cynical demagoguery masking self-aggrandizing interests and unlawful warmongering. Criticism can be also leveled at the futile efforts to democratize at gunpoint, and at the neoconservatives' misunderstanding of the essence of democracy. Additionally, critics can point to the unjust distribution of burdens in American society of fighting and financing the war, as well as the unequal distribution of the profits arising from oil revenues and the reconstruction of Afghanistan and Iraq, or they can point to the immorality of aggressiveness, invasions, and occupations.

However, a different kind of criticism emerges from the discussion on the political representations of the democratic peace thesis in the neoconservative grand strategy. Efforts to grasp the basis for the neoconservative worldview, especially its advocacy of a hard-line policy of world democratization, leads to internal criticism that explores the neoconservative idea structure and uncovers its internal incoherencies. Such incoherencies may prove irremediable, invalidating the ideology and destabilizing the strategy based on it. They can help us to understand some of the sources of the failure of the Bush Doctrine, and in particular the failure to forcefully bring democracy to Iraq. Two powerful internal criticisms of neoconservative ideology and aggressive democracy promotion are: (1) the conservative belief in the power of culture and tradition and their mistrust of "social engineering," and (2) the conservative fear of dictatorial concentration of power.

Conservatives and neoconservatives alike look askance at "social engineering." They believe in the gradual evolution of societies, trusting the wisdom of what already exists, as in Hegel's "what is rational is actual and what is actual is rational" (Hegel 1952:10). Conservative programs of change rely on incremental reforms that take into account the historical—even organic—nature of society. Dismantling a social structure in a quick attempt at change is seen by them as radicalism based on the hubris of the Enlightenment—an excessive belief in human rationality inevitably leading to destabilization. In this light, neoconservatives view welfare policies and other centrist governmental programs as "social engineering" that is bound to fail and cause damage.

But doesn't democratizing other countries involve at least as much trust in rationalism and "social engineering" as the domestic welfare state? Isn't the idea of building democracy in a country that never experienced anything like it, founded on the same Enlightenment presumptions? Is this not an exercise in radicalism and hastiness, involving hubris of the worst kind? If true to their credo, the neoconservatives can only answer these questions affirmatively. Indeed, Fukuyama was quick to criticize this type of neoconservative democracy-promotion agenda, pointing to its incoherence and the need to return to conservative humility (Fukuyama 2004:60). In 2006, pursuing this line of argumentation further led Fukuyama to renounce his allegiance with neoconservatism (Fukuyama 2006).

It is this conservative fear of unchecked power noted earlier that underlies their minimalist, elitist concept of democracy. Indeed, in the domestic arena they uphold the virtues of checks and balances, and in the global arena, balance of power (Ish-Shalom 2006a). Ostensibly, these structures offset dictatorial concentrations of power and foster prudential politics. Nonetheless, the neoconservatives showed a reluctance to respect other global powers, and not only called on the United States to act unilaterally, but favored unipolarity: a world in which the United States was sole hegemon, unchecked and unbalanced.[14] The Bush Doctrine followed suit with a concerted effort to prolong the unipolar moment (White House 2002:29), and assure America's ability to establish structural democracies around the world that would liberate their citizens from unbalanced and unchecked domestic rulers, thus enhancing U.S. security by forging democratic zones of peace.

The internal contradiction is evident and did not escape the conservative Huntington's notice (Huntington 2005)[15] or—as the previous section shows—the notice of the realist theoreticians. If domestic checks and balances to prevent concentrated power are the aimed at instrument, the same precautionary mechanism is necessary globally so that no single power can rule without prudence-inducing restraints. After all, the logic of Lord Acton's warning that "Power tends to corrupt, and absolute power corrupts absolutely,"[16] applies globally, as well as domestically.

These two internal inconsistencies emerge once we understand how the neoconservatives came to adopt the democratic peace thesis, how they transformed it into political representations—both as public conventions and political convictions—what they mean by democracy and democratic peace, and what roles those political representations played in shaping and marketing the democracy-promotion agenda. Their grand strategy of promoting democracy for national security reasons based on the politicization of the academic structural theories of democratic peace suffers from acute internal incoherencies. On consideration of these incoherencies we cannot be surprised at the critical problems that arose when this grand strategy was implemented in Iraq.

Another reason for the failure in Iraq is the rigidity of the policy blueprints inferred from the requisiteless version of the democratic peace structural theories. As we saw, when a theory migrates from academia it is stripped of the four requisites of theorization and transformed discursively into a different idea entity. It is simplified, and at times trivialized and politicized into a political conviction that is discursively conveyed by a political avowal vernacular, the ultimate result being an absolutist account of the thesis with its high level of self-assurance and lack of all sense of cautiousness and self-criticism. The account is also totalistic in that it ignores the conditionality of the democratic peace thesis and its probabilistic nature. According to the political representation of the democratic peace thesis, democracies are less belligerent than nondemocracies, and by definition do not employ terrorism or weapons of mass destruction. The politicized form of the democratic peace thesis also ignores the finding that states that are in the process of consolidating democratically can be more aggressive than nondemocratic states. This is the kind of finding that complicates the absolutist and totalistic nature of political convictions and weakens the rhetorical forcefulness of the political avowal vernacular, which is why they are ignored by ideologues. Politics, it seems, does not try to purge prejudices as academia supposedly does—rather, it utilizes prejudices to serve its purposes and erect obstacles to thwart opponents.

The outcome is not just a distorted absolutist, totalistic account of a theory, since ideologues and politicians also infer policy blueprints from the distorted accounts. And just as the accounts are absolutists and totalistic, so are the inferred policy blueprints dogmatic and rigid. For example, neo-conservative Max Boot declares how he understands the democratic peace:

> Echoing one of President Bush's speeches, it [the *National Security Strategy*] says, "Freedom is the non-negotiable demand of human dignity; the birth right of every person—in every civilization." The strategy is so emphatic because the administration embraces the theory of a "democratic peace"—the notion that liberal democracies are unlikely to use weapons of mass destructions, sponsor terrorism, and undertake other activities that threaten their neighbors and the United States. (2003:27)

This is, of course, a political misrepresentation of the democratic peace theories conveyed using the political avowal vernacular. But no less important is what Boot infers from his account of the theories: "Therefore, the United States has a vital stake in fostering the spread of representative government" (2003:27). There is no flexibility in his proposed blueprints. The stakes are vital, and the United States must act, forcefully if needed.

President Bush was no less convinced and dogmatic than Boot, having clearly understood the lessons of the requisiteless version of democratic peace thesis. In his September 7, 2006, address, he firmly acknowledged the lessons of history:

> We know from history that free nations are peaceful nations. We know that democracies do not attack each other, and that young people growing up in a free and hopeful society are less likely to fall under the sway of radicalism. And so we're taking the side of democratic leaders and reformers across the Middle East ... We will replace violent dictatorships with peaceful democracies. We'll make America, the Middle East, and the world more secure. (2005d)

The dogmatism, rigidity, and self-confidence that characterized Bush and Boot's declarations contributed to the disasters caused by America's policy in Iraq. They blinded the neoconservatives and the Bush administration and prevented them from realizing the complexities, foreseeable difficulties,[17] and needs of the postwar reconstruction effort. The United States that stepped into Iraq was bedazzled by a set of convictions that, among other things, stemmed, from a rigid reading of theory.

The dogmatism and rigidity of this reading were no coincidence, but simply the product of an intrinsic feature of the political representations of theories. After all, political representation is the representation of a representation. A theory is a parsimonious explanatory scheme of a highly multifaceted and contextual reality, and, as a preliminary step toward constructing an explanatory scheme, it casts a patterned and sparing picture on the complexity of reality. In other words, a theory is a representation of reality. It is only by developing a representation of reality that a theoretician can construct a parsimonious explanatory scheme. Thus, theories can be described as theoretical representations of reality. And as long as the four requisites are in place, the theoretician understands that he or she must treat his or her theoretical representation cautiously, and without arrogance. Theoreticians who recognize the representational nature of their theories, will realize that they do not purport to be an exact duplication of reality, and that reality is far more complex, multifarious, and contextual than theories show. They may also realize that, as representations of reality, theories are best at capturing the past and present, and that even though sophisticated statistical tools are available for identifying patterns of change, future change is hardly predictable. Theoreticians who are attentive to complexity, time, and the unpredictability of future transformations, will heed the need for pragmatism and flexibility while applying their theories to reality. They will also be adamant about stating the need to shape policies pragmatically and execute them flexibly—for it is only when theories go hand in hand with pragmatism and flexibility that they can help to generate reasoned and reasonable policies.

But, what actually happened with the democratic peace thesis was that its political representation; that is, the political representation of the theoretical representation, was stripped of its controlling requisites by the neoconservative ideologues. It therefore lost that inbuilt modesty and cautiousness with which theories analyze and explain the world (or at least the ideality of inbuilt humility and caution), so that dogmatism replaced pragmatism, and rigidity replaced flexibility. Instead of producing flexible policy guidelines that were attuned to the multifaceted contextual nature of the world, the policy recommendations deduced from the thesis's political representations led to rigid dogmatic blueprints that attempted to impose themselves on reality. As in the case of the neoconservative grand strategy of forceful democratization, the result can be unreasoned and unreasonable policies—which ended in failure.

Moreover, the Iraq War—which might have been opposed for being subjective, partisan, and ideological—was presented as being part of a scientifically objective, nonpartisan, nonideological policy, allowing its backers to disarm and dissuade potential adversaries in order to reach an almost national consensus. But democracy thrives on disagreement, and in a vibrant democracy disagreement produces public deliberation, which has the potential of generating public reason. Democratically speaking, forestalling disagreement, opposition, and deliberation, causes political harm. The politicization of the democratic peace thesis was therefore an occasion when American democracy was undermined by thwarting the democratic process of deliberation and degrading public reason. In other words, a theory which has the potential to foster public reason and public good in fact undermined American public reason and caused harm to both the American and Iraqi publics by helping to produce a bogged-down foreign policy in the form of forceful democratization. It left in its wake a frustrated democratic polity, and many tens of thousands of dead. These impermissible outcomes raise the issue of theoreticians' responsibilities—an issue that is taken up later in this book.

6

THE THREE FREE WORLD THEORIES

Democratic peace is a theory of democracy, by democracy, for democracy; it is supposed to explain the behavior of democracies, it was conceived in democracies, and its political representations were put into use for the sake of democracies. The focus of this book is a free world theory. But democratic peace thesis is not the only free world theory. There are others; for example, soft power and the capitalist peace theory (or thesis). Soft power is connected to democracy in that its emphasis is on influence by consent, the supposedly democratic approach to influence, rather than by coercion. Though power is not absent from democratic politics, the expectation is that collective decision-making takes place voluntary and freely, so that people reach a collective decision, not coerced by use or threat of force; they should freely consent to the decision. At the heart of democracy lies the concept of rule by consent, which is also the essence of soft power. Put differently, it is a free world theory (or more accurately, a free world theoretical concept). So is the capitalist peace thesis, which focuses on the notion of free-market dynamics. I do not fully subscribe to the common identification of capitalism and democracy as the two can exist separately, and in certain circumstances, they can even exist in a state of tension. But one must admit that today the two generally come together, and are very often thought of as identical, or at the very least, conjoined twins. Moreover, once we expand our discussion from democracy to the free world, the capitalism-democracy relationship becomes more obvious again and less tenuous. Capitalism concerns the freedom to have property, and use it freely. Egalitarian critique would justly point out that those without property do not enjoy this freedom. More cynically, it can be argued that the "have-nots" are free to starve. And yet, capitalism is popularly identified with freedom, and it is an ideology of the free world.[1] So even for those of us who do not fully subscribe to capitalist democracy, the relating of capitalist peace thesis to the free world would come as no surprise. Accordingly, it is quite natural for a book on the democratic peace thesis to discuss soft power and capitalist peace as the three represent three free world theories, as the title of this chapter suggests.

This chapter discusses the political understandings and uses of soft power and capitalist peace in an effort to demonstrate the application of the theoretical model advocated in this book to areas apart from democratic peace. Thus, this chapter's aim is to present support for the contention that democratic peace is not the sole purview of theory as a hermeneutical mechanism.

Soft power came to dominate the Obama administration discourse on strategic matters, and capitalist peace replaced democratic peace in Netanyahu's politics of postponement. As those two cases are relatively new and still in the making, the analysis cannot be developed as thoroughly as the democratic peace analysis. Therefore, this chapter is mostly a preliminary analysis of what is a political work in process, of events that are unfolding before our eyes. As such, the aim of those two analyses is not to write a comprehensive political biography, but rather to hint at the applicability of the analysis and the variations within the hermeneutical mechanism process. The main difference stressed is that the theoreticians who were involved in constructing and developing the theories were also involved in introducing them into the political sphere. Joseph Nye Jr., who coined the term "soft power," has been one of the foremost figures in translating the theory into policy guidelines, and Erik Gartzke, a leading theoretician of the capitalist peace thesis, propagates and advocates the capitalist peace as an effective and valuable policy tool. This is a difference that has some importance, as the following analysis shows.

This chapter opens with a section on the story of soft power in the American political arena. This is followed by a section on the capitalist or economic peace thesis in Israeli politics. The two sections describe the theory, analyze the actions of the relevant theoretician, and then explore the theories' fortunes in the various political spheres.

Obama and Soft Power

Power is an elusive concept. It has been defined and characterized so many times in so many ways, yet still no general agreement exists. It can be, and indeed was, approached from different angles and classified along diverse axes. It is conceived as a mode of interactions, set of resources (quantified or not), or as outcomes; it is categorized as having four faces (the fifth still awaiting discovery), and is dissected along different dimensions.[2] One solution to the perplexity surrounding the concept of power is to claim that it is an essentially contested concept and, moreover, that it is primitive in the sense that "its meaning cannot be elucidated by reference to other notions whose meaning is less controversial than its own" (Lukes 2005). This forceful claim comes from no other than Steven Lukes, one of the foremost theoreticians of power and the originator of the third face of power (Lukes 2004). This essential contestedness makes power a perfect candidate for the hermeneutical mechanism—for a process of migration from academia to the real world involving all the possible meanings that can be attached to the concept.

This is especially so as it is hard to deny that power is a crucial and central phenomenon in the political world in general, and international politics in particular. Notwithstanding the theoretical perplexity of power, the political world keeps practicing and responding to it. There is a high demand at the political end from the suppliers of theoretical insights at the academic end. Enter into this demand-supply axis, Joseph Nye, one of the most successful political scientists of our era—a thinker strongly oriented toward the political world and its demands.

Nye has administration experience, having been assistant secretary of defense for International Security Affairs under President Clinton, and quite frequently appearing on Congressional testimonies. He also contributes regular op-eds to American newspapers, in which he intervenes in the public deliberation, introducing his liberal theoretical insights on U.S. foreign policies.[3] He is also an active think tank player, and, along with Richard Armitage, he recently co-chaired the CSIS Bipartisan Commission on Smart Power—the flagship commission of the Smart Power Initiative, launched in 2006 by the Center for Strategic and International Studies (CSIS), one of the more prestigious and influential Washington think tanks. The commission's bipartisan nature is reflected in its membership and chairing—Nye being a liberal previously recruited by the Clinton administration, Armitage a veteran of the Bush administration and deputy secretary of state from 2001 to 2005. The committee's aim is "a smarter, more secure America." In other words, to study the potential and advancement of smart power; smart power being the recent offshoot of Nye's theoretical concept of soft power

(CSIS Commission on Smart Power 2007). Put differently, Nye also acts as a public intellectual. And, it should be noted, is one of the most respectable of these in the United States. Moreover, in a *Washington Post* op-ed of April 2009, following Obama's inauguration, Nye mourned the disinterest of political scientists in the policy world and called for theoreticians to step into this gap (2009b).

From the intricate theoretical discussions on the definition of power and its essence, Nye drew a very attractive conceptualization of power, which he termed "soft power." Soft power refers to one of the many dimensions of power: the part that works not through coercion, but through attraction. Drawing from both the second[4] and third (Gramscian) faces of power, Nye's conception struck the imagination of both the politicians and the academics—at least the policy-oriented academics. Although lacking in originality and theoretical refinement, in less than two decades his notion of soft power had become a catchall theoretical concept, largely praised, and acted upon.[5] What Nye did was to successfully simplify a complex theoretical concept.

I would not attempt to write here a full political biography of the concept of soft power, or complete analysis of the concept and its academic development. Suffice it to emphasize some key landmarks. The first is Nye's 1990 book, *Bound to Lead*, in which he introduces the concept of soft power. The second is his 2004 book, *Soft Power*, where he develops the concept further. The two books, academic as they are, are always with an eye to the world of decision makers, to whom they offer theoretical insights on leading the world, or at least the free world. This is most evident in the second book's subtitle: *The Means to Succeed in World Politics*. The practical disposition is also evident in Nye's 2008 book, *The Powers to Lead*, which supposedly draws insights from the failed administration of President George W. Bush, and offers itself as a policy guide for the next administration. In the two decades following the publication of his first book, Nye took the theoretical concept of soft power in various directions, linking it to numerous issues, including leadership, security, and public diplomacy. He also ties soft power to a different concept—namely, smart power—which he defines as "The ability to combine hard and soft power effectively" (2008a:107). Regarding smart power, there is uncertainty over who developed the concept: was it former National Security Council member, Antony Blinken; was it Nye himself; or was it Suzanne Nossel, a former deputy to the ambassador for

UN Management and Reform at the U.S. mission to the United Nations. Blinken mentions it fleetingly in a 2002 article in the *Washington Quarterly*. Nye mentions it in his 2004 book *Soft Power,* and Nossel refers to it in an article in *Foreign Affairs* (2004), and again in 2004 (see Rozen, 2009). But whoever its parent, the concept is an offshoot of the idea of soft power, and a theoretical reaction to the Iraq War and the Bush administration's over emphasis of military means (read, "hard power").[6] It is also clear that with smart power at hand, Nye had a complete policy blueprint, founded on his theoretical concept, which, as noted earlier, is a simplified articulation of a complicated theoretical discussion.

The following few paragraphs analyze Nye's theoretical concept based mainly on one of his most recent articles, *Public Diplomacy and Soft Power* (2008). Out of his countless "soft power articles" I have especially chosen this one as it explicitly identifies soft power as a major component of public diplomacy; a theme which, as we soon see, also features significantly in Obama's speeches. Furthermore, as one of Nye's later references to the concept, it is also one of his most articulated, refined, and fully developed. As one of his latest, it also supposes to address the most urgent contemporary needs of the United States (and the free world, more generally), at the time that was defined by President Bush as the Global War on Terror, and by some of the neoconservatives as World War Four (Podhoretz 2002a). It is important to note how differently Nye conceptualizes the problems of the day and the instruments needed to deal with those problems. Most noticeably, Nye sees the Iraq War itself as threat to U.S. soft power, rather than a means of defeating the enemy. As he and Armitage explain in their introduction to the CSIS report, "At the core of the problem is that America has made the war on terror the central component of its global engagement" (Armitage and Nye 2007:11; see also Nye 2008a:96). Later in the chapter I demonstrate how Nye's ideas indeed migrated to the political sphere and informed Obama's discourse and perspective, as well as those of his senior secretaries, Hillary Clinton and Robert Gates.

According to Nye's definition, soft power is "getting others to want the outcomes that you want—co-opts people rather than coerces them" (2008a:95). As such, it perfectly fits democratic politics. To use Nye's words, it is "a staple of daily democratic politics" (2008a:95). It works through influencing and shaping people's preferences and by "setting the agenda and determining the framework of a debate" (2008a:95). In more traditional theoretical terms, this is the second face of power. Nye is quick to stress that rather than use force (hard power), soft power uses values, culture, and a good example in foreign policy, "The soft power of a country rests primarily on three resources: its culture (in places where it is attractive to others), its political values (when it lives up to them at home and abroad), and its foreign policies (when they are seen as legitimate and having moral authority)" (2008a:96). It is, in other words "attractive power" (2008a:95). Nye terms it attractive power in the sense of the use of attraction over foreign people and nations. But it is attractive also in the sense of being attractive to politicians. A typical feature of soft power is that its target audience is the wider public, not just the elites; it addresses itself toward the whole of civil society, not just the tip, the political system (2008a:95, 108). Hence, it involves public diplomacy in its broadest sense: not merely as the obverse side of secrecy, but also of having in mind and addressing the whole public. To do that, public diplomacy should operate on three levels: the first involves daily communication with foreign societies to convey U.S. policy decisions and their rationale. The second concerns the underlying approach of this daily communication. It should be fashioned strategically and present "a set of simple themes much as a political or advertising campaign does. The campaign plans symbolic events and communications over the course of the next year to reinforce central themes or to advance a particular government policy" (2008a:102). Thus, Nye proposes precisely what I term "political avowal vernacular." Though values are the core of soft power, the means to convey them are forceful rhetoric. In Habermasian terms, Nye proposes strategic action, rather than communicative action. This advice again points to Nye's keen political eye. The third level, or instrument, of soft power involves developing lasting relationships with the target audience through "scholarships, exchanges, training, seminars, conferences, and access to media channels" (2008a:102).

Though rhetoric is important in Nye's scheme, soft power must not settle for appearances. If the United States wants to lead, its conduct must be exemplary; it must exchange its customary double standard for setting a moral standard. There must be coherence between rhetoric and practice, values and policies (2008a:102). Abu Ghraib and Guantanamo draw accusations of hypocrisy and seriously undermine U.S. soft power (2008a:101). The United States must also listen to and understand the values, culture, and concern of the people it wishes to lead. Soft power is not only about talking, it is also about listening (2008a:103). Although a commitment to the spread of democracy is an essential component of soft power, the approach cannot be forceful and coercive, "It is easier to attract people to democracy than to coerce them to be democratic" (Armitage and Nye 2007:6–7). Thus, and only thus, can the United States employ soft power. And since hard power is not obsolete (Armitage and Nye 2007:11), in order to succeed in world politics, it is no less important to possess smart power; namely, the capacity and wisdom to efficiently combine soft and hard power.

Put differently, Nye's work on soft power can be read as a simplification (though not trivialization) of an academic theory. Nye's presentation of soft power is not valuable for its originality or sophistication: quite the reverse. The value of Nye's work lies in its simplification of a highly complex theoretical academic discussion. Soft power is the translation of academic discourse into political discourse. In fact, Nye himself combines both theoretical explanatory vernacular and political avowal vernacular in his writing. The latter can be seen for example in his appendix to *The Power to Lead*, entitled "Leadership: A Dozen Quick Take-Aways" (2008b:147–48). Those brief takeaways are a learning guide, strategically articulated—to use Nye's own words—as "a set of simple themes much as a political or advertising campaign does" (2008a:102). Thus, Nye delivers academic insights regarding power in an adaptable fashion for political use. But, and this is a big "but," he intends his simplification of power as an alternative to force. Nye's notion of power is far from a simple-minded simplification. It is a skillfully planned and executed simplification constructed according to liberal convictions, and organized around multilateral principles aimed at replacing the usual, unilateral coercion practiced in international politics. For Nye, soft power is a remedy academia can offer to international politics. It is aimed at legitimizing peaceful means, rather than forceful ones. Therein lies its attraction vis-à-vis the imagination and practice of liberal policymakers and liberal academics—an attraction which grew stronger, especially after the war in Iraq, and the militarist unilateral policies of the Bush administration. Although soft power had immigrated to the public sphere well before Obama's political breakthrough, in the 2008 presidential campaign, political conditions were ripe enough for soft power discourse to take over and provide a respectable, academia-originated alternative to the democratic peace, which legitimized the use of impermissible force and had become politically tainted.

In a sense, the election of Obama as president of the United States was the incarnation of soft power—of a merger between the American values of political equality, and the realities of the American political system with its prejudiced practices. At long last a black (though not exactly an Afro-American) man (and not yet a woman) was elected to lead a nation, which since its establishment had preached, but not practiced, the ideal and value of political equality. Since the early days of his political career, Obama had symbolized this very possibility, and understood how to emphasize the value of political equality and its importance for the American polity. Thus, at the 2004 Democratic National Convention, Obama declared:

> Tonight, we gather to affirm the greatness of our nation, not because of the height of our skyscrapers, or the power of our military, or the size of our economy. Our pride is based on a very simple premise, summed up in a declaration made over two hundred years ago, "We hold these truths to be self-evident, that all men are created equal. That they are endowed by their Creator with certain inalienable rights. That among these are life, liberty and the pursuit of happiness." That is the true genius of America, a faith in the simple dreams of its people. (2004)

But besides being himself the incarnation of soft power, Obama appears also to have taken on board the insights of soft power and its prescription, almost step by step. Soft power, so it seems, came to constitute Obama's political convictions, framing his strategic thinking. First, he diagnoses Iraq and America's involvement in it as the malady undermining the country's moral authority and standing in the world, hampering its ability to lead the free world. For Obama, the way to assume world leadership is through consent, not coercion. As he stated in his celebrated Cairo Address on June 4, 2009, "So no matter where it takes hold, government of the people and by the people sets a single standard for all who would hold power: You must maintain your power through consent, not coercion" (2009e). This statement can of course be rephrased in terms of Nye's concept of soft power: the way to lead the nation and the world is by soft power, not hard power. For Obama, as for Nye, this conceptualization of power is intimately linked with democracy, and with the stern commitment to support democracies abroad. Again, Obama's remarks in Cairo are revealing.

I know—I know there has been controversy about the promotion of democracy in recent years, and much of this controversy is connected to the war in Iraq. So let me be clear: No system of government can or should be imposed by one nation by any other. That does not lessen my commitment, however, to governments that reflect the will of the people. Each nation gives life to this principle in its own way, grounded in the traditions of its own people. (2009e)

Obama makes a point of stressing that democracy is much more than just elections: "We do need to stand for democracy. And I will. But democracy is about more than a ballot box, and that it should not and cannot be imposed from the outside" (2007a). Therefore, as Obama informed the United Nations on September 23, 2009, the United States would no longer be involved in imposing democracy. "Democracy cannot be imposed on any nation from the outside. Each society must search for its own path, and no path is perfect. Each country will pursue a path rooted in the culture of its people and in its past traditions . . . United States of America will never waver in our efforts to stand up for the right of people everywhere to determine their own destiny" (2009f). So democracy promotion would no longer be conducted in neoconservative fashion, at gunpoint. Democracy is no longer understood as only a structure, an elite-driven project. Accordingly, the target of American efforts is the nondemocratic society in general, and not just its leaders. The purpose of American programs is to democratize and facilitate civil society by offering "programs that advance U.S. interests by strengthening democracy and civil society, enhancing economic development, and dealing with international health issues—in addition to curbing the nonproliferation threat" (2005). A policy also applied to a traditional American ally such as Pakistan: "This is why I stood up last summer and said we cannot base our entire Pakistan policy on President Musharraf. Pakistan is our ally, but we do our own security and our ally no favors by supporting its President while we are seen to be ignoring the interests of the people . . . That is why we should dramatically increase our support for the Pakistani people—for education, economic development, and democratic institutions" (2008b).

For Obama, as for Nye, values and culture are fundamental, and the struggle for the hearts and minds of nondemocratic civil societies can be won through the example of American values and culture. "And to all those who have wondered if America's beacon still burns as bright—tonight we proved once more that the true strength of our nation comes not from the might of our arms or the scale of our wealth, but from the enduring power of our ideals: democracy, liberty, opportunity, and unyielding hope" (2008d). And the policies of the United States should conform to those great values even when the going is tough, "but part of what makes us, I think, still a beacon to the world is that we are willing to hold true to our ideals even when it's hard, not just when it's easy" (2009c). The United States, Obama believes, should provide a role model and stand by its values instead of practicing the double standards commonly identified with the Bush days, "It's time to restore our moral leadership by rejecting torture without equivocation; by closing Guantanamo; by restoring habeas corpus; and by again being that light of justice to dissidents in prison camps around the globe" (2008a).

Thus, like Nye, Obama places his faith in public diplomacy, which was hampered in Iraq, and which is seen as the apparatus for America regaining the world's leadership (2007b, 2009d). Obama also targets the unilateralism of the neoconservatives and the Bush administration, offering instead the remedies of multilateralism, international alliances, and international organizations. Multilateralism, he argues, will help the United States in Iraq, and all over the world (2009d). He also preaches the specific policies recommended by Nye, including exchange programs (2009e), listening to what the others have to say, and paying attention to the things that concern them (2009a). During his first year as president, Obama announced a couple of initiatives that involved listening and building bridges. One was the decision to nominate an American ambassador to Syria (Robert Ford) following five years of American absence; the other was the nomination of Rashad Hussain as special envoy to the Organization of the Islamic Conference. Both of these initiatives follow soft power recommendations, preferring dialogue and respect over ostracization.

In this general scheme, military power is applied when necessary with other sorts of power to create the kind of unison Nye would have called "smart power." This is Obama's new strategy for confronting what is for him a new world. "Such a strategy would join overwhelming military strength with sound judgment. It would shape events not just through military force, but through the force of our ideas; through economic power, intelligence and diplomacy" (2008c). Or, as he declared in Trinidad and Tobago on April 19, 2009:

And I think that's why it's so important that in our interactions not just here in the hemisphere but around the world, that we recognize that our military power is just one arm of our power, and that we have to use our diplomatic and development aid in more intelligent ways so that people can see very practical, concrete improvements in the lives of ordinary persons as a consequence of U.S. foreign policy. (2009b)

Indeed, we have here almost an exact political description of Nye's soft and smart power. Although Obama does not use these exact terms, it is nevertheless quite clear that he advocates policies highly informed by Nye's conceptualization. What he does not do—that is, call it by its name—his secretaries of state and defense, Hillary Clinton and Robert Gates, respectively, explicitly do.

On November 26, 2007, Gates declared at Kansas State University:

But, my message today is not about the defense budget or military power. My message is that if we are to meet the myriad challenges around the world in the coming decades, this country must strengthen other important elements of national power both institutionally and financially, and create the capability to integrate and apply all of the elements of national power to problems and challenges abroad. In short, based on my experience serving seven presidents, as a former Director of CIA and now as Secretary of Defense, I am here to make the case for strengthening our capacity to use "soft" power and for better integrating it with "hard" power.

One of the most important lessons of the wars in Iraq and Afghanistan is that military success is not sufficient to win: economic development, institution-building and the rule of law, promoting internal reconciliation, good governance, providing basic services to the people, training and equipping indigenous military and police forces, strategic communications, and more—these, along with security, are essential ingredients for long-term success. Accomplishing all of these tasks will be necessary to meet the diverse challenges I have described. (2007)

When he gave this address at Kansas State University, Gates was still secretary of defense under Bush, a position he entered in December 2006, succeeding Donald Rumsfeld. By then, he had numerous opportunities to learn this lesson in Iraq. Gates, it should be remembered, survived the administration changes and, in a bipartisan nomination by Obama, stayed in office, where he had better chances of implementing those lessons.

Hillary Clinton, in turn, stressed smart power over soft power, perhaps in the belief that it sounded less weak—a trait with which no Democrat, and especially no female Democrat, would like to be identified.[7] In her January 13, 2009, confirmation speech, Clinton urged the United States to adopt smart power policy, "I believe that American leadership has been wanting, but is still wanted. We must use what has been called 'smart power': the full range of tools at our disposal—diplomatic, economic, military, political, legal, and cultural—picking the right tool, or combination of tools, for each situation" (2009). Repeating the term "smart power" four times, she related it to diplomacy, multilateralism, partnering with NGOs, and the importance of values and providing an example. In Clinton's words, "America must be an exemplar of our values" (2009).

Incidentally, Nye likes to quote these declarations by Clinton and Gates, implicitly taking credit for their new insights (see, for example, 2007, 2009a, 2009e; *Economist* 2009). And this credit should not be taken lightly; Nye's soft and smart power are indeed the new theory-originated political convictions, and, as such, represent the new framers for American decision makers in their dealings with the world and the problems that face them—problems at least partly due to the politicization and trivialization of the democratic peace thesis.

A final note. As we saw earlier, soft power aims to find a liberal alternative to the overuse of force and threats in the international arena. This explains its attraction within liberal circles in academia and the policy elites. Nye skillfully designed it to put forward liberal foreign policies and guide a liberal administration with non-militaristic foreign policy tools. But does this mean soft power is immune to public misunderstandings and political misuse? I would say that immunity is too strong an expectation in the political sphere. After all, the democratic peace thesis was also conceived and thought of as "a force for peace," and it too has liberal aspirations and the expectation of presenting a helpful academic instrument for curbing violence in the international arena. As we saw, these liberal foundations, aspirations, and expectations have not prevented the political misuse and abuse of the democratic peace thesis or its instrumentalization in the service of impermissible force. Regretfully, this option always lurks in the political world.

And if we try to figure out Nye's Achilles' heel; that is, the part of his view most vulnerable to misuse and abuse, then I think it would be smart power.[8] Although smart power is a later addition to the soft power literature, and somewhat auxiliary part of it, its role in this literature is by no means insignificant. Smart power is what completes the potentiality of soft power as a policy blueprint. Policymakers cannot forsake a priori the tools of coercion and force. They need them in their arsenal, and Nye provides this with smart power, and the endorsement that hard power may still be needed.

> The threat from terrorists with global reach and ambition is real. It is likely to be with us for decades. Thwarting their hateful intentions is of fundamental importance and must be met with the sharp tip of America's sword. On this there can be no serious debate. But excessive use of force can actually abet terrorist recruitment among local populations. We must strike a balance between the use of force against irreconcilable extremists committed to violent struggle and other means of countering terrorism if we want to maintain our legitimacy. (CSIS Commission on Smart Power 2007:11)

Though admittedly a necessary facet of soft power, it is also inherently vague, fuzzy, and unspecified. It seeks an undefined balance between soft and hard power. This indeterminacy is theoretically understandable as balance is very much context dependent and contingent on countless real-world circumstances. However, this indeterminacy can also fall prey to political needs, and political circumstances can pull it this way or that, emphasizing hard power needlessly at the expense of soft power. As theoreticians who are sensitive to our social and political responsibilities, and who are aware of the political, we must be alert to this potential to misuse and abuse soft power politically through smart power.

Netanyahu and the Capitalist Peace

When Netanyahu returned to office in March 31, 2009, the democratic peace thesis had lost much of its rhetorical capital and rhetorical appeal. The failure of the Bush Doctrine discredited the public convention of democratic peace and rendered its political conviction untenable. Hamas' electoral victory in January 2006 had the same effect by demonstrating that elections cannot alone guarantee the consolidation and institutionalization of democracy, and that they can in fact empower antidemocratic forces. Thus, the politics of postponement needed a new rhetorical device, and now, as then, Netanyahu seized an attractive academic theory to help him rhetorically. The irony is that this new theory was the academic contender of the democratic peace thesis; that is, the theory of capitalist or economic peace.

The historical relationship between the democratic and capitalist peace theories is complex and ranges from mutual disregard, to mutual empowering, and all the way to contentiousness. Mutual disregard is hardly surprising, because, after all, the same can be said about much of the literature in both international political economics and international relations, which more often than not exist in parallel. It is not surprising to find Solomon Polachek, one of the leading economic theoreticians of the capitalist peace complaining that "To an economist both theories [the normative and the structural theories of the democratic peace] seem *ad hoc*, and neither are based on economics principles" (Polachek 1997:296). This feeling of suspicion runs both ways. Many, though by no means all, democratic peace theoreticians, fail to pay enough attention to the economic literature, not even the international political economic literature. And when they do, it is mostly because it suggests a rival thesis that needs refuting (see, for example, Oneal and Ray 1997; Maoz and Russett 1993; Dixon 1994). Some, however, do not ignore international political economics and try to integrate economic reasoning in their preferred explanation. Chief of these is Bruce Russett who, in his latter writings on the democratic peace, endeavors to base the democratic peace on a tripartite foundation of democracy, membership in international organizations, and international trade (see, for example, Oneal and Russett 1997; Russett, Oneal, and Davis 1998; Russett and Oneal 2001).[9] This tripartite account has come to be known as the liberal peace, and represents the theoretical marriage between the political and economic variables of democracy and capitalism, as the joint constituents of modern liberalism, to produce a coherent theoretical account. In the terms introduced in this chapter, these two theories are known as free world theories. It should also be remembered that since Kant's first posited the theory (or his version of it, the republican peace) the democratic peace thesis has been intimately linked to the economic reasoning of calculating interests in terms of wealth.

> If, as must be so under this [republican] constitution, the consent of the subjects is required to determine whether there shall be war or not, nothing is more natural than that they should weigh the matter well, before undertaking such a bad business. For in decreeing war, they would of necessity be resolving to bring down the miseries of war upon their country. This implies: they must fight themselves; they must hand over the costs of the war out of their own property; they must do their poor best to make good the devastation which it leaves behind; and finally, as a crowning ill, they have to accept a burden of debt which will embitter even peace itself, and which they can never pay off on account of the new wars which are always impending. On the other hand, in a government where the subject is not a citizen holding a vote, (i.e. in a constitution which is not republican), the plunging into war is the least serious thing in the world. For the ruler is not a citizen, but the owner of the state, and does not lose a whit by the war, while he goes on enjoying the delights of his table or sport, or of his pleasure palaces and gala days. He can therefore decide on war for the most trifling reasons, as if it were a kind of pleasure party. Any justification of it that is necessary for the sake of decency he can leave without concern to the diplomatic corps who are always only too ready with their services. (Kant 1903:122–23)

Nowhere is the contentious nature of the relationship between the democratic peace and the capitalist peace more evident than in the writings of Polachek himself, and the distance he traveled between his 1980 and 1997 articles. In the former, Polachek presents an economically based theory that diadically explains how mutual dependency, measured in terms of international trade, leads to what he calls "natural peace" (Polachek 1980). He makes no mention of the democratic peace, as one would expect, since in those days it was a barely recognized concept outside the little-known articles of Dean Babst. Interestingly too, Polachek does not even mention the term "democracy" in that earlier article. His explanation of how this "natural peace" is achieved is purely economic, and democracy is not considered a variable worth mentioning. But fast-forward to 1997, and his article is basically an attempt to suggest an alternative theoretical framework to what was by then a leading IR theory—the democratic peace. The theories are now in competition, and Polachek reasons that democracies do not fight each other because: "Democratic dyads trade more than nondemocratic dyads, and as such exhibit less conflict and more cooperation" (1997:296).

This is also the thrust of Erik Gartzke's arguments. Gartzke argues that the peace between democracies is actually a capitalist peace, and is explained by free-market mechanisms that create a conflation of policy goals, which reduces the security dilemma between capitalist states, and consequently mitigate the chances for armed conflicts and wars between them (Gartzke 2007; Gartzke and Hewitt 2010). Accompanying Gartzke is a host of writers such as Michael Mousseau (2003, 2009, 2010), Håvard Hegre (2000), Erich Weede (1995, 2005), and Patrick McDonald (2007, 2010). Although each of them proposes a somewhat different theory, they all emphasize the economic and capitalist explanatory variable over the political and democratic variable. In other words, just as several theories try to explain the democratic peace thesis, there are several theories that try to explain the capitalist peace thesis. Just as the democratic peace theories are lumped together in the popular mind, so have the differences between the various capitalist theories disappeared en route. Moreover, in its current form, the capitalist peace thesis has come to rival the democratic peace, and is seen in academic circles as its greatest theoretical challenger, at least within the liberal paradigmatic frame (Gleditsch 2008; see also Schneider and Gleditsch 2010). However, as we see later, in the public and political discourse, the two theses of the capitalist and democratic peace are conceived and treated as one; namely, liberal peace. Put differently, this is a case of different theoretical constructions cohering through a hermeneutical mechanism into a single public convention that could also become (if it has not yet) a single political conviction.

It is too early to determine whether the capitalist peace has yet achieved the status of a public convention, or for that matter, political conviction status, although some points can be made quite confidently in this regard. First, the hermeneutical mechanism is underway. Second, like the democratic peace, the capitalist peace is a theory that tones well with the self-identification of those who rightly or wrongly perceive themselves as part of the free world. It is especially appropriate to the United States and to the American public with its almost unwavering commitment to capitalism. Third, ideologically speaking, capitalism and democracy are traditionally seen in the United States as a pair of conjoined twins, where one contributes to the other, and neither can exist without its partner. This is especially so where liberty is defined, as it is in the United States, mainly as a negative—as the freedom from arbitrary intervention in one's life, decisions, and property. Thus, capitalism is held up as the economic system for giving one control over one's property, while democracy is pinpointed the political system allowing one control over one's decisions. Together, they constitute liberalism in the sense of individual liberty from the earlier-mentioned arbitrary intervention, which, after all, is the mainstream ideological view in the free world, especially in the United States. So theories that place democracy or capitalism at their center are able to publicly be seen as similar, or even identical, no matter how intricate their theoretical relations really are.

The capitalist peace, then, is not confined to an ivory tower. On the contrary, efforts to export it to the public and political realms have succeeded. And apart from ongoing efforts by think tanks, we also find one of its leading theoreticians, Erik Gartzke, actively participating in the efforts. Cooperating with several think tanks working on the free-market economy, Gartzke serves as a public intellectual propagating the word. The Cato Institute libertarian think tank published a policy paper by Gartzke in October 2005 called "Future Depends on Capitalizing on Capitalist Peace" (2005b).[10] In it, Gartzke tries to translate the capitalist peace into a policy blueprint and market it as forcefully as possible. The piece is often read as an exercise in political avowal vernacular, moderated only slightly by Gartzke, the theoretician, who drops in a word of caution now and then. One of the important steps Gartzke takes is to differentiate capitalist theory from democratic thesis, and try to convince the public that the democratic peace is wrong, and that it is a spurious correlation caused by the free-market institutions of capitalism. He thus writes, "The 'democratic peace' is a mirage created by the overlap between economic and political freedom. Democracy and economic freedom typically co-exist. Thus, if economic freedom causes peace, then statistically democracy will also appear to cause peace" (2005b). He explicitly goes after the democratic peace in its public conventions format, reasoning that, "The conventional wisdom is that democracy fosters peace but this claim fails scrutiny. It is based on statistical studies that show democracies typically don't fight other democracies" (2005b). This is even more pronounced in the longer version of the article published by the Australian conservative think tank Institute of Public Affairs in December 2005, two months after the original policy paper was published. The purpose of the article, titled "Capitalist Peace or Democratic Peace?" is to contrast the two theses. In it, Gartzke warns against adopting policies based on the democratic peace, rather than on the capitalist peace: "Policies predicated on inaccurate associations between democracy and peace, for example, seem destined to create as many problems as they solve" (2005a:13). It is certainly no easy task to attempt to separate the two theses in the popular mind since they have already cohered into one public convention. Nevertheless, Gartzke tries his best because as a theoretician he is aware of the differences between the two, and he believes in the superiority of the capitalist over the democratic peace. It should also be noted that as much as this belief in the superiority of the capitalist over the democratic peace is supported by theoretical and methodological rigor, it is also based on Gartzke's libertarian moral commitments and ideological convictions—libertarian moral commitments and ideological convictions that are evident in his collaboration with the previously mentioned think tanks and their commitment to promoting libertarian policy.

In his effort to establish the thesis in its academic, public, and political formats, Gartzke capitalizes on some of the rhetorical assets of the theory of capitalist peace, taking advantage of its rhetorical capital. First, Gartzke emphasizes constantly the scientific nature of his claim, and the objective nature of the findings.

> When democracy and economic freedom are both included in a statistical model, the results reveal that economic freedom is considerably more potent in encouraging peace than democracy, 50 times more potent, in fact, according to my own research. Economic freedom is highly statistically significant (at the one-per-cent level). Democracy does not have a measurable impact, while nations with very low levels of economic freedom are 14 times more prone to conflict than those with very high levels. (2005b)

But no less important, he links his theory to such prominent figures of the glorious liberal past such as Montesquieu, Adam Smith, John Stuart Mill, Richard Cobden, and Norman Angell. These preeminent thinkers are supposed to provide the same prestige as Kant does to the democratic peace. The capitalist peace is thus at once historically and intellectually grounded, but also scientifically based, refined, and allegedly proved. In the shorter version of the article, Gartzke, of course, fails to mention Angell's failed predictions, portraying the founding fathers and the history of the thesis as flawless. Only in the longer version of the article does he add a note of precaution regarding Mill's predated optimism, and even then he does so quite fleetingly, ensconcing it in words of praise (2005a:14). Furthermore, Gartzke surrounds this precaution with cheerful optimism as to the validity of the thesis today, its predictions, and its potential strength as a policy blueprint.

Where Gartzke does provide a more nuanced analysis is in his reading of the limits of the capitalist peace—or, put differently—in admitting that it is probabilistic and bounded. The theoretician in Gartzke forces him to agree that "Economic freedom is not a guarantee of peace. Other factors, like ideology or the perceived need for self-defense, can still result in violence. But, where economic freedom has taken hold, it has made war less likely" (2005b). At least in this regard Gartzke does not cross the Rubicon, and does not totally transform into an ideologue and orator. However, that does not stop him from concretizing the abstract thesis and translating it into beneficial policy blueprint that ought to be implemented.

> Research on the capitalist peace has profound implications in today's world. Emerging democracies, which have not stabilized the institutions of economic freedom, appear to be at least as warlike—perhaps more so—than emerging dictatorships ... The way forward is to capitalize on the capitalist peace, to deepen its roots and extend it to more countries through expanding markets, development, and a common sense of international purpose. (2005b)

Here is where Gartzke's efforts are most evident, where he does his best at being a public intellectual, offering theoretical insights into public debate and initiating (or at least supporting) the hermeneutical mechanism through which theory migrates outside academia and into the public and political spheres. Moreover, Gartzke is very sensitive to the ideological baggage of the capitalist peace, and highly aware of the ideological explosives he must diffuse when publicly advancing the capitalist peace thesis. Accordingly, he transposes that component of capitalism which is negatively perceived; namely, greed as the motor of wealth accumulation, and changes it into a positive and harmonious policy mechanism. With the help of Adam Smith's Invisible Hand, Gartzke retorts that, "The flowering of economic freedom, what some have derisively labeled 'greed', has begun to dampen the fires of war that to many seemed perennial and inherent, a product of civilization itself" (2005a:16). Greed is rhetorically equated with economic freedom, hence stripped of its negative connotations of being a selfish desire, and assumes the positive connotations inherent in the political concept of freedom as both a moral value and a mechanism for associative harmony. More than a theoretical move, this idea has ideological implications. It serves to initiate the migration of the academic thesis into the public and political spheres where the thesis can become a political actor; where ideological interpretations of the thesis are more dominant than academic nuances, and where political avowal vernacular is more practical and efficient than theoretical explanatory vernacular.

In chapter 7 I argue that theoreticians have a democratic imperative to participate in the public debate, and to introduce their theoretical insights into the deliberation to enrich public reason. They have a political responsibility and democratic imperative to act as theoretician-citizens. It may seem at first glance that Gartzke indeed discharges our democratic imperative as theoreticians, and by introducing the capitalist peace thesis into the public discourse in popular terms he indeed acts as a theoretician-citizen. However, Gartzke performance as public intellectual is flawed for two crucial accounts that run counter to the theoretician-citizen's role description. First, more than simplifying the thesis in a way that would make it publicly comprehensible, Gartzke is involved—as we have seen—in politicizing the thesis and trivializing it by conveying it rhetorically in slogan-like fashion; he discursively uses the political avowal vernacular. Accordingly, rather than making it more difficult for politicians to rhetorically misuse and abuse the thesis, he facilitates its politicization and the misuse and abuse of its rhetorical capital. Second, when politicians misuse and abuse the thesis—as Netanyahu, for example, does—Gartzke fails to stand up publicly to refute and denounce the thesis politicization. How can he, when he is deeply involved in its politicization? He seems satisfied with initiating the migration process, but then gladly cooperates with the thesis politicization. Gartzke, then, fails to discharge the real dictates of our political responsibility and falls short of acting as a theoretician-citizen. The outcome is that whereas in the past the democratic peace thesis was pitted against the realist theories, nowadays, the capitalist peace is measured against its sister free-world theory—the democratic peace. And this process is being executed by a coalition of theoreticians and libertarian think tanks which have a shared theoretical and ideological agenda in common.

These efforts by the coalition were commandeered by Netanyahu. Netanyahu, though, altered some of Gartzke's themes, and politically and rhetorically accommodated them to the exigencies of the political circumstances in which he operates. First, the cohering of the two theses into one concept of liberal peace in the popular mind served his purpose. The actual intricate theoretical relations between the two theses posed no problem to think of, nor was this a challenging rhetorical hurdle. For Netanyahu, the theses were hardly more than rhetorical and political instruments to be adapted to political necessity. As the general public came to identify the two as one, Netanyahu could rotate between them without arousing serious suspicion from the lay public. And as the first; namely, the democratic peace, was overused and discredited, Netanyahu's natural inclination was to turn to the second; namely, the capitalist peace. Netanyahu started to toy with the ideas of the capitalist peace, or to use his terminology, the economic peace, sometime around 2003, while serving as Ariel Sharon's finance minister. The venue he chose to air his new ideas was the Herzliya Conference on the Balance of Israel's National Strength. The Herzliya Conference is an annual conference, which started in 2000, and now draws many of Israel's policy elite and renowned international guests. The event has become a highly prestigious platform, with many politicians describing their visions in their Herzliya address. The best-known case was Sharon's surprise announcement of his unilateral disengagement plan at the fifth Herzliya Conference in December 2004. A year earlier, at the fourth Herzliya Conference, Netanyahu publicly articulated an idea on the theme of economic peace. In that address, Netanyahu repeated his claim that Palestinian society has been poisoned by hatred toward Israel, and that there is no real partner on the Palestinian side for peace negotiations. Hence, any negotiation efforts at the present stage will be doomed to fail. A moderate, pragmatic Palestinian leadership must emerge before any breakthrough can occur. Netanyahu held up the economic sphere as the possible key. Only when individuals desire stability can we expect pressure from the bottom up, and the emergence of a moderate pragmatic leadership (Netanyahu 2003). This is a rudimentary articulation of the theoretical position that trade and economic growth generate an interest in peace; that they make war a costly alternative that no rational being will choose. Economics, then, is the key to peace.

However, that was only an initial and undeveloped engagement with those ideas. Furthermore, in 2003, Netanyahu was still using democratic peace rhetoric to stave off negotiation. It took Netanyahu five more years to return to the ideas of the economic peace and fully develop them. By 2008, Netanyahu was ready to seek reelection, by which time the democratic peace thesis had lost much of its rhetoric appeal. Hamas won (semi-) democratic elections in January 2006, the United States found itself dragged into a prolonged war in Iraq, which was at least partly driven by the democratic peace thesis, and Barack Obama sat in the White House with little patience for either democratic peace rhetoric or Netanyahu. These developments disarmed the democratic peace thesis as a rhetorical tool and led Netanyahu to refresh his rhetorical arsenal with the help of the economic; namely, capitalist, peace. It is amazing to note how Netanyahu stopped altogether referring to the democratic peace phenomenon and theory. What he formerly saw as the panacea for war was deserted quite abruptly and totally substituted with another idea. Netanyahu felt no need to explain or excuse himself. He concluded quite rightly that not many would hold him to his former commitments, especially as the two theses were perceived in the popular mind as closely related, even identical.

In 2008, Netanyahu again chose the Herzliya Conference as the venue for presenting his fully developed economic peace theory. He was opposition leader at the time, with a brilliant comeback campaign in mind to win him the prime ministership for a second time. Netanyahu targeted the unilateral disengagements from southern Lebanon and Gaza, and argued against any further premature territorial concessions. His view was that all prior peace endeavors had failed miserably because they were based on false expectations. According to Netanyahu, economic peace was the only way forward. Market forces and regional economic cooperation in agriculture, industry, and tourism can create islands of prosperity and hope. Thus, the Palestinian public can truly believe that there are prospects for improving their own and their children's lives. These dreams would halt the advance of radical Islam, while regional economic cooperation would provide an economic foundation leading to future peace negotiations, and the stable peace and security Israel had always craved (2008). Note that it is no longer democracy that impedes radical Islam, but rather trade, economic development, and prosperity. We are witnessing here a rhetorical flip-flop from one kind of theory to another.

This flip-flop was completed during his election campaign, and reached its culmination in the early days of Netanyahu's prime ministership, in the spring and summer of 2009. In his swearing-in-ceremony speech, Netanyahu stressed the role of economics in achieving peace.

> My Government will act vis-à-vis the Palestinian Authority to achieve peace on three parallel tracks: economic, security and political. We strive to assist with the accelerated development of the Palestinian economy and in developing its economic ties with Israel. We will support a Palestinian security mechanism that will fight terror, and we will conduct ongoing peace negotiations with the P.A., with the aim of reaching a final status arrangement. (2009a)

Though the tracks are parallel, we can witness in this address the primacy of economics in bringing about the other tracks. Again, economic betterment is the locomotive that will haul the rest of the processes toward peace.

On June 14, 2009, two and a half months into his term, Netanyahu gave a very dramatic speech in response to Obama's Cairo University speech. This time, Netanyahu chose Bar Ilan University as the location for his speech. Bar Ilan University, founded and populated by the national religious sector, is symbolically appropriate, as it mirrored the academic location of Obama's speech, and is considered the furthest right of all the Israeli campuses. Making his first-ever declaration of support for a Palestinian state, in their university, was almost an act of co-opting the rightist national religious sector. In this speech, too, the economic peace takes central stage.

> I call on the Arab countries to cooperate with the Palestinians and with us to advance an economic peace. An economic peace is not a substitute for a political peace but an important element in achieving it. Together we can undertake projects that overcome the scarcities of our region, like water desalination, or maximize its advantages, like developing solar energy, and exploiting our geographic location by laying gas and petroleum lines and establishing transportation links between Asia, Africa and Europe. (2009b)

Netanyahu was quick to stress that this is the key for peace, "I believe that a strong Palestinian economy will bolster peace. It will strengthen the moderates and weaken the radicals" (2009b). But Netanyahu also added two provisos that made his audience believe he was still the old Netanyahu, and still seeking a politics of postponement. Netanyahu stressed that as a precondition for negotiations the Palestinians must recognize Israel as a Jewish state (he later moderated this), and that the Palestinian state must be demilitarized, a proviso that undermines Palestinian sovereignty, and is unacceptable to them. The two provisos added to the concern of those who were already suspicious of Netanyahu; they fiercely attacked his vision as a result.

While Netanyahu's rhetorical use of the democratic peace thesis was prolonged and very successful, the same cannot be said about his rhetorical use of the capitalist peace. Shortly after his Bar-Ilan address, Netanyahu all but abandoned his former approach. He hardly, if ever, alludes to the economic peace, and declared (though has not followed through) with various strict measures regarding the settlements (like the Freezing Construction Decree), offering these measures as new incentives for renewing negotiations with the Palestinians. Those (unimplemented) measures left no room for the rhetorical use of the capitalist peace. Why was this so? What led to the failure of Netanyahu's rhetorical campaign on this occasion? The answer is that this time the experiences of his previous round as prime minister were against him, and he was surrounded by a general mood of suspicion. Contributing to the failure of Netanyahu's economic peace rhetoric was the new American administration, which—at least initially—felt more committed to halting the settlements. This atmosphere of suspicion united people from journalism, academia, and politics, and encouraged them to publicly criticize Netanyahu's proposed policies. Many of those critics focused on Netanyahu's notions of economic peace. On the journalism front, Akiva Eldar, the prominent Haaretz publicist, took the lead in targeting Netanyahu's economic peace. On November 18, 2008 he wrote:

> Now the "new" Netanyahu is proposing an improved path: It is called "economic peace." Mr. Privatization promises that once economic growth in the Palestinian Authority reaches 10 percent annually, and the change is seen and felt, we will achieve stability on the ground. Instead of discussing issues such as the Temple Mount, borders and refugees, he will talk to the Palestinians about building a civil society. (2008)

The academic world also had its criticism, including in the daily newspapers. From different disciplines such as economics (Kleiman 2008), psychology (Strenger 2009), political science (Dror 2009), and international political economics (Feldman 2009), various academics pointed out the futility of Netanyahu's vision of economic peace. However, I wish to focus on two interesting academic critics, whose criticisms relate directly to the issues just raised. The first is Carlo Strenger, a psychology professor at Tel Aviv University, who perceptively reminded his readers of Netanyahu's earlier rhetorical experimentation with the democratic peace, pointing out the inherent contradiction between the democratic and the economic peace theories (Strenger 2009). The second was Nizan Feldman, a Tel Aviv University researcher at the Institute for National Security Studies (INSS), who analyzed Netanyahu's economic peace with an eye to the conditionality of the theory's validity. As argued earlier, one of the four requisites for sound theorization is acknowledging the terms of conditionality that specify the restrictions of the theory's validity and applicability. Feldman did just that: he stated the restrictive conditions under which, and only under which, the economic peace theory can be valid. Feldman specified that the economic peace theory is only valid between two sovereign states, not in cases where one of the parties still seeks independence, as in the case of the Palestinian Authority and Israel. In such cases, the national cause can overtake economic calculations, and people are willing, both individually and collectively, to sacrifice their economic interests and tolerate hardship for the sake of national independence (2009:23). In this case, the economic peace theory is not valid as an explanatory apparatus, nor can we deduce policy blueprints from it regarding the Israeli-Palestinian conflict. Feldman also took aim at Netanyahu's other failure to meet the requisites of sound theorization—namely, the requisite of being bound by logical stipulations when inferring probable outcomes from theory.

> [T]he thrust of the theoretical underpinnings supports the claim that economic growth or cooperation between states reduces the probability that they will go to war with one another, but does not address the possibility of these economic elements leading to conclusions of peace treaties. (2009:21)

In other words, Netanyahu's stated goal for the economic peace; that is, a peace treaty with the Palestinians, is not a valid inference and expectation from the theory of economic peace. Feldman reasons that under the current conditions of the conflict a reasonable and probable outcome is not peace between Israel and the Palestinians, but an improved economic and political infrastructure in the Palestinian Authority that will enable Prime Minister Salam Fayyad to opt for a unilateral declaration of a state (2009:25),[11] which is hardly the vision Netanyahu envisages with his economic peace. Feldman's nuanced theoretical analysis thus exposes the internal weaknesses, even contradictions, of the political misuse of a theory.

Combined with the other points previously raised, it seems that we have here, once again, not a case of merely political misuse, but rather that of abuse: the rhetorical harnessing of a theory to a political agenda (the politics of postponement), that does not sit well with the theory's underpinnings. But this time, academics confronted the political world and would not concede Netanyahu the opportunity to mobilize the economic peace's rhetorical capital. In this way, theoreticians discharged their political responsibility and democratic imperative to act as theoretician-citizens and warn against the misuse and abuse of theories.

Neither was the political world blind to the feebleness of Netanyahu's economic peace theory and the possible hidden agenda that motivated it. In the Israeli political system, Tzipi Livni the opposition leader and former foreign minister, was especially active in criticizing Netanyahu's economic peace. On December 18, 2008, still foreign minister, but deep into her election campaign, she avowed:

> An Israel that speaks in terms the world no longer holds valid, such as economic peace instead of political peace, hoping that no one will ask it to move on to other channels that would create peace with real substance. That way leads us into a corner and does not generate any kind of joint solution. (2008)

Livni lost the February 20009 elections and became head of the opposition, where she kept targeting Netanyahu's economic peace, highlighting its international unacceptability (see for example, Livni 2009). She indeed proved right. The Palestinians utterly rejected Netanyahu's new peace plans that were rationalized by, and fashioned on, economic peace theory (Eldar 2009). So did the international community, represented by Tony Blair, the Quartet Envoy to the Middle East, and George Mitchell, Obama's special envoy to the Middle East. Both of them remarked that developing the Palestinian economy is fine, but it is not a substitute for real diplomatic negotiations, and that an economic peace cannot come in place of a political process; that the two must progress in parallel (Mozgovaya 2010; Ilani 2009). The Palestinians and the international community pushed for something more.

Interestingly enough, in the Israeli political system, Nachman Shai, MK from the opposition party Kadima, joined the criticism by offering soft power as an alternative to economic peace. Shai, who received a PhD in political science and communication in 2009, declared in his first Knesset speech:

> Professor Jo Nye, Dean of the Kennedy School for Government at Harvard University, presented in the 90s a new theory of power and its uses in the international arena. Besides hard power, military and economic force, he presented a new kind of power—soft power. Which according to his definition is the possibility of a state to shape another state and society's preferences not by forceful means. What are those things? Values, culture, political institutions. And the instruments of achieving it are creating exemplary model, addressing common values and goals, diplomacy.
>
> Hard power we know well, and we had to use it again and again in the history of the State of Israel, but what about soft power? Currently I complete an academic research in Bar Ilan University, which study the events of Geut Vashefel[12]—2000–2005—in which Israel successfully confronted a terror campaign. With the help of this research I wish to learn how can Israel build its soft power and use it with its neighbors, primary the Palestinians, but also the Arab States, the Muslim States, and if possible—with the whole world.
>
> For this purpose Mr. Chair and Members of Parliament, I initiated the establishment of a lobby for the advancement of public diplomacy of Israel—this thing we often call "Hasbara", and in its center the empowering of soft power. And I shall repeat: values, culture, policy, political institutions. (2009)

Evident in Shai's speech are the rhetorical capital of theory and the awareness by Shai, a former journalist and spokesperson, of this rhetorical capital. This is why it was important for him to emphasize the academic origins of this policy option, and the very prestigious academic source of it—Professor Nye, dean of a Harvard University school. Later, Shai, as Nye before him, refocused his interest and energies toward smart power (2010).

In this constellation of opposing alert forces, Netanyahu's rhetorical maneuverability was narrowed down, and moreover, once his former rhetorical flirtation with the democratic peace was aired by critics with better memories than the wider public, Netanyahu's odds diminished. Netanyahu and his economic peace were in the spotlight, and almost doomed to fail. Political circumstances, together with past experiences, are a crucial component in rhetorical success. This time the political circumstances were against Netanyahu, and turned his mobilization of the rhetorical capital of the capitalist peace thesis into a failure.

Conclusions

The two cases covered in this chapter are still ongoing. It is hard to tell if and how they will continue to unfold. This is especially so with Nye's soft power which, so it seems, is still gaining momentum. Implied by President Obama and explicitly praised by Clinton and Gates, soft power stands a good chance of becoming the political conviction of the Obama administration. As such, it can replace the political convictions originating with the democratic peace thesis, which was discredited after the Bush administration became bogged down implementing it in Iraq and elsewhere in the Middle East. The case of the capitalist peace thesis, though other theaters may adopt it, basically seems closed in Netanyahu's case. Still trying to practice his politics of postponement with the Palestinians, he abandoned the democratic peace, which had been emptied of its rhetorical assets and lost its rhetorical capital. In its place he started to mobilize a theoretical new contender: the capitalist, or economic, peace. But, facing Netanyahu were critics from journalism, academia, and politics, alerted by their previous poor experience with him. Confronting the opposition, Netanyahu quickly abandoned the economic peace as well for more substantive measures toward the Palestinians. Consequently, the economic peace theory has not gained the status of political convictions. Nevertheless, it is too early to mourn the capitalist peace as by now it has probably achieved public convention status among large sections of the free world—not the least due to the efforts of theoreticians like Gartzke, who is one of its leading theoreticians. This role and function was shared also by Nye with soft power and facilitated the theories' migration outside of academia through the hermeneutical mechanism process.

Together, democratic peace, capitalist peace, and soft power constitute the three free-world theories supposed to explain the behavior of democracies, which were conceived in democracies, and whose political representations were implemented for the sake of democracies. With them, we conclude the theoretical and empirical sections of this book, and the ground is now ready to lay out its normative dimension: the establishment of a theory of theoreticians' responsibilities for the real-world ramifications of their theories, and for the process of hermeneutical mechanism.

7

THEORIZING AND RESPONSIBILITY

Tumultuous are the lives of theories. Conceived in the serenity of academy, they may find themselves forced into the real world and subjected to the vicissitudes of politics. This migration of theories from academia to the real world is what raises the question of theoreticians' responsibility. Are the theoreticians responsible for the real-world ramifications, political harms, and moral wrongs resulting from their theorizing, and what sort of responsibility do they bear? The political biography of the democratic peace thesis discussed earlier in the book will help us answer these questions.

This chapter basically argues that social science theoreticians[1] are not morally responsible for their theories' ramifications in the sense of blame responsibility. However, they are socially responsible in the sense of task responsibility (Goodin 1998:148). They also bear political responsibility ensuing in democratic imperative and scholarly responsibility ensuing in theoretical imperative. The ramifications of theories in the real world are mostly the result of political uses and, sometimes, political abuses. Politicians and ideologues harness theories to their political agendas often ignoring the theory's actual content. In other words, it is not the theoreticians who affect reality, and it is not even theories that affect reality: it is the public and the political representations and misrepresentations of the theories that affect reality. Representations and misrepresentations of theories occur when theories are altered by being publicly misinterpreted and even distorted by political abuse. This may lead to two kinds of political harms as described in earlier chapters. The first is the exploitation of a theory's rhetorical capital to forestall disagreement, political opposition, and public deliberation, and ultimately to degrade the public reason. The second form stems from the rigidly dogmatic policy blueprints caused by the political misrepresentation of theories, leading to policies vulnerable to failure due to the intricate, multifaceted nature of social reality. Both harms can be identified in the context of the democratic peace thesis and its public and political representations and misrepresentations, both of which have contributed to actual moral wrongs such as the organized and impermissible violence of the Iraq War. Those political harms and moral wrongs instigate the responsibilities discussed in this chapter.

Politicization is essentially unpredictable, so theoreticians cannot be held accountable for the real-world ramifications of their theories. They cannot be ascribed with blame responsibility for the political harms and moral wrongs which were brought about by their theories. And although some may find it tempting, it is senseless to blame democratic peace theoreticians for the war in Iraq, or blame them for the problems with the Israeli-Palestinian peace process. But, it would be perfectly reasonable to ask theoreticians to evaluate if theorization and theory in fact have any intrinsic features that make them susceptible to public misinterpretation and political abuse. Theoreticians—including democratic peace theoreticians—should ask themselves whether there is something in the democratic peace theories (and theories in general) that predisposes them to misinterpretation and abuse. They should ask themselves if perhaps they created a theory that was open to misinterpretation and abuse and because of that helped engender the war in Iraq and extend the Israeli-Palestinian conflict. Should they identify such elements, they must be duty bound to address their theory's susceptibility and vulnerability. This is then the theoreticians' task responsibility.

I wish to propose that, yes, theories do have several intrinsic features that render them susceptible to public misinterpretation, and lay them open to political abuse. These features, as we have already seen, are the structural duality of the accessibility and incomprehensibility of theories overlaid with the prestige of objectivity. Together, these generate the rhetorical capital of theories, which is a useful resource for politicians and ideologues to mobilize for political and ideological ends. To discharge their task responsibility and work against their theories' vulnerability, theoreticians must renounce the principle of objectivity and instead adopt a normative ethic. This would make it harder for politicians to abuse their theories, and theoreticians would be able, and morally obliged, to use theories to benefit society. But I must qualify this. The social responsibility which is ascribed to theoreticians is not individual, but rather, collective. Similarly, some of the measures which they are required to undertake in order to discharge their responsibility, are required of them as community. Later, however, the conclusion argues that responsibility should revert back to theoreticians as individuals, since it is they who must actualize and practice the normative ethics called for in this book.

I would also like to discuss two further responsibilities. The first is the political responsibility ensuing in a democratic imperative. The second is the scholarly responsibility ensuing in a theoretical imperative. For different reasons, each type of responsibility burdens theoreticians with the imperative (both democratic and theoretical) to show more concern and involvement in the political destinies of their theories, and participate more actively in the public deliberations that shape policies. Hence, whereas political actors bear the moral responsibility for the political harms and moral wrongs, theoreticians—as process enablers—are allocated with the political and scholarly responsibilities and democratic and theoretical imperatives to disable the structural duality, thus precluding harms and wrongs. To disable the structural duality and discharge the democratic and theoretical imperatives, theoreticians must abandon positivist-like objectivity, with its requirement of detachment, and adopt a more proactive stance in the public and political spheres in which their theories are distorted, and policies are sometimes informed by these distorted understandings. In other words, they should act as theoretician-citizens in the public sphere and through civil society.

The argument proceeds in several phases. The first describes the need for a general theory of theoretician responsibility by demonstrating the theoretician's distinctive social role among the generators of social ideas. The second section goes on to refute both the univocal "yes" responses and the univocal "no" responses to whether theoreticians should be responsible by arguing that both responses demand too much and too little, respectively, from theoreticians. I then proceed to discuss why the forward-looking type of responsibility—task responsibility—would be appropriate for theoreticians. The third section analyzes the structure of theory and theorizing, and examines how a theory's rhetorical capital renders it vulnerable to political use and abuse. The fourth section establishes the responsibilities theoreticians should accept and the measures needed to discharge them—these include both the democratic and theoretical imperatives to act as theoretician-citizens and the more fundamental and far-reaching obligation to renounce the principle of objectivity so as to participate actively in the moral and social construction of society.

The Theoretician as a Distinct Social Role

The first step toward developing a general theory of social science theoreticians' social responsibility is to evaluate the need for one. I show that theoreticians and/or their products (theories) share qualities relating to their dealings with the real world, which place them in a category of their own and necessitate the kind of general and special theory of responsibility we are discussing. This section then deals with the distinct characteristics theoreticians have that justify a general theory of social responsibility for theoreticians. In a later section, the features in theories that actually justify such a theory are explored. Theoreticians share two distinct characteristics that greatly affect their dealings with the real world: the first is the nature of the theoretician's social role; the second is the institutional nature of the role, and the theoretician's occupational ethic.

Social science theoreticians occupy a social role as producers of social ideas; they are not alone in producing social ideas. Intellectuals and experts, too, occupy a similar social role. Yet, there are differences between the three groups.[2] Intellectuals possess and produce general and unspecific knowledge, sometimes cynically disparaged as non-required knowledge. As Jean-Paul Sartre wrote, "Now, it is a fact that an intellectual is someone who fails to mind his own business" (quoted in Szacki 1990:231). Experts, on the other hand, possess and produce definite, concrete, and applicable knowledge relating to a particular subject matter. Along this continuum, theoreticians occupy a middle ground. They are experts, but their expertise lies in producing theories. Theory is an intellectual construction committed to the explication and explanation—following strict methodological rules—of the patterned relations between different phenomena. Theories are essentially general and abstract.[3] Accordingly, they do not offer specific concrete knowledge, nor are they off-the-shelf suggestions to be applied in the real world. To apply theories to specific phenomena, a mechanism is needed to translate them into policy guidelines applicable to them.

This translation can be made by experts (in the conventional sense referred to above), who may be either policy or regional experts. Such experts operate then as mediators, or as Joseph Lepgold suggested (1998), a transmission belt between the abstract general world of theory and the specified kind of knowledge required by policymakers. The translation can also be performed by the theoreticians themselves acting as mediators by taking a more public role; for example, the role of public intellectuals. In the role of public intellectual, however, the theoretician steps out of his or her regular social role, and for a moment assumes the role of the intellectual with its set of specific characteristics. Sometimes, it is the ideologues or policymakers who translate theories into policy. For example, from the theoretical abstract proposition that democracies do not (or rarely) fight each other, the neoconservative pundit Max Boot did not hesitate to infer "Therefore, the United States has a vital stake in fostering the spread of representative government" (2003:27). And with that, Boot the ideologue, took a leap of application, and committed the abstract theory to a concrete policy guideline. Occupying, as they do, this middle ground between intellectuals and experts places theoreticians in the unique position of contributing indirectly, though sometimes substantially, to the policy-making process.

Another occupational characteristic of theoreticians, which sets them apart from other producers of social ideas (mainly intellectuals), is that the social role of theorizing is institution-based. Contrary to the fuzziness that shrouds the intellectual, the theoretician normally works at an academic institution, and more importantly, is committed to a relatively strict occupational ethic. One of the main tenets of this ethic is a commitment to objectivity. Hence, it is one thing to ask an intellectual to be committed to morality; it is altogether different to demand that the theoretician commit his or her theorizing—contrary to the established ethic—to moral standing. It is against this background of occupational ethic that commits the theoretician to objectivity that one has to labor in advancing the argument made here.

We have already discussed how a general theory of theoreticians' social responsibility is needed due to the theoretician's social role. A second reason why a general theory is needed concerns the nature of theory. Certain features of theories as both processes (theorizing) and products (theory) make them susceptible to public misunderstanding and vulnerable to political abuse. It is because of the susceptibility and vulnerability of theories that a general theory of theoreticians' social responsibility is needed which would allow us to avoid public misunderstanding and prevent the political abuse of theories. The third section, therefore, deals extensively with these features, but in the meantime, let us examine two common views regarding theoreticians' responsibility and propose an alternative.

Two Common Views and Another Option

The stories are familiar: evolutionary theory provides arguments for genocide; modernization theories nurturing military dictatorships; realist theories of international relations frame Cold War policies; democratic peace thesis—the paradigmatic example taken up here—legitimate aggressive policies of forceful democratization. As these examples and many others show, theories seem to affect the world they intend to explain; theories may have real-world ramifications. But should we ascribe theoreticians with responsibility for the real-world ramifications of their theorizing? In International Relations (IR)—the parent discipline of the democratic peace thesis—the answers range from a univocal "yes" from critical theoreticians, to a univocal "no" from adherents of positivism, especially neorealists. Immanuel Wallerstein, for example, is the exemplar of critical theoreticians. Applying Marxist critique to the contemporary capitalist World System, Wallerstein assigns theoreticians the Gramscian role of Organic Intellectuals. He assumes that social science theories have emancipatory potential, "The process of analysis and the process of social transformation are not separate. They are obverse sides of one coin. Our praxis informs, indeed makes possible, our analytical frameworks. But the work of analysis is itself a central part of the praxis of change" (1979:65). The responsibility, therefore, lies with the theoreticians to fulfill this potential, "the intellectual tasks before us are important ones, that our intellectual responsibilities are moral responsibilities" (Wallerstein 1984:184). Other IR critical theoreticians turn their focus to the flipside phenomenon of emancipation and change. They accuse mainstream IR theories and theoreticians—mainly realists and neorealists—of serving the status quo, and fostering a conflictual world dominated by powers and superpowers. This accusation is advanced most forcefully by Richard Ashley, "Neorealist structuralism lends itself wonderfully well to becoming an apologia for the status quo, an excuse for domination" (1986:289; see also Ashley 1987:418). More recently, Steve Smith declared in his International Studies Association 2003 presidential address that "International Relations has been one voice singing into existence the world that made September 11 possible" (2004:500). The theoretical accounts of both Ashley and Smith are based on the assumption that theories (and ideas, more generally) have a real and substantial impact on world reality; they have actual power. Following these assumptions, it makes sense for Wallerstein to ascribe theoreticians with moral responsibility.[4]

At the other end of the spectrum are the neorealist theoreticians who deny that theories have influence and power, or that theoreticians have responsibility for world problems. Firstly, neorealists abide by the positivist detachment assumption that sees theoreticians as detached from the subject matter of their theorizing—in other words, the social world. Theoreticians, they insist, do not and should not be involved in shaping this world.[5] Added to this is the neorealist theoretical assertion that what matters in global politics is the division of material capabilities and resources, and what we get is a total dismissal of theories (and ideas, more generally) as agents of change or the status quo. Theories, in neorealism, have no real consequences outside academia, no substantial real-world ramifications. Consequently, theoreticians as theoreticians have nothing (outside academia) to be accountable for. The question of responsibility, in other words, is solved by sidestepping. Kenneth Waltz, the godfather of neorealism, represents this stand in his defense against Ashley's charges, "How can any theory have these affects? Ashley has a higher regard for the power of theories than I have" (1986:340; see also Waltz 1997:915).

However, this IR dispute is inclined to be emotional and accusing. Each party tends to define itself through its disagreement with the other party, creating ill-defined manifestos as opposed to clear, precise argumentation. There are, however, theoreticians from other disciplines, mainly philosophers, who articulate the question of theoreticians' responsibility in more refined terms. The following analyzes two such paradigmatic responses. The first, that of William Connolly, takes a positive stance: Connolly believes theoreticians are allocated with responsibility overseeing their research. Others, including Marc Fleurbaey and J. R. Lucas take a negative view of the theoretician's responsibility, Lucas, not rating the powers of theoreticians very highly; Fleurbaey blaming politicians for using and abusing theories.

Connolly writes about theoreticians having responsibility.

> Social scientists are not so influential that their conceptual decisions inevitably affect the practices of the polity. But the social scientist's limited influence does not justify his lack of attention to the political import of the conceptual contours commonly accepted within his profession

and his society. If the understanding of conceptual contests in politics elaborated here is at all correct, then the social scientist has an obligation to endorse those ideas that he thinks would help to nourish a politics of responsibility were they to be incorporated into the practices of our polity. One can and must debate just what interpretations of key social and political concepts are worthy of such endorsement, but to deny any intellectual responsibility in this area is to falsify the connection between such contests and the constitution of social and political life. (1993:204)

Fleurbaey, dealing with political philosophers but to the same affect, answers the question of responsibility negatively: "But theorists, admittedly, are not liable for the world events, nor, to some extent, for the use and misuse of their concepts in the public debate" (2001:501). Lucas joins in debate and lumps poets, philosophers, scientists, and artists together in the sense that they "are in no position to do anyone great harm by a bad decision, and are not much good either if they merely keep their noses clean, and take care not to stray from the path of rectitude" (1993:188). But both positions are wrong: Connolly demands too much of theoreticians; Fleurbaey and Lucas are too quick to dismiss them of any responsibility.

Let us take Connolly's stand first, and see where he was wrong. Connolly's thesis is saddled with three shortcomings. The first is that he ignores the political process in which theories are manipulated. The second is his exaggerated belief in theoreticians' powers. The third is his excessive demands from theoreticians.

More often than not, theories do not affect reality in their own terms. At times, the consequences of theories in the real world run counter to the theoretical—and moral—intentions of the theoreticians who constructed them. So it was with the theories of democratic peace, which neoconservatives used to reason and legitimize their project of forcefully democratizing the Middle East. In an ironic twist, academic theories that happily identified a force for peace—namely, democracy—were politically exploited to advance the cause of war. As this example demonstrates, theories do interact with reality. However, this interaction may be hostile to their authors' original intentions. Thus, it would be more accurate to argue that reality is influenced in fact by the theories' public and political representations and misrepresentations. These representations and misrepresentations stem from changes inflicted on theories when they are mistakenly interpreted or deliberately abused. The former involves public representation as it takes place in the public realm; the latter can be referred to as political misrepresentation, as it takes place in the political arena and is carried out consciously by politicians for political reasons. What this means is that theories are politicized more than politics are theorized. Theories and theoreticians are captives of politics. Connolly overlooks this aspect of the politicization of theories prior to their impact on the real world.

The second shortcoming is an outcome of the first. As Peter Berger and Thomas Luckmann wrote "Theoretical thought, "ideas," *Weltanschauungen* are not *that* important in society" (1967:15). Connolly readily admits that social scientists are not overdeterminedly influential. He fails, however, to assess how theoretical thought is only one part of what Berger and Luckmann term "commonsense 'knowledge'" (1967:15), which, according to them, and correctly so, is the central force of social construction; that is, of the impact ideas have on social and political reality. It is not only that theoretical ideas are a relatively small part of the world of ideas, it is also the way they are integrated into the world of ideas: how they are understood, interpreted, politicized, disseminated, and socialized into. The migration process that determines their impact on reality is conditioned on many factors, both material and ideal, so much so that their real influence is significantly trimmed down. Only by acknowledging the conditioning of theories' influence can one really assess the impact of theories (or their representations) on reality, and consequently, the responsibility of theoreticians.

Yet a third shortcoming results from the previous two. Connolly's demands on theoreticians are excessive. Once we accept that a theories' influence on reality depends on other factors (primarily their politicization), the question arises: how can theoreticians forecast their theories' influence? How can a theoretician decide which theoretical ideas can "nourish a politics of responsibility"? In a way, the fate of theories is beyond the theoretician's control, and it is hard to conceive how they would practically set about meeting Connolly's burdensome demands. Unless, of course, we accept John Lyne's "moral imagination," which he defines as "the capacity to envision how a situation can admit of other descriptions and perspectives, how others may be affected, how attributes may be claimed or rejected as part of 'us,' how we understand who is part of our community, how the course of language we unleash may do its work over time" (1998:273). In our context, important in the moral imagination is the capacity to envision the various ways in which a theoretical idea can be integrated into the commonsense knowledge of society, can form part of the world of ideas, and even more so, can be altered to a politically distorted misrepresentation and be abused politically. Taking into account the complexity of the migrating process and the number of factors involved and the skills politicians have to harness whatever they deem helpful to their agendas, it seems utterly unreasonable to expect theoreticians to imagine the fate of their theories. It would be unreasonable to expect them to be able to construct theories with the intention of bringing about designated political and social desired outcomes. Moral imagination would not help us here. Connolly's demands of theoreticians are unreasonable, and his attributing them responsibility is thus flawed.

However, there is a distinct category of cases to which Connolly's scheme of theoretician responsibility does apply. Theoreticians are generally quite passive actors in the politicization of their theories. They might view the process as spectators and potentially they may offer a critique of the process, but they are not in control of it, and more so, they do not initiate it. Most cases fall under this category, and therefore fall out of Connolly's understanding of the responsibility of theoreticians. There are occasions, however, where social science theoreticians are not passive actors, but rather perform an active role as introducing entrepreneurs, as political agents mobilizing their theories. There are those theoreticians who consciously and for various reasons aim to introduce their theories into the world of politics with the deliberate calculated intention of influencing it. As chapter 6 showed, this is what happened with Joseph Nye and Erik Gartzke. Other cases in point are Henry Kissinger, Anthony Giddens, Robert Putnam, and Walt Rostow (Ish-Shalom 2006b). At times, theoreticians of this ilk are moved by a moral desire to help to improve the world. Alternatively, they are driven by a desire for personal power or by a longing for fame and prestige. By deliberately initiating the process and trying to supervise it and affect its results, these theoreticians form a category of their own. Indeed, those in this category do bear a responsibility of the kind Connolly describes, regarding the ramifications of their theories, for they are indeed political agents and conscious initiators of the process. One should note, however, that even in these cases, the political-entrepreneur-type theoretician does not have full command and control of the consequences of his or her agency as the world of politics tends to intervene and spoil intended actions. However, this is a typical and inherent phenomenon resulting from the complexity of the social and political world. We do ascribe responsibility, even though consequences are not necessarily the perfect end result of calculated efforts by agents. Apart from those who believe in the purest, crudest version of consequentialism, there is a moral intuition that people should be held responsible for foreseeable consequences that any reasonable person in their position would have been aware of. As Lucas aptly remarks: "We hold a man responsible not only for the actually foreseen, but for the reasonably foreseeable, consequences of his action, and will not automatically excuse him if he pleads that he did not know that his action would be likely to engender them" (1993:52). It is doubly so in cases of those who voluntarily seek executive office. By taking that office they assume responsibilities for the planned and unplanned consequences of their scheming; this is after all the merits we expect from high-office holders. Again, Lucas's formulation is of help "those who undertake office have to consider not only what ought to be the consequences in an ideal world, but what will be the consequences in this actual world, of what they do or do not do" (1993:189). This moral intuition is not limited to the case of theoreticians-turned-political entrepreneurs, and it does establish that their moral responsibility for their actions is not to be rejected (though in certain circumstances it can be mitigated).

Returning now from this detour to the main thesis of this chapter, one might ostensibly think that by refuting Connolly's argument I have confirmed Fleurbaey or Lucas's case for not making theoreticians responsible for the ramifications of their theorizing. I wish to claim, however, that the arguments advanced by Fleurbaey and Lucas are also flawed. There ought to be a sense in which theoreticians do bear responsibility for the outcomes of their theorizing. It is true that those who are not agents are not to be allocated responsibility, and in as much as it was argued earlier that theoreticians are passive actors rather than active agents in the process of politicizing theories, theoreticians are not to be blamed nor praised for the outcomes of the political misrepresentations of their theories. Whatever is beyond one's control, of one's agency, is also beyond one's responsibility. In that sense, although theoreticians are the creators of theories, they are not to be blamed nor praised for the outcomes of their theorizing in the real world.

This kind of responsibility, though, does not cover the whole span of responsibilities, and it is not what is meant here by ascribing responsibility to theoreticians. Fleurbaey is right in stressing, as he does, the centrality of political abuses when theories are translated into publicly debated items and twisted into political misrepresentations. I wish to argue, however, that since these abuses form a recurring pattern, when theory meets politics, theoreticians should examine the reasons for this pattern. It may, as in fact it is claimed here, that some intrinsic features of theorizing are the enabling factor of the political abuse of theories. The possibility of this suggests another kind of responsibility. What Fleurbaey probably has in mind in denying responsibility of theoreticians is a backward-looking responsibility of the type that deals with allocating blame or praise for actions. It is the kind of moral responsibility T. M. Scanlon calls "responsibility as attributability" (1998:248), and which Robert Goodin calls "blame-allocating sort of responsibility" (1998:148). Under the perimeters of "blame responsibility," it is the politicians who abused or used the theories who are to be blamed or praised for the consequences of theory politicization. Yet a question still begs as to what extent intrinsic features of theory and theorizing are to lend a hand in making theory vulnerable to political abuses. This possibility brings to the fore a forward-looking type of responsibility—the one Goodin calls "task-oriented sort of responsibility" (1998:148). It is the responsibility to tackle problems with the intention of amending them;[6] that is to say, it is the type of social responsibility that is produced by an ethical obligation to try and amend present social and political problems as to avert future undesired outcomes, or the complimentary ethical obligation to maintain a present good state of affairs, and to produce future desired outcomes.[7]

It is this ethical obligation, I would maintain, which ascribes a task responsibility to theoreticians. Theoreticians are not liable, guilty, or blameworthy for the outcomes of their theorizing, but they owe it to themselves—and to other members of society—to examine their own work. Theoreticians need to find out if indeed some intrinsic features of theory and theorizing share responsibility for the political abuse of theories by rendering them vulnerable to such abuses, by being, so to speak, an enabling factor to the political abuse. It is this that allocates theoreticians with task responsibility.

The Structure of Theory

Three-stage action is required by theoreticians to discharge their task responsibility. The stages are sequenced and each depends on its precursor. The first stage is to examine theory and theorizing in order to find out if some of their intrinsic features share responsibility for their political abuses by rendering theories vulnerable to such abuses. Put differently, a thorough examination is warranted to determine if intrinsic features of theory act as enabling factors of political abuses. If such intrinsic features do exist, then a second stage is needed to identify corrective measures aimed at reducing the vulnerability of theories and diminishing the possibility of future political abuse. Theoreticians should also assess if those corrective measures are at all bearable. The third stage would be to try to implement the corrective measures and reduce the vulnerability of theories to politicization and political abuse.

The first stage is the least controversial of all the stages. Surely no one would object to self-examination to determine the sources of political abuse. Some, though, might object to my claim that this self-examination is an ethical requirement—an obligation that amounts to something which ascribes social responsibility. Nevertheless, insofar as intrinsic features that arise from the way we theorize are to some extent accountable for the political abuse, the request for self-examination is an ethical necessity due to what Scanlon calls "substantive responsibility" (1998:248); in other words, the things people are required to do for each other. Theoreticians are, allegedly, accountable to the wider public for the vulnerability of their theories to political abuse and, as such, self-examination is a social responsibility, a task responsibility. It is, in other words, an ethical requirement that ascribes a social responsibility to conduct such self-examination.

When we examine the structure of theories, we see a number of intrinsic features that account for the vulnerability of theories to political abuse. Theories have rhetorical capital, which makes them vulnerable to political abuse. As discussed earlier in detail, rhetorical capital is the aggregate of persuasive resources inherent in theories arising from the intrinsic features of theories; that is, the structural duality of accessibility and incomprehensibility overlaid with the prestige of objectivity.

Theories offer explanations (usually causal explanations) for regularities. It is this basic requirement and expectation of theories that lies at the center of theories' structure; in other words, theories link explanans to explanandum. Surrounding this center are additional structural and auxiliary procedural features. First, there is the principle of objectivity which, according to the positivistic and conventional wisdom, governs theorizing. Supposedly, theories are pursued for the sake of scientific knowledge, and as such should not be influenced by political partisanship, moral conviction, and ideological persuasion. Theories' ability to explain, and the prestige their objectivity bestows, makes theories attractive to politics,[8] as policymakers need causal mechanisms to help them devise efficient policies. No less important than efficiency, causal mechanisms help policies become better accepted and legitimated by the public. By offering causal mechanisms credited with objectivity rather than tainted by partisanship and ideology, theories are a perfect apparatus for fulfilling both of these needs (Shenhav 2005). The previously mentioned features and sources of the rhetorical capital of theories are dependent on their being accessible to the public. Without that accessibility the theories, no matter their real-world implications and their attractiveness to policymakers, would have remained obscured and secluded in the ivory tower. As theorizing is carried out in a public sphere, and as theories are circulated rather freely, they are indeed highly accessible to the public. This accessibility enables the theories' migration to the public sphere, and is a major source of rhetorical capital.

However, we need to distinguish between theories as products, and theorizing as the production process. Accessibility relates to the theory as a product. Theories migrate well. But the theorizing production process does not migrate well. Some of the technicalities and subtleties of theorizing are far from accessible to the wider public and do not migrate well from academia to the public sphere; they make theories incomprehensible to the nonacademic public. In particular, and as was explored and demonstrated extensively in previous chapters, four requisites of theorizing do not fare well in the public sphere and become lost in the process of migration. Because of the importance of these requisites to the question of theoreticians' responsibilities, I will briefly run through them again. The first requisite of theorizing, which is lost in migration, is the cautiousness and (conditioned) criticism built into academic discourse and conduct. When politicians and ideologues refer to it, democratic peace thesis sounds reputable, undisputed, and uncontested, and hence peace among democracies is taken for granted. As quoted earlier, this is George W. Bush's view of peace among democracies, "We know from history that free nations are peaceful nations. We know that democracies do not attack each other" (2006B). Bush saw democratic peace as uncontested; there was no need for complicated subtle theoretical apparatus to infer conclusions from compound reality, democratic peace can be induced simply from observing history and needs no academic caution.

Second, most theories are explicit about the conditions in which they are valid, but lose their terms of conditionality in migration; for example, many democratic peace theoreticians insist that peaceful democratic relations are dyadic, occurring only within pairs of democracies. Moreover, it is now widely acknowledged by theoreticians that these peaceful relations only hold true within pairs of consolidated democracies. Such conditionality disappears in the political sphere where theoretical claims become totalistic assertions. Boot, for example, defines democratic peace theory as "the notion that liberal democracies are unlikely to use weapons of mass destructions, sponsor terrorism, and undertake other activities that threaten their neighbors and the United States" (2003:27). Similarly, Benjamin Netanyahu learns from history that "modern democracies do not initiate aggression. This has been the central lesson of the 20th century" (1996). Outside academia it seems democracies are peaceful not only among themselves; they are peaceful overall. Third, and closely related, theories lose their probabilistic nature and become absolute, law-like statements. This can be seen, for example, in the pronouncement by Lawrence Kaplan and William Kristol that the democratic peace is "a truth of international relations" (2003:104). The statements by Bush and Netanyahu reflect a similar absolute and law-like quality. They do not deal with probabilities: democracies are not less likely than other regimes types to be involved in war; democracies do not initiate war, period. Fourth, and again related to this question of conditionality, is the role of the laws of logic that stipulate what is validly inferred from a theory and what is not. When there are no terms of conditionality, the rules of deducing conclusions from a theory, and of deducing policy guidelines from a theory—which is more relevant in the public arena—are seriously hampered. For example, we cannot infer from the theory that posits that: "consolidated democracies never (or rarely) fight each other," that other kinds of dyads (e.g., democracies and nondemocracies, or nondemocracies and nondemocracies) are necessarily war-prone. Therefore we cannot deduce, which is what the Bush Doctrine did, and which it used to legitimize the war in Iraq, that democratizing Iraq would lead to immediate regional stability, because that would require a willingness to democratize the rest of the region. And even if we did democratize the rest of the region, we would still face a long period of regional destabilization while the newly democratized states struggled through the long and arduous process of consolidating their democracies.

Discarding these four requisites of theorizing ignores the threat of regional destabilization and leads to a distorted reading of the theories, and to political representations and misrepresentations. It also involves a shift from a theoretical explanatory vernacular to a political avowal vernacular; from a subtle complex reading of the theory and its ideas to a political, persuasive, simplistic, slogan-like reading and communication of its ideas. It is a discursive switch in which the theory is politically mobilized by able rhetors.

This structural duality of accessibility and incomprehensibility is in fact what allows the politicization of theory to occur. The coupling of this structural duality with the principle and prestige of objectivity reinforces its political ramifications. As previously noted, the prestige of objectivity increases a theory's attractiveness to politicians forever in quest of rhetorical assets. Objectivity allows politicians to portray their policies as nonideological, and more importantly, non-partisan and non-sectarian. Politicians try to draw on the prestige of objectivity to portray their policies as benefiting the general good of society, rather than some sectarian good. Furthermore, a theories' stated objectivity relieves its theoreticians of any sense of social responsibility to govern the political fortunes of the theories. The principle of objectivity shields the theoreticians in their ivory tower—on their theoretical high ground—where they go about analyzing and theorizing society, in no way accountable to the general public. Their background places them above and outside politics, allowing them to abandon their theories to political abuse, and to feel no obligation to challenge it. The abuse of the theory can thus continue uncriticized and unchallenged.

But insofar as the analysis presented here is correct, theoreticians are ascribed with a task responsibility. They are obliged to examine the intrinsic features of theory and theorizing that comprise the rhetorical capital of a theory, and they are also responsible for finding a way to fend off political abuse, to disable this factor, and to try their best to limit the potential for political abuse. We cannot reasonably expect political abuses to totally disappear, but we must do our best to reduce it. It is warranted by the theoreticians' task responsibility.[9]

Discharging the Theoreticians' Task Responsibility

After establishing that theoreticians are ascribed with task responsibility to take measures against political abuse of theories we need to undertake the second stage—identifying the measures theoreticians are to take to disable the enabling factor. We must identify the Achilles' heel of theorizing that makes theories vulnerable to abuse and misrepresentation. Earlier analysis identified the rhetorical capital of theories as the enabling factor of political abuse. However, we still need to assess which of the three components of rhetorical capital needs to be modified in order to reduce the potential political abuse of theories. So far, the discussion has led us over relatively secure ground—after all, how contentious can defining a problem be? But it is now—when trying to formulate and propose a remedy—that most of the difficulties and controversies can arise. It is here that the terrain becomes much less certain underfoot.

The first intrinsic feature of theory to be explored is theory's accessibility to the wider public. Accessibility, however, is the inevitable outcome of how science is conducted, of science's infrastructure. Science, by nature, is democratic, and as such it is inclusive: it is not only open to its practitioners, but also to the wider public that can access it itself, or more likely, with the help of intermediaries. The problem, as we see shortly, is the nature of those intermediaries. In addition, accessibility is a positive quality of theories, which we should not give up. Accessibility is what connects theoreticians and theories with the public, and as such, legitimates the public funding of science. Most importantly, accessibility enables academia to contribute positively to public deliberation, and thus to a well-governed polity, and academia's capacity to do this should not be given up.

The difficulty with the second intrinsic feature—namely, the incomprehensibility of theorizing—is that it is an inevitable outcome of the complexities, technicalities, and subtleties of theorizing, and of the theoretical explanatory vernacular in which theoretical assumptions and findings are conveyed. One cannot get rid of them simply by deciding to simplify theorizing, as those complexities, technicalities, and subtleties are the bedrock of good theorizing. They constitute the procedural mechanisms and methodologies that allow and guarantee good science. Though they are the reason theorizing is incomprehensible to the wider public, they are a necessary and indispensable element of theorizing. Consequently, as long as academic education remains out of reach for most, theorizing is almost bound to remain incomprehensible to most. What theoreticians can, and ought, to do then is facilitate the public's understanding by intermediating and simplifying theories (for example, by theoreticians acting as theoretician-citizens and offering assistance to science correspondences and popular writers, etc.), which can also help prevent the harmful trivialization of theories by politicians seeking to abuse them. Also note, the problem of incomprehensibility runs deeper than a general academic education can help. Educated as I am in the humanities and the social sciences, I remain dumbfounded by theories from the exact sciences. I suspect that theoretician from the exact sciences will similarly be taken aback by reading a social sciences theory. Thus, and especially due to the exceedingly specialized nature of the academic world, even a general academic education will not suffice, and the problem of incomprehensibility is here to stay.

We are thus left with the third intrinsic feature of theories: the declared objectivity of theorizing, or the prestige of objectivity. Objectivity means quite a few things, ranging from detached impartial conduct (including the conduct of inquiry), to external object-like truth unconditioned by epistemological enquiry, to a more mundane aloofness from party political squabbles. As John Searle rightly maintains, objectivity is used to designate both ontological and epistemological meaning (1995:7–9). This is an important point to which I keep returning. The common denominator of all these understandings is that objectivity stands for disengagement of some sort, which in our context involves the disengagement of theoreticians and theorizing from political and ideological belief systems—an epistemological disengagement that supposedly makes possible discovering an external ontological truth. The epistemological implication of this understanding is that theories are politically neutral and, to no less a degree, morally neutral, and that a distinction exists between fact and value. Allegedly, theories do not rise from values, nor do they have a moral say, or moral implications. An ontological upshot of this understanding is that the truth theories establish do not depend on values, and is external to the mode of theorizing. Hence, the ethic of objectivity (and its accompanying prestige of scientific objectivity) encompasses both the epistemic and ontological senses of objectivity: social science's vocation is the objective quest for the objective truth. This is the heritage of positivism, which advocates the principle of objectivity as the warranted method of theorizing.

It is this positivist understanding that eases the political and rhetorical abuse of theories by politicians who can expediently present a distorted reading of any theory to support any ideological and political program. Objectivity shields theoreticians from the need to involve themselves in politics; supposedly it relieves them of the kind of social responsibility arising from being ethically accountable for their theories' ramifications in the real world. Moreover, by being relieved of social responsibility, theoreticians are not obliged to unveil political abuses of their theories, as the principle of objectivity dictates their aloofness from the political world. They thus hold the theoretical high ground. So, it is not surprising that there were no public protests from prominent democratic peace theoreticians regarding the political uses, misuses, and abuses of the democratic peace thesis by the neoconservatives and the Bush administration. When Bruce Russett did criticize the rhetorical misuse of his theory by the Bush administration, he did so in the rather publically obscure academic journal *International Political Perspectives* (2005), far from the public view.[10] However, if theoreticians are ascribed with social-task responsibility, this will not do. Theoreticians are accountable to the wider public, and ethically obligated to deal with the political ramifications of their theories—including those stemming from the political abuses of their theories, as in the case of democratic peace thesis and the Israeli campaign against the Oslo accords and the American war in Iraq.

There are several preliminary and limited measures that can be taken by theoreticians to stand for their social obligations to the public. First, they could follow Max Weber's advice and make sure their research agendas responded to pressing social dilemmas (1949:21–22, 61). Or, as Ward Jones argues concerning philosophers, they should be responsible to their contexts: "Philosophical communities and individual philosophers should be sensitive to—attuned to and concerned with—the practically and theoretically relevant issues that are salient in their nonphilosophical surroundings, and at least some of their work should be motivated by a concern for those issues" (2006:631). Failure to be motivated by the issues around them may result in justified accusations of neglect. Connolly, in one of his earlier papers (1973), suggests a second possible measure: when evidence to decide between several alternative theories is inconclusive, theoreticians may opt for the more moral alternatives.

A third preliminary measure was suggested by Wesley Widmaier—that theoreticians should act as public intellectuals and explain the theories in their own voice (2004). This measure is indeed called for, though it should also be admitted that it has its limits. First, many theoreticians are reluctant to speak out, and in any case, they are not all good at doing this. In a media environment that calls for short sound bites to explain profound theoretical ideas, probably the most able articulators among the theoreticians would fall short of the oratorical capabilities of the able politicians.[11] Probably, it was this media environment that led to the failure of several initiatives by theoreticians to prevent the war in Iraq. Two prominent groups—the Coalition for a Realistic Foreign Policy and Security Scholars for a Sensible Foreign Policy—attempted what Patrick Thaddeus Jackson and Stuart Kaufman called Weberian Activism (2007; see also Payne 2007). Yet, in a media environment that rewards short sound bites and oratorical capabilities such scholarly Weberian Activism proved insufficient. Second, as discussed earlier, the social roles of theoreticians and intellectuals are two distinct roles, each with its own characteristics. The proposal presented here relates to theoreticians as theoreticians. By trying to assume the role of intellectuals, theoreticians might abandon some of their specific characteristics that render them unique. In that case, the role of theoretician would risk being stripped of its meaning. Put differently, there is nothing wrong with stepping into the public intellectual role as long as the theoretician understands that this is an altogether different role requiring different qualities (oratorical ones, for example), and, if undertaken incautiously, could impinge on his or her theoretician qualities. However, and as discussed further momentarily, the political harms and moral wrongs that threaten society as a result of the politicization of a theory outweigh these caveats and professional stakes, and therefore burden theoreticians with the somewhat similar role to public intellectuals—the role of theoretician-citizens.

A fourth limited measure is for theoreticians to assist the public's understanding, by helping science correspondences to explain theories by simplifying, rather than trivializing them. A fifth limited measure is for theoreticians to take note if their theories are used politically, evaluate the moral implications and, if necessary, act as whistleblowers, warning the public of dangers posed by the misrepresentations of their theories.

These preliminary measures add up to a dictate, a democratic (and theoretical) imperative, for theoreticians to act as theoretician-citizens. A theory is an intellectual accomplishment, rich in analytically processed informative knowledge about the unfolding of human conduct and social relations. It can be very helpful in shaping policies, which, after all, are public tools for coping with the complexities of the social world. This beneficial potentiality ascribes theoreticians, as the constructors of theories and as citizens of their polity, with the political responsibility of participating in the political process of policy shaping. In a democracy where policies are formed publicly, and where they consider citizens' inputs, this responsibility takes the shape of a democratic imperative—a civic commitment to contribute to the democratic deliberation process.

Although the democratic imperative is ascribed to all citizens in a democracy,[12] two factors make it all the more necessary for theoreticians to uphold: The first is the informative insights with which theories abound; the second is the process of politicization and trivialization that theory sometimes undergoes. Even though theoreticians may potentially be able to contribute beneficially to the democratic process of policy shaping, because their theories are sometimes hijacked by politicians and ideologues, and politicized and trivialize (at times, at least), their contribution may be detrimental to reason and policy shaping. So it is with the democratic peace thesis. Rather than contributing reason to American policy-making, it led to rigidity and dogmatism and the Iraq War. Rather than contributing to the public understanding in Israel of the stakes and gains involved in the peace process with the Palestinians, the politicization of the democratic peace thesis led to antagonism (both in Israel and the United States) toward any territorial concession to a polity that was not yet established, based on the problematic claim that this not-yet-established polity was nondemocratic, and therefore an unreliable partner for peace. Both factors commit theoreticians to serving in the role of theoretician-citizens (in contrast to Plato's philosopher-king).

In their capacity as theoretician-citizens, theoreticians should help translate theoretical insights into inputs for democratic and public deliberation. It is in this translation of theoretical insights that theoretician-citizens differ from public intellectuals; the theoretician-citizens' offerings to democratic and public deliberations rest in and arise from their expertise (albeit, abstract expertise) rather than from some nonspecific knowledge as with public intellectuals. In their public contribution, theoreticians as theoretician-citizens should not bow their academic integrity to the dictates of political avowal vernacular. Instead, they should skillfully—and I admit that I have no clear answer how this is done—steer a course to enable them to simplify their theoretical insights without falling into the attractive (rhetorically wise) trap of unwittingly trivializing and politicizing them. Only thus can they show respect to themselves, their academic vocation, and to the political faculties of their fellow citizens.

Theoretician-citizens must also protect their theories against politicization and trivialization by ideologues and politicians, and ensure their theories are not politically hijacked, and do not assume a life of their own and influence policy-making against their maker's intentions. Through participation as theoretician-citizens and involvement in their theories' migration into the real world, theoreticians can guarantee that their theoretical insights are understood flexibly and executed pragmatically, and they could warn against rhetorical misuse and the political dogmatic misapplication of their theories.

Nevertheless, a potential criticism can be leveled against assigning the role of theoretician-citizen to theoreticians. Though the thrust of my general arguments is in line with the deliberative and participatory model of democracy, assigning the role of theoretician-citizen to theoreticians might be somewhat patronizing. Even more problematic, assigning theoreticians with this role may seem like elitism—like helping institutionalize democracy as an elitist project in which different privileged and powerful groups divide the responsibilities between them, leaving the rest of the public out, and perhaps also share between them the spoils of government. In that case, there is an internal tension, even a contradiction, between a role that might seem elitist and patronizing, and the general thrust of my argument, which is deliberative and participatory. However, this criticism does not hold. Being a theoretician-citizen does not imply elitism or patronizing the public. Being a theoretician-citizen means recognizing the theory's merits, rather than the merits of the theoretician. It relates to the aforementioned beneficial potentiality of a theory to addressing a sociopolitical complexity which ascribes theoreticians, as the constructors of theory and as citizens of their polity, with the political responsibility and democratic imperative to participate in the political process of policy shaping. It is for their beneficial potentiality that theories ought to be brought to bear on policy-making, and no one is better positioned to execute this task than theoreticians. It is for this deliberative and participatory reasoning that theoreticians are expected to take upon themselves the role of theoretician-citizens.

Accordingly, theoreticians should be more active in civil society, offering their theoretical insights to public deliberations, enriching public reason. This point is worth stressing: the appropriate and democratic route of beneficially employing theoretical insights is not through the political system and through the policy establishment. As we can learn from the 2010 ISA annual convention theme, "Theory vs. Policy? Connecting Scholars and Practitioners," International Relations scholars are too obsessed and preoccupied with building bridges with policy elites. However, this should not be the theoreticians' principal vocation. Rather, they should be more concerned with building bridges with the public, or better still, taking down the walls of academia and forming partnerships with civil society. They should concern themselves with contributing their theoretical insights to the public, and do so in the public sphere where the arguments will be scrutinized and valued based on their merits, and not by the academic credentials of their proponents.[13] This is how the academia internal meritocracy would not be used and exploited in order to institutionalize elitism, and this is how theoretician-citizens would not (generally speaking) be tempted by the futile prospects of becoming philosopher-kings.

Accordingly, theoretician-citizens should be involved in the public sphere by making modest and honest offerings of their theoretical insights; offerings intended to fulfill two tasks. The first is as input to policy-making, to improve its output—in other words, to directly improve policies. This task also covers the function of whistle-blowing in cases where theoreticians identify a misuse and abuse by politicians of the rhetorical capital embedded in their theories. However, the second task is more fundamental and operative in the long run, and involves improving the policy-making process by helping to enrich the citizens themselves and invigorating their political faculties—not by imposing answers, and not so much by coaching them to give the right answers, but by the nourishment of asking questions, of doubting, and no less important, encouraging them to assume responsibilities. It is with this educational—I fear to use the word enlightening—task that the democratic imperative of acting as theoretician-citizen burdens us as theoreticians; theoreticians, mind you, privileged by public resources.

Furthermore, it is in the act of participation in the public sphere that the ability to simplify theory without trivializing and politicizing it can be cultivated. Participation in the public sphere means engagement in what Jürgen Habermas calls the lifeworld. According to Habermas, the lifeworld is where taken-for-granted public conventions are constructed and maintained; the social and cultural background against which argumentation operates. As Habermas wrote with somewhat Gramscian undertones, "the lifeworld appears as a reservoir of taken-for-granteds, of unshaken convictions that participants in communication draw upon in cooperative processes of interpretation" (Habermas 1987:124). Therefore, I would expect that participating actively in the public sphere and engaging the lifeworld help to foster awareness and intimate knowledge with societies' sensitivities, understandings, worries, hopes, practices, values, and norms. Fostering such intimate knowledge results in learning how reasoning operates in the social arena, and how to tailor theory-based arguments in a socially tangible manner—one which able to generate the required outcomes. Of course, that means there is no generalizable method for simplifying theory without trivializing and politicizing it, but rather localized practices, each with its own specific normative setting, social locale, political culture, and democratic functioning that varies from one society to another.[14]

Positivism notwithstanding, by forsaking positivist-like objectivity (in the sense of neutrality and detachment), theoreticians could avoid the political harms and moral wrongs previously described; they could enable theory to fulfill its full potential of benefiting decision making by enriching public deliberation with theoretical insights that generate public reason and advance reasoned and reasonable policies. This is the outward-bound dictate of the democratic imperative arising from the political responsibility ascribed to theoreticians.

There is another concern that lends force and immediacy to the requirement for theoreticians to be involved in the public and political destinies of their own theory. This concern is more inward-bound toward the academic vocation itself, and thus I shall call it a theoretical imperative. Nowadays, there are many questions regarding theoreticians' responsibilities in the wake of the Iraq War. The theme of the 2007 annual convention of the International Studies Association was "Politics, Policy and Responsible Scholarship," and one of the many questions in the call for papers was "Do we scholars bear responsibility for how our ideas are understood and used outside our immediate social and academic context?" One of the main panels, "The Study of War: Data Collection, Theory Building and Responsible Scholarship," convened by Lothar Brock, dealt explicitly with the responsibility of democratic peace theoreticians for the Iraq War. During the panel, Bruce Russett responded to the issue of responsibility by stressing that the only responsibility of theoreticians is theoretical responsibility; namely, theorization along strict methodological lines. I disagree with this opinion and argue that theoreticians do have other sorts of responsibilities, and that even theoretical—or as I call it, scholarly—responsibility charges them with broader obligations than simple adherence to strict methodological rules. As the case of the democratic peace thesis demonstrates, scholarly responsibility also charges theoreticians with the theoretical imperative to guard their theories against political misuse or, in other words, against the manipulation of their theories for political goals, which are antagonistic to their theories' intent and content.

To substantiate my claim, I would like to consider Tony Smith's book, *A Pact with the Devil* (2007). In it, Smith apparently blames the democratic peace theoreticians for helping to bring about the Iraq War. He ascribes them with moral responsibility for its concomitant blame and praise.[15] Smith claims that these liberal theoreticians willfully cooperated with the neoconservatives, offering them the theories and ideas that produced the Bush Doctrine (2007:51). He asserts that their theories were "a loaded gun put into the hand of whoever would pick it up" (2007:91), and that "Together they [the neoconservatives and the neoliberals, democratic peace theoreticians included] would march to conquer Baghdad" (2001:176). Overlooking the process of politicization and trivialization that the thesis underwent independently of the theoreticians' actions and intentions, Smith erroneously concludes that the theoreticians are to blame for the Iraq War as they consciously and purposefully signed a pact with the devil.

Smith mostly presents a political indictment of the neoliberal intellectuals in the 1990s who advanced liberal internationalist ideas to legitimate interventionism. Prominent among these were the democratic peace theoreticians, and Smith targets Russett personally along with (more awkwardly) John Rawls and Andrew Moravcsik. The book is a paradigmatic example of the hazards posed to theories by their political misuse. Smith does not satisfy himself by erroneously blaming Russett and others for the Iraq War. He also refutes the theoretical and scientific status of the democratic peace thesis, calling it "a pseudo-scientific account of world affairs" (2007:xii, 108). More troubling still is his misreading of the thesis, which he understands as follows: "Their [the democratic peace theoreticians] essential claim was that a world order dominated by liberal democracies would by its very character necessarily be one of peace. By the same token, democratic peace implied that nondemocratic states were inherently aggressive and would likely be hostile to the liberal world for the very freedom it enjoyed" (2007:95). Evident here, especially in the second part of the quotation, is a misreading of the democratic peace thesis not unlike the politicized misinterpretation explored earlier.[16] Though this may be due to the political nature of the book, which renders it prone to political biases, we cannot dispense with Smith simply by holding up the political nature of his book. As much as Smith's purpose is political, he is also a respected, sophisticated, and well-read IR scholar.

How can we explain Smith's misreading of the thesis? In my opinion, he fell into the intellectual trap of reading the theory backwards. Smith was not sensitive enough to the politicization and trivialization the thesis underwent prior to its "realization" by President Bush in the Iraq War. Reading many political texts, Smith grew to identify the thesis with its political representation and misrepresentation that framed the strategic thinking of many of the neoconservatives, and with the political avowal vernacular used discursively and intentionally by some of them to rationalize the Bush Doctrine. Being engrossed as he was in rebuffing the doctrine, he meshed together the two distinct idea entities and discursive genres, and criticized the thesis for what it is not.

Smith is a paradigmatic example of the current trend that manifested itself in the 2007 ISA annual convention as well. It seems that by abandoning their theories to their political destiny, the democratic peace theoreticians opened the door to a renewed theoretical attack on the validity of their theories; an attack which is proving to be as intensive as the criticism leveled against the thesis in its early days. It is too early to judge the outcome of the new attack on the thesis. Will this trend grow, and will it undermine the current broad acceptance of the thesis? The future of the attack is dependent to a large extent on America's fortunes in Iraq. What is clear from the earlier-cited account is that letting the theory become politicized and trivialized carries implications regarding its academic and theoretical legitimacy. Theoreticians wishing to spare themselves this erroneous (but humanly understandable) outcome need to be more aware of the possible political destinies of their theories. In other words, it is a theoretical imperative, as well as a democratic imperative, to guard against the politicization and trivialization of one's theory.

However, important as both the democratic and theoretical imperatives are, they do not cover the full range of responsibilities covered by the phenomenon analyzed here, of the political biography of the theories of democratic peace. Moreover, the measures dictated by the democratic and theoretical imperatives are only partial. They mostly entail the rejection of neutrality in favor of moral commitment by theoreticians, and they are an improvement on the positivist efforts to maintain neutrality. Yet they are preliminary and limited as they only respond to the epistemological aspect of objectivity. They fail to acknowledge its ontological side. According to Avner de-Shalit, an advocate of this stance, "objectivity is the ability to reach a position where I realize that the world does not center on me; neutrality, if it is possible, is the ability not to be motivated by matters that are politically important to me when I write and teach" (2006:30). What is important to note is that de-Shalit focuses on "me." The world, according to de-Shalit, is not centered on the individual. Or put differently, the world is not the product of subjective acts. I happily endorse this claim. Yet, this individualist option does not encompass the whole range of alternatives available to objectivity. Rejecting subjectivity does not automatically leave us with objectivity, as de-Shalit wrongly assumes. Rather, we are left with a third option: that of intersubjectivity as advanced by phenomenology, as well as by social constructivism. This is an understanding that, while there is around us something that is real, it requires our interpretation of it to really matter. The social world, to a degree, is socially constructed. Thus, and contrary to de-Shalit's stance, understanding that "the [social] world does not center on me," does not lead automatically to the endorsement of objectivity. It still leaves us the option of rejecting objectivity and endorsing intersubjectivity. This option is more appropriate to the understanding that objectivity, or the lack of it, is an attribute of the social world (ontological objectivity), as well as it is an attribute of the human mind (epistemological objectivity). What is more, rejecting objectivity is not only philosophically suitable, it also the sound inference from the analysis of the rhetorical capital of theory as the enabling factor of its political abuse. Hence, rejecting neutrality cannot suffice, and I propose the more comprehensive argument of the need for rejecting objectivity for the sake of the normative social science ethic.

Committing theoreticians morally and explicating the moral groundwork of a theory constitutes a normative ethic. Normative ethic also includes the derivative principles of evaluating theories according to their moral standards and according to the morality of their possible ramifications in the real world (imperfect as such an evaluation is). In other words, the customary evaluation of theories—which is limited to appraising their explanatory strength, parsimonious properties, and prospects of additional hypotheses—is inadequate; it should be supplemented with moral evaluation. On top of that, a normative ethic involves a commitment from theoreticians to contribute to society and ensure that their theories benefit society. If theoreticians renounce the objectivity principle and acknowledge their theories' moral groundwork, as well as their moral implications, this will diminish the possibility of political abuse. Abuse will also become more evident. It is not that politicians will stop trying to abuse the rhetorical capital of theories, but they may find it harder once the articulators (the theoreticians) openly explicate the moral groundwork of theories and their moral implications. The overt moral groundwork will also commit theoreticians to countering any distorting abuse of their creation, the theory. They would not be shielded by the moral dodging explicated, for example, by Waltz, Fleurbaey, and by Lucas.

Introducing this normative ethic to the social sciences to replace the existing objective ethic would fulfill theoreticians' task responsibility of modifying theorizing and protecting theories against political and rhetorical abuse and the resulting undesired ramifications. Moralizing theory would not only reduce the possibility of political abuse, it would also enable academia to contribute more fruitfully to public deliberation. By reducing theory's vulnerability to political abuse, academia could contribute to political deliberation in a much more reasonable and beneficial fashion. It would allow theoreticians to bring to political deliberation theoretical insights which—being based on rigorous research, intellectualism, scholarship, knowledge, and sound logic of inference—could help to elucidate ends and means, and hence promote rational deliberation. Moreover, and as was previously explored, objectivity is not achieved (or rejected) exclusively in the epistemic realm. Objectivity stands and falls on the two senses of epistemology and ontology. Therefore, renouncing the principle of objectivity for the sake of a normative ethic carries with it an ontological equivalent. In the social world, truth is not an object-like entity. Truth is not external to the way we explore, understand, and theorize it. To some extent, truth is constructed theoretically, and to theorize about reality is to participate in reality's construction, and hence to be implicated in moral consequence. By shielding their theories from misrepresentation, theoreticians can ensure that their contribution to the construction of the social world is as close as it can be to what they intended it to be; that when identifying democracy as a "force for peace," their theories are not mobilized to rationalize and legitimize war, not commandeered in its service.

We need to consider one more point before finally establishing that theoreticians' task responsibility indeed necessitates substituting objectivity with morality as the proper way to theorize. Even supposing that moralizing offers all the benefits I claim it does, is the price worth paying? It may be that by abandoning objectivity as the foundation of theorizing we will bring science to an end. If objectivity is an essential part of theory it is indispensable, and any attempt to rid ourselves of it will result in substituting theory with ideology. If this is indeed the cost of moralizing theory, we certainly cannot allow it. Better to pay the price of being vulnerable to political abuse than to take science apart and become ideologues ourselves.

This surely is the position of positivists, who see objectivity as the defining quality of science. Yet this perception is misguided. As Hilary Putnam (2002), among others, effectively demonstrated, the distinction between fact and value is metaphysically inflated. Science is entrenched with values and norms, and facts are entangled with values.[17] I would also add that every human thought is so entrenched with values and norms and, moreover, it is warranted that human thought is so entrenched. We ought not to try and relegate morality to a secluded domain where its influence would be limited; we should celebrate the existence of moral reasoning in other forms of human thought, theoretical thought included. Furthermore, social reality is not an object-like entity which passively awaits discovery by an external observer; it is a realm that is being actively and continuously constructed and reconstructed by those participating in it, including social scientists (along with their values). Positivism and the endorsement of the objectivity ethic are just not equipped to understand social reality.

Science is not ideology, however, and theoreticians should take great pain to guard against ideologizing science and theory. Yet to do so they should not disregard their moral commitments. Rather they should follow the procedural mechanisms that guarantee those moral commitments will enrich theorizing, rather than trivialize theory into ideology. They should maintain and reinforce the scientific culture of questioning and self-critique, and uphold the laws of inference. Norms and values are among the constitutive building blocks of theory, but the laws of inference dictate how to theorize from those building blocks in such a way as to maintain academic rigorousness. Beside the warranted academic rigor, intellectualism, scholarship, and knowledge, the normative ethic obligates social science theoreticians to be active participants as theoretician-citizens in the moral construction of society.

It should be clear that this task responsibility is a collective one; it belongs to the social scientists as a whole.[18] There are a couple of reasons for this collective responsibility: first, there are the three factors discussed in chapter 1: public conventions, positivist confidences, and individual blind spots. By undermining the theoreticians' capacity for self-reflection and self-criticism, these factors obstruct the individual theoretician from discharging this task responsibility. Second, it is beyond the capacity of any one individual theoretician to single-handedly invalidate the principle of objectivity; nor is it in the authority of individual theoreticians to do so; neither is it a simple act of individual volition to discredit the prestige of objectivity. Introducing a new scientific ethic, a normative one, is a collective endeavor that requires a tremendous collective effort and time. In the terminology used earlier, it is a collective effort of reaching a new intersubjective understanding of the meaning of social science.

As the required measures are collective in essence, so is the social responsibility that necessitates those measures. It is especially so because task responsibility is forward-looking. Theories nowadays are reputed to be objective, and even though it is preferable for each theoretician to disclose his or her theory's moral groundwork, it is not required by the collective social task responsibility. It is preferable for each theoretician to disclose his or her theory's moral groundwork for two reasons. First, the original articulators of theories are best situated for disclosing the moral groundwork as they are the most informed about their theories. Second, they are the ones who may be publicly identified with the theories; hence, they may be acknowledged as the legitimate authority to renounce their presumably objective nature (and additionally to disclose the political abuse of their theories). Yet, though preferable at times, we should also note three qualifications to the desirability of the original articulators to be the ones who disclose their moral groundwork. First, the original articulators of a theory may be unconvinced by the arguments presented here. They may remain die-hard positivists advocating objectivity. The community of theoreticians should not be held hostage by positivists in its quest to discharge its task responsibility. Second, many theories are the product of a collective endeavor of many theoreticians through several generations. There may not be one identifiable theoretician to be given the task of disclosing the theory's moral groundwork. Third, some original theoreticians are long gone, and it would be absurd to ascribe them with task responsibility of reforming the social science ethic. Additionally, disclosing the moral groundwork of a theory is only one—albeit crucial—aspect of the new normative ethic advocated here (which is instrumental, let us be reminded, in discharging our task responsibility). Other components of the normative ethic—such as examining the normative ramifications of theories, exposing and struggling against political abuse of theories and, in general, a more active participation in the public arena—cannot be assigned to a single theoretician. It involves a collective endeavor arising from a collective responsibility. For all these reasons, task responsibility— including the struggle against the political abuse of theories—is a collective responsibility.

Conclusions

This chapter dealt with the question of social science theoreticians' responsibility for the ramifications of their theories in the real world, and for the ensued political harms and moral wrongs. After rejecting both the univocal "yes" and univocal "no" responses to the question, I have employed the notion of task responsibility to present a general theory of theoreticians' social responsibility. Task responsibility is the kind of forward-looking social responsibility for tackling problems, with the intention of amending them. Task responsibility is especially apt in the case of theoreticians and the ramifications of their theories, as the ramifications, as well as the political harms and moral wrongs, are mostly the outcomes of public and political representations and misrepresentations of theories, not of theories themselves. It is the doings of politicians and ideologues who so use and abuse the representations and misrepresentations of theories, and actually bring about the ramifications, political harms, and moral wrongs. Consequently, it is unreasonable to blame (or praise) theoreticians for the ramifications of their theories, and it is unfair to ascribe them blame responsibility for the political harms and moral wrongs brought about by their theories. It is more likely—and fair—to allocate the blame (or praise) with the decision makers who so use and abuse theories and bring about the ramifications, along with the political harms and moral wrongs. Nevertheless, it is perfectly reasonable and fair to ask theoreticians to carry out self-examination to see if the way they conduct theorization renders theories vulnerable to political use and abuse, and if they find it does, they bear the burden of finding a reasonable solution to the problem of vulnerability and implement it. In other words, theoreticians are allocated with a collective task responsibility.

In the course of this chapter, the vulnerability of theories in general, and of the democratic peace theories in particular, to political use and abuse was located in the rhetorical capital of theories; that is, the aggregate persuasive resources inherent in theories. It was also argued that the rhetorical capital of theories arises out of intrinsic features of theories; namely, the structural duality of accessibility and incomprehensibility, overlaid with the prestige of objectivity. Henceforth, it was claimed that to discharge their task responsibility theoreticians should renounce the principle of objectivity and substitute the ethic of objectivity with a normative ethic.

Some preliminary measures were suggested regarding the substitution of the ethic of objectivity with normative ethic. Those preliminary measures added up to what was termed the political and scholarly responsibilities along with their democratic and theoretical imperatives, respectively. Each of these imperatives lends additional forcefulness and immediacy to the obligations arising out of the social-task responsibility, obligating the theoreticians to show greater concern and involvement in the political destinies of their theories and to participate more actively, as theoretician-citizens, in the public deliberations that shape policies. Moreover, being active in the public sphere and through civil society, theoretician-citizens would help to enrich citizens and improve the process of policy making.

On top of the democratic and theoretical imperatives to act as theoretician-citizens was the more fundamental and far-reaching social task responsibility and its ensued obligation to explicate the moral groundwork of theories and their moral implications. It was also argued, against positivist accounts of social science, that this measure is reasonable and worth pursuing. Moreover, it was argued that it is the ethical obligation of theoreticians that arises out of their collective task responsibility, and that substituting the ethic of objectivity with a normative ethic would contribute to the moral construction of society.

I wish to conclude this chapter by raising yet another question. Could it be that failing to stand to their social, political, and scholarly forward-looking responsibilities will ascribe theoreticians with blame responsibility? Could their failure to perform the third and final stage of their social, political, and scholarly responsibilities—the actual implementation of their imperatives; namely, substituting the ethic of objectivity with a normative ethic—will generate in the future the moral backward-looking type of responsibility that carries with it moral culpability? Would the public then be right to blame theoreticians for failing to discharge their social, political, and scholarly responsibilities and moralize theorizing?

CONCLUSIONS
Zooming In, Zooming Out

Though faltering at times, the democratic peace theories have thriving lives. The aim of this book has been to trace those lives, understand them theoretically, and assess them in normative terms. Theoretically, the migration of theory to the nonacademic world was conceptualized through the hermeneutical mechanism model. By focusing on a theory's internal structure as an assemblage of political concepts, this book conceptualizes theories as theoretical constructions, a form of idea entity, and moreover, a form of political thought: a configuration of decontested political concepts arranged together, each conferring meaning on the others and receiving meaning from them. Thus, theories as political thought presents us with meaningful political concepts, functioning explicitly or implicitly, originally or derivatively, primarily or secondary, predominantly or partially to stir us to political action. Another point the hermeneutical mechanism model stresses is the metamorphosis of theory outside academia, its transformation from one form of idea entity to others; from a theoretical construction, to a public convention, to, finally, a political conviction. We defined public conventions as general background knowledge concerning the world that is taken for granted and which shapes the commonsensical codes of thinking and behavior. Political conviction was defined as specific knowledge engendering a strong, opinionated view that necessitates political action. Those two forms of idea entity are, in essence, the public and political representations and misrepresentations of academic-born theoretical constructions.

This book's theoretical framework analyzed the metamorphosis and focused on changes theories undergo during migration and how the four requisites of sound theorizing fall by the wayside as theories becoming increasingly politicized and dogmatized. First, there is a loss of the caution and sense of (conditioned) criticism that is built into academic culture and discourse. Second to disappear are the terms of conditionality. Third to go, is the probabilistic nature of theories as their public and political representations and misrepresentations become absolute, law-like statements. Fourth, the laws of logic that stipulate what can and cannot be validly inferred from a theory, do not necessarily function in the public and political spheres. These combined losses result in a simplistic yes-no version of theories in the form of their public and political representations and misrepresentations; in other words, theories end up as public conventions and political convictions that originated with the theoretical constructions.

No less important are the discursive changes, involving the various discursive genres used to convey the different forms of the idea entities. Theoretical constructions are conveyed through the theoretical explanatory vernacular; or in other words, meticulous claims of the relations between different phenomena, articulated to deliver the subtlest minutia of a theory's contentions established through strict and careful theorization. This vernacular functions to convey theoretical discoveries and the logic of explanation and verification. Public conventions, on the other hand, circulate through the discursive genre of a commonsensical descriptory vernacular, which is: the loose expression of unreflective accounts that unfold the narratives in which the world is captured and figured out by the public common sense. This vernacular affirms and reaffirms the commonsensical depiction of reality. Political convictions are conveyed using the discursive genre of the political avowal vernacular; in other words, forceful declarations rhetorically uttered in slogan-like fashion to confirm and convey political stands. This discursive genre functions to justify and legitimize ideological beliefs and political actions. Politicization and dogmatization are again evident here. With the help of pundits, ideologues, and politicians, the (at least partially) critical examination and reflexivity with which the political concepts are assembled in theoretical constructions facilitate a doxic and dogmatic acceptance of meanings; meanings which, being reassembled doxically as public conventions and dogmatically as political convictions, eventually frame and dominate the public common sense. The theoretical constructions are altered and at times distorted, thereby engendering their public and political representations and misrepresentations. They are transformed into public conventions and political convictions which, more than the theoretical constructions themselves, are the true movers and shakers in the real world. The public conventions and political convictions are responsible for producing the real-world ramifications explored in the empirical section of this book.

The empirical analysis traces the migration of the democratic peace thesis' theoretical constructions starting in the 1990s, which intensified in the early 2000s, when these constructions transformed into public conventions and political convictions. It also explores the political convictions of the democratic peace thesis in the Israeli-Palestinian conflict and the Iraq War. The former demonstrates the political mobilization of the rhetorical capital of the democratic peace thesis; the latter shows how the theory's political misrepresentation (as a political conviction) framed the neoconservative and Bush administration's strategic thinking, leading them to believe in the strategic merits of democratization. Rhetorical capital refers to the aggregate persuasive resources inherent in entities, including theories. We identified several resources of the rhetorical capital of theories, some general and shared by all theories, others particular and specific to the democratic peace theories. There is one general resource, which is shared by most theories; namely, the structural duality of accessibility and incomprehensibility overlaid with the prestige of objectivity. There are four additional specific resources: (1) the democratic peace thesis' status among policy elites as a public convention; that is, as a law-like phenomenon governing the realm of world politics; (2) two distinct families of theories—one structural the other normative—which try to explain the phenomenon and can be misused to deliver separate political messages; (3) policy implications of subscribing to the conclusions of the democratic peace thesis; namely, a political commitment urging the democratization of nondemocratic states for the sake of national security, and (4) the long and prestigious heritage of the thesis, being ascribed rightly or wrongly to Immanuel Kant. All these resources were mobilized rhetorically by both Benjamin Netanyahu in his politics of postponement, and Natan Sharansky in his politics of avoidance. Both successfully used a political avowal vernacular, and, armed with the thesis' rhetorical capital, managed to secure their political agendas.

In the case of the American neoconservatives it was different. It was not a case of rhetorical manipulation, but an example of the thesis' political representations and misrepresentations as public conventions and later as political convictions framing the neoconservatives' (and other policy elites) understandings of the world and world politics. As a consequence, the political convictions produced by the democratic peace as theoretical constructions helped generate the neoconservative grand strategy of promoting democracy abroad, including forceful democratization, carried out at gunpoint by the American Armed Forces. Accordingly, the Iraq War was rationalized, legitimized, and marketed, among other things, as an effort to democratize Iraq and supposedly serve American strategic interests of a secure stable Middle East as a zone of democratic peace.

The empirical section of this book also analyzed the political biographies of two more free world theories: soft power and capitalist peace. The analysis demonstrates the general applicability of the model of theory as an hermeneutical mechanism, showing that the model is not only valid for democratic peace theories, but can also be generalized to other theories operating in the democratic world. The analysis of the two cases is quite preliminary as their migration to the world outside academia is still in progress. However, the preliminary analysis suffices to show that these cases also involve an interaction between academia and the political world. In both cases, too, the nature of the relationship between academia and the political world is somewhat different from the introduction of the democratic peace theories into the political world. This difference concerns the active role of leading theoreticians in translating their own theoretical constructions into public conventions and political convictions: Joseph Nye in the case of soft power, and Eric Gartzke in the case of capitalist peace thesis. Their efforts seem successful, and their theoretical constructions have been translated into real-world ramifications. In the former case, soft power became a pillar of President Barack Obama's administration's understanding of world politics, and a roadmap for operating properly and efficiently in it. Soft power wishes to present and legitimize a liberal alternative to gunpoint democratization—an alternative that reaffirms American commitment to democratization, but moves the core of effort for democratization from military power to the power of example and cultural attraction, and the onus of responsibility from the American Armed Forces to local domestic civil society groups. In the latter case, capitalist (or economic) peace became the center of Netanyahu's failed rhetorical efforts to pursue his politics of postponement. The denuded rhetorical capital of the discredited democratic peace thesis was substituted by the economic peace and conveyed in Netanyahu's customary political avowal vernacular. Rhetorically, the aim was to convince the international community that rather than moving forward with the defunct political process with the Palestinians (which necessitated territorial concessions), it was better to concentrate on the economic track, which would allegedly lead to the much-awaited peace. However, for the political reasons and circumstances described in chapter 6, Netanyahu's political mobilization of the capitalist peace's rhetorical capital proved short-lived and unsuccessful. Both political biographies, whether successful or not, lend additional urgency and importance to the normative analysis of the implications of theories' political fortunes considered in the normative section of this book.

The normative section analyzed theoreticians' responsibilities for the real-world ramifications of their theories. This mainly referred to the political mobilization of their theories' rhetorical capital as an obstacle (one of many) to the peace process between Israel and the Palestinians, and as a cause (one of several) of a war fought by the United States far from home. In other words, the democratic peace theories were used for the reasons hostile to their raison d'être, which was to identify a hidden force for peace. For democratic peace theoreticians, and chiefly Dean Babst, their work had at long last accomplished the principal task of International Relations: to find a cure for war. Accordingly, the normative task of this book was to provide a moral account for this discrepancy between the theories' raison d'être and their inverted function and ramifications. I argued that (as a rule) we cannot ascribe theoreticians with moral responsibility; we cannot blame or praise them for those ramifications. Exceptions are cases in which theoreticians like Walt, Mearsheimer, Gartzke, and Nye have acted as political agents in and through the political system in a deliberate effort to translate their theoretical constructions into public conventions and political commitments. Usually, though, this is not the case. The migration of a theory into the political world is a complex sociopolitical process where theoreticians play a secondary role, if any. This was the way it was with the democratic peace thesis and theories. However, even in those more complex cases, theoreticians should be ascribed with scholarly, political, and social task responsibilities. These responsibilities share a common aim: for theoreticians to be more involved in their theories' political fortunes. They should assume the role of theoretician-citizens, and as such, be more active in civil society, adding their theoretical insights to the public deliberation and enriching the public reason. This point is worth doubly underscoring: the appropriate and democratic principal route for using theoretical insights to society's benefit is not through the political system and the policy establishment; it is rather through modest and honest offerings of the theoretical insights in the public sphere and to the wide public— offerings to be publicly scrutinized and valued not according to the credentials of the theoreticians who brought them forward, but rather according to the merits of the insights. The academic meritocracy can in this way serve the public deliberation and public reason without being used and exploited to institutionalize elitism. This is the true and real meaning of serving as a theoretician-citizen and not being carried away with hubris at the thought of being a philosopher-king.

I also argued that theoreticians should relinquish the ethic of objectivity in favor of explicating the normative commitments informing their theories. This will limit politicians' opportunities to politically and rhetorically misuse and abuse theories in the service of political and moral agendas that stray from the theories' moral groundwork. It will also lead to theoreticians participating morally in the world's social construction. But if theoreticians fail to discharge these scholarly, political, and social task responsibilities they open themselves to charges of moral culpability.

Zooming In, Zooming Out

The question now is: what next? How can we avoid charges of moral culpability? In conclusion I would like to go further than my previous two calls for collectively explicating the normative commitments that inform our theories and assuming the social role of theoretician-citizens. The road ahead lies in combining three of the main themes presented in the book; namely, the centrality of political concepts, the essential contestedness of the political concepts, and the normative underscoring of the responsibilities of theoreticians. Emphasizing the centrality and importance of political concepts as the building blocks of theoretical constructions as well as their moral and political contestedness brings to the fore a strategy for coping with the normative dilemmas we face and for discharging our responsibilities toward the wider public. I call this strategy *Zooming In, Zooming Out*. It is in fact a double-faceted strategy where we zoom into the internal components of our theoretical constructions; namely, the political concepts, and at the same time define and conceptualize them normatively and with moral sensitivity while taking note of their effect on society outside academia. It is a strategy that empowers individual theoreticians and helps them to discharge their collective responsibility. Therefore, after chapter 7, which dealt with theoreticians collectively, I now need to bring the individual theoretician back to center stage and make the individual the principal agent of the normative ethics, which I espouse here. Because although it is the collective social responsibility of the community of theoreticians to denounce objectivity and embrace normative ethics, it is through the individual theoretician's work that this new normative ethics becomes actualized and practiced.

The first action, which focuses on the construction of concepts (*Zooming In*), is not that novel taken alone. We are expected to take our concepts seriously, and we receive methodological training to define them accordingly. Definitions should provide us with as precise as possible description of the relevant concepts; a description that enables us to clearly identify any social object which falls under our study, and filter out those social objects that do not. For this purpose, a definition must be exhaustive in the sense of including all social objects supposedly captured by the concept, and exclusive in the sense of ruling out all social objects outside the concept's domain. Another criterion fundamental to theory construction is definition operationalization. This means that the definition will be helpful in making the theories and/or hypotheses testable, refutable, and also, if possible, instrumental in measuring the phenomenon being investigated. Together, exhaustiveness, exclusiveness, and operationalization provide us (or so the conventional wisdom goes) with a razor-sharp scientific apparatus with which to develop and test hypotheses. Moreover, as definitions are supposedly transparent and neutral, they are disposed to a rational and objective concurrence among the theoreticians; a concurrence that is free of any moral commitments and political convictions.

But if this depiction of defining our concepts is true and accurate, then why are those very concepts contested? For it is that contestedness that plagues our studies and, as we saw in chapter 2, embeds theoretical constructions within moral commitments and political convictions—from which they were supposedly free. Answering this puzzling question marks the first stage in justifying Zooming In, Zooming Out. In the social world, definition is the bounding and rounding of that which is unbounded and unrounded. In the social world, things do not fall that neatly into human-made concepts. Boundaries are fuzzy at best. Social objects are related to each other by various comparable features and separated by other distinct features. Hence, definition is about establishing an arbitrary delineation between social objects, whether phenomena, processes, or what have we. It inflates the importance of certain differences in order to separate certain phenomena and processes (rounding), and undermines and even ignores the relevancy of other differences to combine other phenomena and processes (bounding). This is the only way to arrive at definitions in the social world, and therefore definition involves the social construction of social categories.

Think of peace and democracy. The figure of 1,000 deaths is an obvious arbitrary boundary[1] that differentiates between conflicts where there are 1,000 dead and so are identified as wars and conflicts where only 999 are killed, and so are not identified as wars. (As if one death can make all the difference between war and no war). And a Polity II score of 6 serves the same purpose, of arbitrarily differentiating democracies from non-democracies (see, for example, Dixon 1994). There is nothing exogenously obvious about these conceptual (and measurable) boundaries—a conclusion that lends further backing to the argument defended here regarding the contestedness of political concepts. Boundaries between concepts and categories are not objective (in the ways noted in chapter 7); they are embedded within moral commitments and political convictions. Definition is a moral and political act, even though not necessarily a conscious one. Hence, is the moral and political content of those concepts which are taken as neutral; hence, is the contestedness of that which was supposed to act as the foundation for rational and objective concurrence and scientific repeatability.

However, the concepts' contestedness and their moral and political contents are neither perceptible to the public eye, nor largely to the scholarly eye and, among other things, are hidden by the definition's operationalization. Operationalization entrusts research with the language of scientific objectivity and works to hide the moral commitments and political convictions of the concepts that form the building blocks of theoretical constructions—moral commitments and political convictions that are at work whenever a researcher defines the concepts he or she is working with (e.g., democracy and peace); when he or she theoretically constructs the social categories he or she will later gear into a rigorous research program. Hence, operationalization obfuscates theories' normative underpinnings. Moreover, it encourages theoreticians to seek measurable variables, even when these variables do not exactly conform to their theoretical framework. This dynamic was especially evident in the case of Zeev Maoz and Bruce Russett, who withdrew to the more measurable proxy criterion of political violence when attempting to prove the power of democratic norms, and in the case of William Dixon, who used structural indicators for testing his normative theory (see chapter 2).

These observations lead me to the second and more novel dimension of my proposed strategy: Zooming Out. More than even the obfuscation of the normative dimensions of theory, theoreticians' responsibilities are what obligate Zooming Out. As was discussed, the concepts we use in our theoretical constructions are political, and one feature of their being political is their contestedness—the fact that they have several possible meanings, each informed and reasoned by a different moral and ideological framework. Notwithstanding the operationalization of the concepts and the language of scientific objectivity used by theoreticians, to choose one meaning is to participate in the political arena and embrace one moral and ideological framework. Furthermore, as this book shows, this choice has real world-ramifications if theoretical constructions migrate outside academia and become public conventions and political convictions. For the above reasons, Zooming Out accompanies and supplements Zooming In. Zooming In asks us to focus our theoretical rigor on better defining the concepts we use. Zooming Out rejects the criteria of exhaustiveness, exclusiveness, and operationalization as inadequate when standing alone. Zooming Out burdens us with the obligation of defining our concepts morally. It asks us to be ready to justify morally the definitions with which we operationalize the political concepts we use when theorizing. To be able to do that we must also reflexively and critically engage with our own moral commitments which inform (sometimes unconsciously) our theoretical definitions. It also calls on us to morally judge the possible real-world ramifications of our theories. It is not that all possible ramifications are foreseeable, but we have to try our reasonable utmost to anticipate any possible real-world ramifications, and evaluate them morally.

Though at first glance this strategy appears quite modest, it carries with it some fundamental implications and outcomes for social research, which will be explored shortly. One obvious outcome of the Zooming In, Zooming Out strategy is improved dialogue between social and political science on the one hand, and moral and political philosophy on the other hand. If, to some within academic social and political science circles, this outcome may seem a devastating blow to their scientific integrity and the soundness of their labor, this is surely not the case with moral and political philosophers. Keen and perceptive philosophers are usually attuned to the realities of the world and to the theories that try to explain them (see Chernoff 2009:161; Enoch 2002:240–43; Taylor 1985:65–66). This is obviously the case with consequentialism, which addresses the outcome of actions (or rules), and requires the ability to forecast somehow those outcomes with the help of causal mechanisms linking acts (or rules) and outcomes. Those causal mechanisms are sought in social and political science theories (see, for example, Singer 1972:241).

The same interest in examining real-world processes through social and political science theories is found in deontological moral theories. Deontologists, too, rely on causal mechanisms borrowed from social and political science. C.A.J. Coady offers this deontological argument: "Even those of us who think that truth, in some substantial sense, does apply to moral discourse need to acknowledge that moral truths are supported by practical reason and are dependent in complex ways on issues of practicality" (2004:788). The complex relationship between moral and practical reasoning—or, in the terms employed here, between moral and political philosophy and the social and political science—are relevant across the different subject matters addressed by both disciplines (each with its own methodology and aims). We find it in just war theory, which argues, "if there is no probability of achieving the just causes, the war's destructiveness will be to no purpose" (Hurka 2005:35); hence, the war will be judged as unjust. We also find it in attempts to justify conscientious objection, which depends also on the prospective outcomes of objecting to legally enacted rules and laws; would conscientious objection "have a devastating effect on the integrity and continued capacity for efficient functioning of the military" (McMahan 2006:387)?[2] If conscientious objection could have such a devastating effect, then moral judgment may condemn it. The ability to predict these outcomes does require reliance and familiarity with the relevant social and political science theories.

But we need not stray far from the democratic peace thesis for an example of political philosophers relying on social and political science theories. A good example of this is John Rawls, who gave the theory of democratic peace as evidence of the practicality of his *Law of Peoples* (1999). He worked hard to try and persuade that his proposal was a realistic utopia, something to which we could reasonably aspire, albeit with great effort and pains. Rawls acknowledges that he has to "offer a reply to political realism as a theory of international politics, and to those who say that the idea of a realistic utopia among people is quixotic. I do so by sketching a view of democratic peace" (1999:44). It is evident that Rawls the philosopher was aware that he also needed to communicate with social and political science theoreticians; that he needed to address their theoretically informed concerns. He did this by basing his arguments on social and political science theories; namely, the theories of democratic peace, which he saw fit to refer to quite extensively (1999:44).[3]

Note that Rawls also tried to accommodate the democratic peace to his own political philosophy, and in doing so reformulated the theories, making them more deliberative. Let us now examine his philosophical move. For now, it is suffice noting that philosophers like Rawls are aware of the work taking place in the social and political science. Moral and political philosophers perceptively rely on causal mechanisms to establish their justificatory schemes; in other words, they keep social science theories in mind when setting up their political theories. Zooming In, Zooming Out calls for social and political scientists to supplement the philosophers' awareness and reliance with a complementary awareness and reliance of their own. To do this, they must be aware of the moral and analytical work moral and political philosophers are undertaking. That is not to suggest they must invent the moral wheel; they just have to be able, self-reflexively, to use moral definitions to back their moral commitments. Note, as discussed earlier, that theoreticians' moral commitments are operative when defining concepts, and during subsequent theorization. Usually, though, (mostly positivist) theoreticians are unaware of any inherent moral aspects involved in defining and theorizing, and hence fail to respond to them. Furthermore, operating in the darkness of unawareness, moral commitments are not fully developed, and at times cause internal weaknesses, clashing as they do with the operationalization requirements of research. Chapter 2 offered ample examples of such internal weaknesses, which are especially evident in Dixon, who substantially conceptualized democracy as deliberative, yet operationalized it procedurally.

Accordingly, Zooming Out obligates a more conscious, reflective, and responsive attitude to the workings and implications of moral commitment. It calls for moral commitments and their implications to be explicit and transparent to both theoreticians and those they theorize about in order to be able to justify morally the definitions theoreticians chose when theorizing and be willing to engage critically with their own normative commitments. By critically engaging with our own normative commitments we can prevail over the impediments of public conventions, positivist confidences, and individual blind spots, and prevent their interference in the academic culture of self-reflection and self-criticism. Such engagement can help us to achieve a deeper and broader level of self-reflection and self-criticism, and contribute significantly to improving and enriching the definitions of concepts we theoreticians employ; improving and enriching in both moral and analytical terms. The result will be to improve our theorizing and its products; in other words, our theoretical constructions. I will not pretend this is an easy task, for it is indeed daunting. But I will insist that it is doable, and that our scholarly, political, and social task responsibilities charge us with this normative mission.

Rawls offers an example of how this works at the philosophical end of the bridging movement embedded in the Zooming In, Zooming Out strategy. Rawls indicates that the peace resulting from the democratic peace is not a temporary balance of forces; rather, it is peace which is gradually stabilized for the right reasons, "a situation in which, over the course of time, citizens acquire a sense of justice that inclines them not only to accept but to act upon the principles of justice" (1999:45). Rawls's understanding of peace is of a stable and positive peace. Furthermore, it is not the interests defined as the political survival of this or that elite that are responsible for achieving a (temporary) peace, as explained by the structural theories of democratic peace. It is justice and its principles functioning as a moral public compass, and achieving this through citizens who internalize and act upon them. Civil society is the anchor of peace, not the political system; the citizens and their values are what establish and guarantee democratic peace, not politicians and their interests.

This definition and conceptualization of democracy inclined toward the normative end of the scale, and indeed Rawls is explicit in embracing the deliberative model of democracy. According to Rawls, contemporary existing democracies may indeed appear as merely pure formal constitutional regimes. However, this is not the democratic ideal for Rawls and, moreover, these are not the democracies that can produce the ideal of democratic peace—stable and positive peace brought about by the right reasons. The democratic ideal we should ceaselessly aspire to, and which will bring about democratic peace, is one that guarantees the public capacity for deliberation. It is a democratic model that enables the production and elucidation of public reason, and hence the translation of citizens' preferences into public policies and public goods. For that a democracy must meet five criteria: "(a) A certain fair equality of opportunity, especially in education and training ... (b) A decent distribution of income and wealth ... (c) Society as employer of last resort through general or local government, or other social and economic policies ... (d) Basic health care assured for all citizens. (e) Public financing of elections and ways of assuring the availability of public information on matters of policy" (1999:50) Rawls is adamant that this definition and conceptualization of democracy is not compatible with libertarianism. He sees democracy going hand with hand with liberalism. Liberalism as the proponent of social welfare principles and a basic structure, which allows citizens to take part in public deliberation and promote public reason along with the public policies and the public goods that dovetail in. Thus, and only thus, can we approach the ideal of democracy and a real and stable democratic peace.

What is evident in Rawls's discussion is that in his thinking, the explanatory dimension is only secondary. He aims for a normative analysis, and it is this normative aim which drives and directs his discussion. The democratic peace theory merely provides an empirically plausible, causally valid foundation on which to build his normative theory. Rawls treats the explanatory dimension of his work functionally, and as such it is quite embryonic. Zooming In, Zooming Out calls for a comparable move by social science theoreticians where they use moral and political philosophy as a morally justifiable and permissible foundation for building an explanatory theory. And, as their main aim and task is explanatory, their treatment of the normative dimension can also be functional and embryonic. According to the Zooming In, Zooming Out strategy, this will suffice, though it is also of fundamental importance.

As a final note, let me draw a preliminary chart of how we can discharge our scholarly, political, and social task responsibilities according to the Zooming In, Zooming Out strategy. I do this taking the democratic peace as the example, though it should be clear that Zooming In, Zooming Out should be employed by all social science theoreticians working with any type of social science theory. First, in this example, we must critically base ourselves on a normative theory of democracy. Problematic though this may be, my moral commitments are linked to the deliberative and participatory models of democracy. These are the models that duly respect our humanity, sociability, the reasonableness of our judgment, and our political faculties. As Avner de-Shalit forcefully argues in support of participatory and deliberative democracy, "we value participation itself, not simply as a means of reaching decisions" (1997:74). Participation and deliberation are the political apparatus that give due respect to the above-mentioned human traits and faculties and, moreover, help to actualize them. This is the source for the moral and political superiority of these models of democracy over the elitist and structural models. They also sit perfectly well with my prescription for the theoretician-citizen. Put differently, there is not much sense in offering a prescription of the theoretician-citizen as a democratic imperative if one does not favor deliberation in the public sphere—by civil society, and for civil society. Theoretician-citizens have a role in the participatory and deliberative models, and not in any other models of democracy. If there are theoreticians who feel more comfortable morally and politically with elitist and structural models of democracy, let them refer to and infer their moral inspiration from the relevant literature.[4]

The same applies to the political concept of peace. We should reexamine how we define peace, and decide if we are morally satisfied with a minimal, negative definition of peace; namely, peace as the absence of war (Waltz 1959:1). Alternatively (as is my choice and consonant with the deliberative conceptualization of democracy), theoreticians can follow Kenneth Boulding, and define peace more positively—as a stable and positive state (1979) brought about by the right reasons: an established social state of affairs in which war is not an option. Accordingly, they should only consider this stable and positive peace as their dependent variable and as the social category worthy of being defined "peace," and of being studied and theorized as such.

Following this initial phase, developed explicitly in our theoretical writing, we must reexamine our operationalized definitions and see if they are compatible with our moral commitments. Remember that defining is a social construction of social categories, and as such is an intellectual and theoretical activity with serious moral implications and political outcomes. Critical reflexivity is therefore necessary when defining and/or applying operationalized definitions; we should take seriously the contestedness of the political concepts that comprise our theoretical constructions and be willing to scrutinize openheartedly and sincerely the morality of the operationalization of the definitions we choose to employ. In case there is no correspondence between our moral commitments and the operationalized definition, we should redefine the latter to correspond to the former. In other words, moral commitments take precedence over operationalization, and hence should govern the act of defining and the ensuing process of theorizing.

Once this normative embryonic phase is over, our task as social scientists is to develop the explanatory mechanism of the democratic peace—a morally and empirically grounded democratic peace theory. As advised here, this theory should center on deliberation and participation as both a moral and explanatory core: how deliberation and participation are morally justified (being the best actualization of our humanity, sociability, reasonable judgment, and political faculties) and causally implicated in bringing about stability for the right reasons—that is, democratic peace.

Lastly, after completing these theoretical assignments, we should be willing to take on the social and political role of theoretician-citizens; contribute our derivative theoretical insights in the public sphere; be participants in the public and democratic deliberation to help invigorate citizens' political faculties; and elucidate public reason, public policies, and public goods. These are the assignments that will discharge our scholarly, political, and social task responsibilities, and these are the measures that will enrich and improve our theorizing and contribute to democratizing and moralizing our own societies, as well as other societies.

NOTES

Introduction

1. More and more studies pointed out in recent years the influence of the democratic peace theories on the world outside academia, see Owen IV (2005), Brock, Geis, and Müller (2006:3), Büger and Villumsen (2007), Smith (2007), Acuto (2008), Desch (2007/08), Hobson (2009:636, 2011), Moses, (2010), Steele (2010), Geis and Wagner (2011).
2. For examples, see chapter 2.
3. For a full discussion, see chapter 7.
4. See chapter 1 for literature review.
5. However, it should be noted that the book's focus is mainly on the political fortunes of the democratic peace thesis in the United States and Israel, not in Europe. A brief Bourdieusian account of the political happenings of the thesis in the context of NATO can be found in Büger and Villumsen (2007).
6. For a very detailed study of the Arab peace discourse as an obstacle to the peace process see Sela (2005).
7. I borrow the term from Emanuel Adler (1997).

Chapter 1

1. There are analogical affinities between my own view of the political biography of theory and Martha Finnemore and Kathryn Sikkink's theory of the life cycle of norms (1998).
2. In that my thinking is in line with Science and Technology Studies (STS). See, for example, Latour 1987; Jasanoff 1990, 2005; Pielke 2007; Longino 2002. For STS in IR, see Büger and Gadinger 2007.
3. Freeden himself distinguishes among genetic, functional, and semantic analysis, claiming that his analysis is semantic. Freeden defines genetic analysis as "how did a particular set of political views come about?" (1996:3). He characterizes functional analysis as questioning "what is the purpose, or role (if unintended), of a particular set of political views?" and that semantic analysis asks "what are the implications and the insights of a particular set of political views, in terms of the conceptual connections it forms?" (3). But this declaration applies to the analysis in his book of the various particular ideologies, as can also be inferred from the above-quoted definitions. On that level Freeden is correct, and he deals with the semantic

meanings of the various particular ideologies, including liberalism, conservatism, Marxism, etc. But on a deeper level, in his theoretical discussion, Freeden is guided by his analysis of ideologies as configurations that decontest political concepts. This is a functional definition of ideology. Moreover, according to Freeden, people act according to their understanding of ideologies. If this is the case, then ideologies are not only semantic configurations but also configurations oriented toward political praxis. In other words, ideologies are action oriented (1996:3, 77). Thus, ideologies have functions, and the definition of the political phenomenon known as ideology, or the more general political phenomenon known as political thought, is a functional definition.

4. See also Adler 2002; Davis 2005; Weldes 1996.

5. See chapter 6.

6. For additional literature on political, policy, or public entrepreneurship, see Checkel 1997; Young 1994:45–46, 114–15; Schneider and Teske with Mintrom 1995; Schneider and Teske 1992; Kingdon 1995:179–83, 204–5; Kirchheimer 1989. Risse and Sikkink (1999) use their terminology of "transitional advocacy networks" to convey a somewhat similar idea. Ethan Nadelmann (1990:482) refers to NGO's as "transnational moral entrepreneurs."

7. Among the many definitions of the concept of agency the one I prefer most is by Anthony Lang, who explicitly links agency to responsibility: "agent capable of formulating and undertaking plans of action for which they can be held responsible" (2008:96).

8. This theoretical move might help to resolve a recent theoretical debate within the Constructivist School of International Relations. While earlier IR theories are inclined to ignore issues of rhetoric and communicative action completely, constructivism analyzes these issues as crucial to the understanding of world politics. However, while most constructivists tend to use a Habermasian framework for analyzing rhetoric and communicative actions, some have moved to analyzing them as manipulative apparatuses, as yet another device of coercion and power relations. By shifting their focus from the rhetors to the assets available to them, theoreticians may abandon the dichotomist reading of rhetoric in world politics. Persuasive resources are out there to be used in a Habermasian or a manipulative way; they could be used manipulatively to mask real interests, or sincerely to elucidate real interests. A more valuable theoretical treatment enabled by focusing on rhetorical capital would involve clarifying the reasons and conditions that both facilitate and lead to each of the two options. On the Habermasian reading of rhetoric in IR constructivism see Payne 1996; Price 1998; Risse 2000; Farrel 2003. For a reading of rhetoric as manipulation, entrapment, and coercion in IR constructivism see Schimmelfenning 2001; Jackson and Krebs 2007. A more balanced and nuanced reading may be found in Payne 2001.

9. The loose nature of social capital is manifested in particular in Robert Put-

nam's seminal work *Making Democracy Work* (1993). Although Putnam attempts to establish a causal relation from social capital to functioning democracy, it remains unclear whether the causal direction is not the reverse: from functioning democracy to social capital. Thus, although Putnam tries to convince readers that effective social networks (the locus of social capital) instrumentally and causally contribute to functioning democracy, it is equally reasonable to infer that functioning democracy is a breeding ground for effective social networks abounding with social capital: see Levi 1996; Lowndes and Wilson 2001; Newton 2001; Tarrow 1996.

10. This is by no means a reification of theories. Attributing theory with rhetorical capital is not the same as claiming theories are somehow conscious entities that rhetorically persuade other entities to achieve their goals. It is only to imply that theories—like other entities, abstract and concrete, conscious and nonconscious—can possess persuasive resources, which rhetors can find useful in their persuasion campaigns: rhetorical capital that rhetors activate and set in political motion. It is, in other words, an analytic concept that is functionally oriented. It highlights the ways rhetors can functionally use diverse entities.

11. This is a problem above all for those interested in quantifying their subject of research.

12. In this section, I use the term "science" broadly as I engage with the literature of the rhetoric of science, which conflates the natural sciences, social sciences, and the humanities, and analyzes them using a similar approach. My focus and analysis are, of course, directed mainly at the social sciences.

13. For a different view that sees rhetoric as an integral and essential part of political theory and philosophy see Finlayson 2006.

14. But neither that science is objective and detached.

15. Or in the language of contemporary feminist standpoint theoreticians: situated knowledge (Haraway 1988; Harding 1991; Tickner 1992, 2005; Potter 2006).

16. A similar, though broader conditionality was introduced by Fareed Zakaria (1997), who maintains that democratic peace is actually liberal peace between constitutional liberal states. He warns against the attempt to build illiberal democracies, namely, democracies that do not respect the rule of law and do not enjoy the pacifying force of liberalism.

17. The simplistic and totalistic yes-no reading of theories tones well with what Thomas Gilovich calls "the bounded rationality of human information processing" (1991:3), those cognitive biases that affect everyday human reasoning when dealing with the complexities that abound in the real world.

Chapter 2

1. Useful historical background can be found in Gleditsch 1992, 2008. The first major publications in the International Relations discipline: Wallenstein 1973; Rummel 1979, 1981, 1983; Doyle 1983a, 1983b 1986; Maoz and Russett 1993.

2. For a contemporary theoretical offshoot see Adler and Barnett 1998.

3. I embrace here the conventional view that deliberative and participatory models of democracy are closely related and complementary. In recent years, however, Diana Mutz (2006) has advanced an opposing and interesting position that sees the two as contrary to each other.

4. On the concept of citizenship and its implications for the democratic peace, see Henderson 2006.

5. *Journal of Peace Research* 29, no. 4 (1992).

6. It should be noted that later in his career, Russett came to embrace a more multifaceted explanation which brings together democracy, international trade, and membership in international organization to explain democratic peace. But even then, he relates it all to the democraticness of the states. See Russett 1988; Russett, Oneal, and Davis 1998; Oneal and Russett 1999.

Chapter 3

1. On their disillusionment with Reagan, see Tyan 2006.

2. The example of Norman Podhoretz demonstrates that this ideological divide is not purely generational. While belonging to the older cohorts, Podhoretz did endorse the democratic peace thesis as we will see below.

3. And also in an op-ed in the *New York Times* and *Washington Post*, on August 17, 1992, signed by Muravchik and thirty-two other centrists and neoconservative foreign-policy experts, claiming Clinton to be committed to standing by democracy.

4. The neoconservative commitment to the agenda of democracy promotion was reaffirmed again in 1997 with the establishment of The Project for a New American Century. This neoconservative think tank, chaired by William Kristol, declared in its statement of principles the "need to promote the cause of political and economic freedom abroad" (1997). The think tank kept calling for democracy promotion, and furthermore linked this cause to the democratic peace. Its September 2000 report, "Rebuilding America's Defenses," called "to secure and expand the 'zones of democratic peace'" (2).

5. The Saudi issue remained a thorny one for neoconservatives, even under President George W. Bush's administration. Actually, the close relationship between the United States and Saudi Arabia became even more problematic for the neoconservatives following the September 11, 2001, terror attacks, as most of the terrorist were Saudis. See for example, Schwartz 2001; Pipes 2002–2003; Alexiev 2003.

6. It could also be safely argued that Thomas Friedman's "Golden Arches Theory of Conflict Prevention" is a satirical twist of the democratic peace. As such, it is based on a familiarity with the theory, and on the assumption that the theory is public knowledge—the necessary public knowledge for there to be a point in

satirizing it. Indeed, Friedman's theory came to be popularly known as the MacDonald's Peace. Friedman's version of the theory can be summed up as: "No two countries that both have a McDonald's have ever fought a war against each other." See Friedman 1996. He later developed it further in his 1999 book *The Lexus and the Olive Tree*.

7. For Krauthammer's proposal see, Krauthammer 2004a, 2004b.

8. Though as I argue in a later chapter, his Smith's argument confuses the ideologues with the theoreticians.

9. According to Schafer and Walker, Blair's belief system is less cooperative than Clinton's with regard to non-democracies. See Schafer and Walker 2001, 2006.

Chapter 4

1. And elsewhere in Europe, as we saw earlier, especially in the cases of Tony Blair and Chris Patten.

2. For an interesting criticism of attributing the democratic peace thesis to Kant, see Tomas Baum (2008), who attempts to locate the moral origins of the thesis in Jeremy Bentham. Others have also criticized the appropriation of Kant by theoreticians of democratic peace (Franceschet 2002; MacMillan 1995).

3. See most forcefully Lars-Erik Cederman (2001).

4. On the relations between political discourse and causality, see Shaul Shenhav (2005).

5. This political mobilization of theory's structural duality is also evident in a different case, namely Al Gore's film *An Inconvenient Truth*. As ruled by Justice Burton on October 10, 2007, "It [the film] is substantially founded upon scientific research and fact, albeit that the science is used, in the hands of a talented politician and communicator, to make a political statement and to support a political programme" (2007).

6. Michael Oren (2002), a senior fellow at the Shalem Center, published an op-ed in the *Chicago Sun-Times* arguing in the spirit of the democratic peace thesis that Israel cannot expect peace with nondemocratic Arab states, including the Palestinian Authority.

7. The social science orientation of Netanyahu's remarks might be attributable to Dr. Uzi Arad, who took over from Hazony and served as Netanyahu's foreign policy adviser when he was prime minister. Arad with his political science and international relations training is well acquainted with the democratic peace thesis. See, for example, his interview to Robert S. Greenberger and Karby Leggett (2003) of the *Wall Street Journal*, where he advocates democratic peace and claims that "the evidence was irrefutable: Democracies do not attack democracies."

8. Netanyahu published the same arguments for the wider public a week later

in Benjamin Netanyahu (2002b), and yet again for the American Jewish public via the Jewish Telegraphic Agency (2002d).

9. It is worth noting that democracy as a cure for terrorism is absent from the book Netanyahu edited in 1987, when the democratic peace thesis was just beginning to emerge, and was far from its current status as a public convention. See Netanyahu (1987).

10. Among the many public addresses where Netanyahu raised the same points were his addresses in Nashville at an International Mass Retail Association (IMRA) conference in June 2000; Columbia Business School in spring 2001; Denver in January 2002; and at Yeshiva University in March 2002. Netanyahu raised the same points before Israeli audiences, for example, at the Herzliya Conference on "The National Balance of National Strength and Security" in January 2001 (see Weizman 2001), and in an interview for *Haaretz* newspaper (see Ari Shavit 1996). He also raised these points in several radio interviews, such as Australian Broadcasting (ABC) in an interview on August 13, 2001, Mark Colvin (2001).

11. For their association, see Andrei Sakharov 1990:468–69; Sharansky 1988:esp.332–33.

12. A play on words meaning both "Israel for Immigration" and "Israel on the Up."

13. See Sakharov's famous three manifestos of 1968, 1970, and 1974. Here, he more or less presents the same reasoning, though he distances himself even further from the Soviet ideology, establishing himself as a fierce dissident of the regime.

14. In "Democracy for Peace," Sharansky (2002b) stated: "Democracy is for everybody. Of course, encouraging democracy does not mean that people's lives, mentality, and culture need to be transformed. 'Democracy' means one simple thing— the ability of people to express their views, thoughts, and beliefs freely, without the fear that they will be imprisoned as a result." This is a minimal and structural definition of democracy, implying that democratization is a formal, structural reform that does not affect culture and norms.

15. See, for example, the applauding articles of two neoconservatives: Charles Krauthammer (2002); Ira Stoll (2002).

16. He offers a similar flattering analysis in (2000a).

17. Sharansky further stressed this point in an op-ed some three weeks later (2002d).

18. Especially, though by no means only, during the final days of Barak's coalition, when the failures of the Camp David summit of July 2000 came to light (Sharansky 2000c).

19. He expressed similar views during speeches to the 145th session of the 15th Knesset on October 30, 2000, and the 170th session of January 1, 2001, when he declared that Jerusalem constitutes Israel's identity as a nation.

Chapter 5

1. A word of caution is in order. As we will see, not all neoconservatives endorsed the structural theories of the democratic peace, and neither do they all advocate democracy promotion. However, some prominent neoconservative thinkers did endorse the theories and the policy of promoting democracy. Furthermore, this policy came to be identified with neoconservatism. Therefore, and for the sake of brevity, I will use the general form of "the neoconservatives" throughout the chapter, rather than the more accurate but cumbersome terminology "some prominent neoconservative thinkers."

2. This term was used by Niall Ferguson (2004:106) to characterize the culture of the Middle East.

3. The two sets of writings began life as (question marked) articles, and three years later were published as books (having shed the self-doubt and question marks): Fukuyama 1989, 1992; Huntington 1993, 1996.

4. Although Kristol opposed democratization policies, his bafflement is typical.

5. On this issue, as on other points, there were also differing voices among the neoconservatives; Irving Kristol, for example, was a fierce opponent of continuing the war. See Kristol 1991.

6. For Sharansky's linkage between democratization and the end of terror, see Sharansky 2002b. For Netanyahu's linkage, see Netanyahu 2002b. For the neoconservatives' linkage, see Gerecht's remark: "the spread of democracy in the Muslim Middle East remains the only cure for the sacred terror of 9/11" (2004a:27). See also Muravchik 2001–2002:15–16; Barnes 2003:9; Taheri 2004:20–22.

7. Huntington was one of the early critics of Fukuyama: see Huntington 1989.

8. Josef Joffe made this point in *Commentary* in criticizing Fukuyama's position: see Joffe 1992.

9. Both were on the editorial board of the prestigious journal *National Interest*—Huntington since the first issue (Fall 1985), Fukuyama since the thirty-third issue (Summer 1994). Both left following a feud with the editors of the *National Interest*, to help form a new journal, *American Interest*.

10. This is also evident in the February 24, 1997, special issue of the *Weekly Standard*, which was devoted to the rising power of China. The issue immediately followed a harsh review article on Huntington's determinism and pessimism as the crux of the neoconservative disagreements with him; see Kagan 1996.

11. Yet, as Edward Mansfield and Jack Snyder have argued, democratization is not necessarily the surest way to achieve stability and peace. If democratization is pursued in the absence of proper political institutions, it might lead to both domestic and international violence. See Mansfield and Snyder 2005.

12. For a careful reading of European and U.S. agreements and disagreements

on the policies of promoting democracy in the Middle East, see Tamara Cofman Wittes and Richard Youngs (2009).

13. In line with Mearsheimer and Walt's public writings "realism" is used here in the generic sense, and includes a whole family of theories, such as classical realism, structural neorealism, and the new kid on the block: neoclassical realism.

14. In an earlier article, Krauthammer called for "nothing short of universal dominion" (1989:49). Since then, he has somewhat moderated his aspirations, Krauthammer 2001, 2004b. See also Boot 2003.

15. Neither was it hidden from the conservative analysts of the Cato Institute. For their critique of the Bush administration's democracy promotion, see for example Carpenter 2006; Hadar 2009.

16. See his famous letter to Mandell Creighton (Dalberg-Acton 1907:504).

17. See for example the warnings issued by *The Project for the Future of Iraq*, initiated by the U.S. State Department (2002), and ignored by the administration.

Chapter 6

1. The academically produced and ideological pinnacle of this identification is Friedrich A. von Hayek (1945).

2. For a good review of the literature see Barnett and Duvall 2005.

3. Several examples are: 2007, 2009a, 2010c, the *Economist* 2009. Nye's contributions are found worldwide. See for example, 2009c (Egypt); 2009d (Kenya); 2010b (South Korea); 2010d (Lebanon).

4. The ability to set the agenda in a way that prevents grievances from becoming political issues. See Peter Bachrach and Morton S. Baratz (1962).

5. It also draws criticism from critical theoreticians. See Janice Bially Mattern (2005).

6. As such, smart power is attractive also to conservatives who were at the front of the struggle against the Iraq War. See for example Carpenter 2008.

7. As suggested by Eric Etheridge in his *New York Times* blog (2009).

8. As indicated by Galia Press-Barnathan (2012), soft power has also contributed to the politicization and securitization of popular culture, making it a power resource to be employed as a foreign policy tool by states trying to improve their international standing.

9. And see also Russett's contribution to a special issue of *International Interactions* (2010).

10. The same paper was also published under the name "The Capitalist Peace," on November 15, 2005, by the Fraser Institute, a conservative Canadian think tank (2005c). A month later, in December 2005, Gartzke published an extended version of the paper, entitled "Capitalist Peace or Democratic Peace?" with the conservative Australian think tank Institute of Public Affairs (2005a).

11. I should also note the cautious language of probabilities employed by Feldman in his forecasts.

12. *Geut Vashefel* means high and low tides. This was the military code name for the second intifada.

Chapter 7

1. "Social science theoreticians" and "theoreticians" will be used interchangeably from now on.

2. This distinction roughly follows Jerzy Szacki's (1990) distinction between several kinds of intellectuals. The first is of cultural intellectuals who are members of a wider group of people who relate to values and ideas. Of these, some assume a political role by entering the political marketplace and pursuing an active political role. Another group of intellectuals are specialists, or "concrete" intellectuals. Regrettably, the remaining articles in this edited volume do not follow suit, and by conflating the different social roles into one category they miss many of the subtleties of the responsibilities of intellectuals.

3. Although the democratic peace theories are routinely accused of being American ethnocentric. For example, Ivie 2005; Oren 1995; Tsygankov 2003.

4. Later in the chapter we see that Tony Smith does the same thing regarding democratic peace theoreticians.

5. Though as Rodger Payne demonstrates neorealists do at times act as public intellectuals, for example in their campaign opposing the war in Iraq (and described in chapter 6). Payne correctly identifies it as "an apparent contradiction in realist theory and practice" (2007:509). Suitably, Payne titles his article "Neorealists as Critical Theorists."

6. An alternative terminology is "remedial responsibility," which, as David Miller points out (2001, 2004), is the kind of responsibility assigned to an agent who is in a position to offer remedies to harms. Goodin's terminology of task responsibility, however, better captures the forward-looking nature of the kind of social responsibility I propose here.

Another alternative is found in Iris Maryon Young's account of political responsibility (2004). Following Hannah Arendt, Young develops the notion of political responsibility as a type of responsibility that belongs to the wider family of moral responsibilities and is directed to political processes of rectifying. As such, it is also forward-looking. However, as Young indicates, political responsibility is more apt to issues of justice; hence, it is not suitable to our current discussion.

7. Compare also to Jerzy Jedlicki who, in the context of inherent collective responsibility argues, "If it is [collective responsibility] to mean the inheritance of blame and a curse as well as the right—man's or god's—to punish children for the sins of their fathers, this understanding cannot be reconciled with the individual-

izing principle of justice. It is another matter if we understand responsibility of the community as the inheritance of obligations. For the principle that the debts and obligations of the testator fall on the heir to a legacy is not inconsistent with the principle of individual justice" (1990:60).

8. Along with intellectualism, scholarship, and knowledge that are commonly attributed to theorizing and theoreticians.

9. A corresponding responsibility may be ascribed to the wide public; the responsibility to try and protect theory against misrepresenting and abusing, or, to put it differently, the public should be committed to a responsible reading (and responsible "consuming") of theories. The theoreticians and public's responsibilities do not contradict each other, and do not rule out one the other. It will be very interesting to discuss also the public's responsibility, but it is beyond the scope of the present book. I owe this point to Shlomi Segall.

10. A notable exception is John M. Owen IV who criticized the Bush administration's misuse of the thesis in the more publicly oriented *Foreign Affairs* (2005).

11. On the rhetorical difficulties of academics to write short op-eds to newspapers, see Douglas A. Borer (2006).

12. Though individuals should have leeway within the framework of democratic imperative to enjoy "the freedom not to get involved in politics" (Pollak 2007:94).

13. There are several interesting initiatives of academy-community partnership, such as legal clinics and the International Science Shop Network, whose mission is to provide "independent, participatory research support in response to concerns experienced by civil society." The blogosphere provides us with another opportunity for such contributions.

14. For the importance of local norms to the transfer of ideas, see Acharya 2004.

15. Smith's move is seconded by Brent Steele (2010).

16. A comparable scholarly misreading of the democratic peace thesis can also be found in Edward Demenchonok's work (2007).

17. In IR see Mervyn Frost (1996:20–23). For an earlier account, see Gunnar Myrdal (1969).

18. By collective responsibility I do not have in mind the responsibility of collective entities but the kind of responsibility "in which each of a number of individuals might be held (or hold themselves) to account for the actions of one or more of their number" (Graham 2000:49). Transmuted to task responsibility terms used here, we may say that collective task responsibility is the kind of responsibility in which each of a number of individuals might be held (or hold themselves) in charge of amending problems in the actions of one or more of their number.

Conclusion

1. The exact and nuanced definition given in the Correlates of War is: "an interstate war must have: a) sustained combat, involving b) regular armed forces on

both sides and c) 1,000 battle fatalities among all of the system members involved" (Sarkees and Schafer 2000:125).

2. See similar reflections by John Rawls on civil disobedience (1999:328).

3. This reliance on the thesis is the basis for Tony Smith's rash accusations of Rawls being a democratic peace theoretician, and hence among those morally implicated in bringing about the Iraq War (2007:106–7).

Rawls is not the only political philosopher who relies on the democratic peace theory to justify a normative argument. See for example Allen Buchanan (2007:279–80), as well as legal scholar Anne-Marie Slaughter (1995:504–5).

4. Apart from the elitist writers referred to in the book (such as Joseph Schumpeter and Walter Lippmann), one can consult the 2009 special issue of *Comparative Sociology*, which is dedicated to elitist models of democracy (volume 8, number 3).

REFERENCES

Acharya, Amitav. 2004. "How Ideas Spread: Whose Norms Matter? Norm Localization and Institutional Change in Asian Regionalism." *International Organization* 58 (2): 239–75.

Acuto, Michele. 2008. "Wilson Victorious? Understanding Democracy Promotion in the Midst of a 'Backlash.'" *Alternatives* 33 (4): 461–80.

Adamson, Walter A. 1980. *Hegemony and Revolution: A Study of Antonio Gramsci's Political and Cultural Theory.* Berkeley and Los Angeles: University of California Press.

Adler, Emanuel. 1992. "The Emergence of Cooperation: National Epistemic Communities and the International Evolution of the Idea of Nuclear Arms Control." *International Organization* 46 (1): 101–45.

Adler, Emanuel. 1997. "Seizing the Middle Ground: Constructivism in World Politics." *European Journal of International Relations* 3 (3): 319–63.

Adler, Emanuel. 2002. "Constructivism and International Relations." In *Handbook of International Relations*, edited by Walter Carlsnaes, Thomas Risse, and Beth A. Simmons, 95–118. London: Sage.

Adler, Emanuel, and Michael Barnett, eds. 1998. *Security Communities.* Cambridge: Cambridge University Press.

Adler, Emanuel, and Peter Haas. 1992. "Conclusion: Epistemic Communities, World Order, and the Creation of a Reflective Research Program." *International Organization* 46 (1): 367–90.

Alexiev, Alex. 2003. "Hatred's Kingdom by Dore Gold." *Commentary* 115 (5): 70–71.

Alker, Hayward R., Jr., and Bruce M. Russett. 1965. *World Politics in the General Assembly.* New Haven: Yale University Press.

Aristotle. 1909. *The Rhetoric of Aristotle.* Edited by John Edwin Sandy, translated by Sir Richard Claverhouse Jebb. Cambridge: Cambridge University Press.

Armitage, Richard L., and Joseph S. Nye Jr. 2007. "Introduction: How America Can Become a Smarter Power." In *CSIS Commission on Smart Power: A Smarter, More Secure America.* Washington, DC: The CSIS Press, 5–14.

Ashley, Richard K. 1986. "The Poverty of Neorealism." In *Neorealism and its Critics*, edited by Robert O. Keohane, 255–300. New York: Columbia University Press.

Ashley, Richard K. 1987. "The Geopolitics of Geopolitical Space: Toward a Critical Social Theory of International Politics." *Alternatives* 12 (4): 403–34.

Babst, Dean V. 1964. "Elective Governments—A Force for Peace." *Wisconsin Sociologist* 3 (1): 9–14.

Babst, Dean V. 1972. "A Force for Peace." *Industrial Research*. April, 55–58.
Bachrach, Peter, and Morton S. Baratz. 1962. "Two Faces of Power." *American Political Science Review* 56 (4): 947–52.
Baker, James A. 1992a. "Securing a Democratic Peace—Statement by Secretary of State James to Senate Foreign Relations Committee." April 9, http://findarticles.com/p/articles/mi_m1584/is_n15_v3/ai_12272837.
Baker, James A. 1992b. "Press Briefing by Secretary of State James Baker." June 15, http://www.fas.org/spp/starwars/offdocs/b920615.htm.
Baker, James A. 1992c. "From Cold War to Democratic Peace." June 29, http://findarticles.com/p/articles/mi_m1584/is_n26_v3/ai_12504744/?tag=content;col1.
Baker III, James A., with Thomas M. Defrank. 1995. *The Politics of Diplomacy; Revolution, War, and Peace*. New York: G. P. Putnam's Sons.
Barber, Benjamin. 1984. *Strong Participatory Politics for a New Age*. Berkeley and Los Angeles: University of California Press.
Barnes, Fred. 2009. "A Real Peace Process." *Weekly Standard*, May 5, 9.
Barnett, Michael, and Raymond Duvall. 2005. "Power in International Politics." *International Organization* 59 (1): 39–75.
Bates, Thomas R. 1975. "Gramsci and the Theory of Hegemony." *Journal of the History of Ideas* 36 (2): 351–66.
Baum, Tomas. 2008. "Quest for Inspiration in the Liberal Peace Paradigm: Back to Bentham?" *European Journal of International Relations* 14 (3): 431–53.
Berger, Peter L., and Thomas Luckmann. 1967. *The Social Construction of Reality: A Treatise in the Sociology of Knowledge*. New York: Anchor Books.
Berman, Paul. 2003. *Terror and Liberalism*. New York: W. W. Norton.
Beer, Francis A., and Robert Hariman, eds. 1996. *Post-Realism: The Rhetorical Turn in International Relations*. East Lansing: Michigan State University Press.
Berlin, Isaiah. 1969. "Two Concepts of Liberty." In *Four Essays on Liberty*, edited by Isaiah Berlin. London: Oxford University Press.
Blair, Tony. 2003. "Address to the Joint Session of Congress." July 17, http://www.murphy.house.gov/index.cfm?sectionid=52&parentid=24&sectiontree=23,24,52&itemid=818.
Blinken, Antony J. 2002. "Winning the War of Ideas." *Washington Quarterly* 25 (2): 101–14.
Boggs, Carl. 1976. *Gramsci's Marxism*. London: Pluto Press.
Boot, Max. 2003. "What Next? The Bush Foreign Policy Agenda beyond Iraq." *Weekly Standard*, May 5, 27–33.
Borer, Douglas A. 2006. "Rejected by the *New York Times*? Why Academics Struggle to get Published in National Newspapers." *International Studies Perspectives* 7 (3): vii–x.
Boulding, Kenneth. 1979. *Stable Peace*. Austin: University of Texas Press.

Bourdieu, Pierre. 1986. "The Forms of Capital." In *Handbook of Theory and Research for the Sociology of Education*, edited by John G. Richardson, 241–58. New York: Greenwood Press.

Boyle, Michael. 2004. "Utopianism and the Bush Foreign Policy." *Cambridge Review of International Affairs* 17 (1): 81–103.

Brands, Hall. 2008. *From Berlin to Baghdad: America's Search for Purpose in the Post–Cold War World*. Lexington: University Press of Kentucky.

Brock, Lothar, Anna Geis, and Harald Müller. 2006. "Introduction: The Theoretical Challenge of Democratic Wars." In *Democratic Wars: Looking at the Dark Side of Democratic Peace*, edited by Anna Geis, Lothar Brock, and Harald Müller, 3–12. Basingstoke, England and New York: Palgrave Macmillan.

Brown, Seyom. 1994. *The Causes and Prevention of War*. 2nd edition. New York: St. Martin's Press.

Buchanan, Allen. 2007. *Justice, Legitimacy, and Self-Determination: Moral Foundations for International Law*. Oxford: Oxford University Press.

Bueno de Mesquita, Bruce, James D. Morrow, Randolph M. Siverson, and Alastair Smith. 1999. "An Institutional Explanation of the Democratic Peace." *American Political Science Review* 93 (4): 791–807.

Büger, Christian, and Frank Gadinger. 2007. "Reassembling and Dissecting: IR Practice from a Science Studies Perspective." *International Studies Perspectives* 8 (1): 90–110.

Büger, Christian, and Trine Villumsen. 2007. "Beyond the Gap: Relevance, Fields of Practice and the Securitizing Consequences of (Democratic Peace) Research." *Journal of International Relations and Development* 10 (4): 417–44.

Burton, Michael J., Mr. Justice. 2007. "Between: Stuart Dimmock and Secretary of State for Education and Skills" (now Secretary of State for Children, Schools and Families). http://www.bailii.org/ew/cases/EWHC/Admin/2007/2288.html.

Bush, George W. 2002. "President Bush Delivers Graduation Speech at West Point." June 1, http://www.georgewbush-whitehouse.archives.gov/news/releases/2002/06/20020601-3.html.

Bush, George W. 2003. "President Bush Discusses Freedom in Iraq and Middle East." November 6, http://www.georgewbush-whitehouse.archives.gov/news/releases/2003/11/20031106-2.html.

Bush, George W. 2004. "President Bush Discusses Importance of Democracy in Middle East." February 4, http://www.georgewbush-whitehouse.archives.gov/news/releases/2004/02/20040204-4.html.

Bush, George W. 2005a. "Inauguration 2005." January 20, http://georgewbush-whitehouse.archives.gov/news/releases/2005/01/20050120-1.html.

Bush, George W. 2005b. "State of the Union Address." February 2, http://georgewbush-whitehouse.archives.gov/news/releases/2005/02/20050202-11.html.

Bush, George W. 2005c. "President Discusses Freedom and Democracy in Kyoto, Japan." November 16, http://georgewbush-whitehouse.archives.gov/news/releases/2005/11/20051116-6.html.

Bush, George W. 2005d. "President Discusses War on Terror and Upcoming Iraqi Elections." December 12, http://georgewbush-whitehouse.archives.gov/news/releases/2005/12/20051212-4.html.

Bush, George W. 2006a. "State of the Union Address." January 31, http://georgewbush-whitehouse.archives.gov/news/releases/2006/01/20060131-10.html.

Bush, George W. 2006b. "President Bush Discusses Progress in the Global War on Terror." Cobb Galleria Centre, Atlanta, Georgia, September 7, http://georgewbush-whitehouse.archives.gov/news/releases/2006/09/20060907-2.html.

Cammett, John M. 1967. *Antonio Gramsci and the Origins of Italian Communism*. Stanford, CA: Stanford University Press.

Carpenter, Ted Galen. 2006. "The Imperial Lure: Nation Building as a US Response to Terrorism." *Mediterranean Quarterly* 17 (1): 34–47.

Carpenter, Ted Galen. 2008. *Smart Power: Toward a Prudent Foreign Policy for America*. Washington, DC: Cato Institute.

Carroll, Susan J., and Linda M. G. Zerilli. 1993. "Feminist Challenges to Political Science." In *Political Science: The State of the Discipline II*, edited by Ada W. Finifter, 55–76. Washington, DC: The American Political Science Association.

Cederman, Lars-Erik. 2001. "Back to Kant: Reinterpreting the Democratic Peace as a Macrohistorical Learning Process." *American Political Science Review* 95 (1): 15–31.

Checkel, Jeffrey T. 1997. *Ideas and International Political Change: Soviet/Russian Behavior and the End of the Cold War*. New Haven: Yale University Press.

Chernoff, Fred. 2009. "Conventionalism as an Adequate Basis for Policy-Relevant IR Theory." *European Journal of International Relations* 15 (1): 157–94.

Christopher, Warren. 1993. "Securing US Interests While Supporting Russian Reform." March 22, http://dosfan.lib.uic.edu/ERC/briefing/dossec/1993/9303/930322dossec.html.

Christopher, Warren. 1998. *In the Stream of History: Shaping Foreign Policy for a New Era*. Stanford, CA: Stanford University Press.

Clinton, Hillary Rodham. 2009. "Statement of Senator Hillary Rodham Clinton Nominee for Secretary of State, Senate Foreign Relations Committee." January 13, http://www.state.gov/secretary/rm/2009a/01/115196.htm.

Clinton, Bill. 1996. *Preface to the Presidency: Selected Speeches of Bill Clinton, 1974–1992*. Compiled and edited by Stephen A. Smith. Fayetteville: University of Arkansas Press.

Clinton, William J. 1993a. "Speech by President to Korean National Assembly." July 10, http://archives.clintonpresidentialcenter.org/?u=071093-speech-by-president-to-korean-national-assembly.htm.

Clinton, William J. 1993b. "Address by the President to the 48th Session of the United Nations General Assembly." September 27, http://archives.clintonpresidentialcenter.org/?u=092793-speech-by-president-address-to-the-un.htm.

Clinton, William J. 1994a. "State of the Union Address." January 25, http://archives.clintonpresidentialcenter.org/?u=012594-speech-by-president-sotu-address.htm.

Clinton, William J. 1994b. "Remarks by President on CNN Telecast of a Global Forum with Clinton." May 3, http://archives.clintonpresidentialcenter.org/?u=050394-remarks-by-president-on-cnn-telecast-of-a-global-forum-with-clinton.htm.

Clinton, William J. 1994c. "Presidential Press Conference on China MFN Status." May 26, http://archives.clintonpresidentialcenter.org/index.php?u=052694-presidential-press-conference-on-china-mfn-status.htm.

Clinton, William J. 1994d. "President Interviewed by Haiti Wire Reporters." September 14, http://archives.clintonpresidentialcenter.org/?u=091494-president-interviewed-by-haiti-wire-reporters.htm.

Clinton, William J. 1995. "Remarks by President at Nuremberg Symposium." October 15, http://archives.clintonpresidentialcenter.org/?u=101595-remarks-by-president-at-nuremberg-symposium.htm.

Clinton, William J. 1996. "Speech by President at Human Rights Day Event." December 10, http://archives.clintonpresidentialcenter.org/?u=121096-speech-by-president-at-human-rights-day-event.htm.

Clinton, William J. 2000a. "Speech by President to the Indian Parliament." March 22, http://archives.clintonpresidentialcenter.org/index.php?u=032200-speech-by-president-to-the-indian-parliament.htm.

Clinton, William J. 2000b. "Speech by President to the People of Pakistan." March 25, http://archives.clintonpresidentialcenter.org/index.php?u=032500-speech-by-president-to-the-people-of-pakistan.htm.

Clinton, William J. 2000c. "Speech by President to the University of Warwick, England." December 14, http://archives.clintonpresidentialcenter.org/?u=121400-speech-by-president-to-the-university-of-warwick.htm.

Coady, C. A. J. 2004. "Terrorism, Morality, and Supreme Emergency." *Ethics* 114 (4): 772–89.

Cohen, Raymond. 1994. "Pacific Union: A Reappraisal of the Theory that 'Democracies Do Not Go to War with Each Other.'" *Review of International Studies* 20 (3): 207–23.

Colvin, Mark. 2001. "Netanyahu Defends Israeli Policy." August 13, http://www.abc.net.au/pm/stories/s345664.htm.

Connolly, William E. 1973. "Theoretical Self-Consciousness." *Polity* 6 (1): 5–35.

Connolly, William E. 1993. *The Terms of Political Discourse*. 3rd edition. Princeton, NJ: Princeton University Press.

Cox, Michael. 2003. "The Empire's Back in Town: Or America's Imperial

Temptation—Again." *Millennium—Journal of International Studies* 32 (1): 1–27.

Craig, David J. 2003. "Human Rights Champion Sharansky: Palestinian Democracy Key to Peace." September 19, http://www.bu.edu/bridge/archive/2003/09-19/sharansky.html.

CSIS Commission on Smart Power. 2007. *CSIS Commission on Smart Power: A Smarter, More Secure America*. Washington, DC: CSIS Press.

Dalberg-Acton, John E. E. 1907. *Historical Essays and Studies*. Edited and with an introduction by John N. Figgis and Reginald V. Laurence. London: Macmillan.

Davidson, Alastair. 1977. *Antonio Gramsci: Towards an Intellectual Biography*. London: Merlin Press.

Davis, James W. 2005. *Terms of Inquiry: On the Theory and Practice of Political Science*. Baltimore: Johns Hopkins University Press.

Demenchonok, Edward. 2007. "From a State of War to Perpetual Peace." *American Journal of Economics and Sociology* 66 (1): 25–47.

de-Shalit, Avner. 1997. "On Behalf of 'The Participation of the People': A Radical Theory of Democracy." *Res Publica* 3 (1): 61–80.

de-Shalit, Avner. 2006. *Power to the People: Teaching Political Philosophy in Skeptical Times*. Lanham, MD: Lexington Books.

Desch, Michael C. 2007–2008. "America's Liberal Illiberalism: The Ideological Origins of Overreaction in U.S. Foreign Policy." *International Security* 32 (3): 7–43.

Deutsch, Karl W., Sidney A. Burrell, Robert A. Kann, Maurice Lee Jr., Martin Lichtermann, Raymond E. Lindgren, Francis L. Lowenheim, and Richard W. Van Wagenen. 1957. *Political Community and the North Atlantic Area*. Princeton: Princeton University Press.

Diamond, Larry. 2000. "Promoting 'Real' Democracy." January 1, http://www.ppionline.org/ppi_ci.cfm?knlgAreaID=115&subsecID=900026&contentID=1328.

Dixon, William J. 1994. "Democracy and the Peaceful Settlement of International Conflict." *American Political Science Review* 88 (1): 14–32.

Dobriansky, Paula. 2004. "Advancing Democracy." *National Interest* 77: 71–78.

Donnelly, Tom, and William Kristol. 2004. "More Caissons Rolling Along." *Weekly Standard*, February 9, 7–8.

Doyle, Michael. 1983a. "Kant, Liberal Legacies, and Foreign Affairs, Part I." *Philosophy and Public Affairs* 12 (3): 205–35.

Doyle, Michael. 1983b. "Kant, Liberal Legacies, and Foreign Affairs, Part II." *Philosophy and Public Affairs* 12 (4): 323–53.

Doyle, Michael. 1986. "Liberalism and World Politics." *American Political Science Review* 80 (4): 1151–69.

Drolet, Jean-François. 2011. *American Neoconservatism: The Politics and Culture of a Reactionary Idealism*. London: Hurst & Company.

Dror, Yehezkel. 2009. "A New Peace Paradigm." *Haaretz*, February 9.

Drury, Shaida B. 1997. *Leo Strauss and the American Right*. New York: St. Martin's Press.
Dryzek, John S. 2002. *Deliberative Democracy and Beyond: Liberals, Critics, Contestations*. Oxford: Oxford University Press.
Eberly, Don. 2008. "Civil Society: America's Most Consequential Export." June 10, http://www.ppionline.org/ppi_ci.cfm?knlgAreaID=450004&subsecID=900020&contentID=254663.
Economist. 2009. "Five Questions for Joseph Nye." January 20, http://www.economist.com/blogs/democracyinamerica/2009/06/five_questions_for_joseph_nye.
Ehrman, John. 1995. *The Rise of Neoconservatism: Intellectuals and Foreign Affairs 1945–1994*. New Haven: Yale University Press.
Eldar, Akiva. 2008. "Hamas is waiting for Netanyahu." *Haaretz*, November 18.
Eldar, Akiva. 2009. "Palestinian PM: Settlement Building Will Destroy Peace Process." *Haaretz*, March 7.
Elster, Jon. 1998. *Deliberative Democracy*. Cambridge: Cambridge University Press.
Enoch, David. 2002. "Some Arguments Against Conscientious Objection and Civil Disobedience Refuted." *Israel Law Review* 36 (3): 227–52.
Ephron, Dan, and Tamara Lipper. 2002. "Sharansky's Quiet Role." *Newsweek*, July 15.
Ericson, Magnus. 2000. "Birds of a Feather? On the Interactions of Stable Peace and Democratic Research Programs." In *Stable Peace among Nations*, edited by Arie M. Kacowicz, Yaacov Bar-Siman-Tov, Ole Elgstrom, and Magnus Jerneck, 130–49. Lanham, MD: Rowman & Littlefield.
Etheridge, Eric. 2009. "How 'Soft Power' Got 'Smart.'" January 14, http://opinionator.blogs.nytimes.com/2009/01/14/how-soft-power-got-smart.
Etzioni, Amitai. 2007. *Security First: For a Muscular, Moral Foreign Policy*. New Haven: Yale University Press.
European Union. 2003. "European Security Strategy." December 12, http://europa.eu/legislation_summaries/justice_freedom_security/fight_against_terrorism/r00004_en.htm.
Farber, Henry S., and Joanne Gowa. 1995. "Polities and Peace." *International Security* 20 (2): 123–46.
Farrell, Henry. 2003. "Constructing the International Foundations of E-Commerce—The EU-U.S. Safe Harbor Arrangement." *International Organization* 57 (2): 277–306.
Fearon, James D. 1994. "Domestic Political Audiences and the Escalation of International Disputes." *American Political Science Review* 88 (3): 577–92.
Featherstone, Mark. 2007. "The End of History." *Journal of Classical Sociology* 7 (1): 109–26.
Feldman, Nizan. 2009. "Economic Peace: Theory versus Reality." *Strategic Update* 12 (3): 19–28.
Femia, Joseph V. 1981. *Gramsci's Political Thought: Hegemony, Consciousness, and the Revolutionary Process*. Oxford: Clarendon Press.

Ferguson, Niall. 2003. "Hegemony or Empire?" *Foreign Affairs* 82 (5): 154–61.
Ferguson, Niall. 2004. *Colossus: The Price of America's Empire*. New York: Penguin Press.
Finlayson, Alan. 2006. "'What's the Problem?': Political Theory, Rhetoric and Problem-Setting." *Critical Review of International Social and Political Philosophy* 9 (4): 541–57.
Finlayson, Alan. 2007. "From Beliefs to Arguments: Interpretive Methodology and Rhetorical Political Analysis." *British Journal of Politics and International Relations* 9 (4): 545–63.
Finnemore, Martha, and Kathryn Sikkink. 1998. "International Norm Dynamics and Political Change." *International Organization* 52 (4): 887–917.
Fleurbaey, Marc. 2001. "Egalitarian Opportunities." *Law and Philosophy* 20 (5): 499–530.
Franceschet, Antonio. 2002. "Moral Principles and Political Institutions: Perspectives on Ethics and International Affairs." *Millennium—Journal of International Studies* 31 (2): 347–57.
Freeden, Michael. 1996. *Ideologies and Political Theory: A Conceptual Approach*. Oxford: Clarendon Press.
Friedman, Thomas L. 1996. "Big Mac I." *New York Times*, December 8, 15.
Friedman, Thomas L. 1999. *The Lexus and the Olive Tree*. New York: Farrar, Straus and Giroux.
Frost, Mervyn. 1996. *Ethics in International Relations*. Cambridge University Press.
Fukuyama, Francis. 1989. "The End of History?" *National Interest* 16: 3–18.
Fukuyama, Francis. 1992. *The End of History and the Last Man*. New York: Free Press.
Fukuyama, Francis. 1999. "Second Thoughts: The Last Man in a Bottle." *National Interest* 56: 16–33.
Fukuyama, Francis. 2004. "The Neoconservative Moment." *National Interest* 76: 57–68.
Fukuyama, Francis. 2006. *America at the Crossroads: Democracy, Power, and the Neoconservative Legacy*. New Haven: Yale University Press.
Gadamer, Hans-Georg. 1989. *Truth and Method*. 2nd and revised edition. Translated and revised by Joel Weinsheimer and Donald G. Marshall. New York: Crossroad.
Gallie, W. B. 1956. "Essentially Contested Concepts." *Proceedings of the Aristotelian Society* 56: 167–98.
Gartzke, Erik. 2005a. "Capitalist Peace or Democratic Peace?" http://www.ipa.org.au/library/57-4-capitalistpeaceordemocraticpeace.pdf.
Gartzke, Erik. 2005b. "Future Depends on Capitalizing on Capitalist Peace." http://www.cato.org/pub_display.php?pub_id=5133.
Gartzke, Erik. 2005c. "The Capitalist Peace." http://www.fraseramerica.org/commerce.web/product_files/TheCapitalistPeace.pdf.

Gartzke, Erik. 2007. "The Capitalist Peace." *American Journal of Political Science* 51 (1): 166–91.

Gartzke, Erik, and J. Joseph Hewitt. 2010. "International Crises and the Capitalist Peace." *International Interactions* 36 (2): 115–45.

Gat, Azar. 2005. "The Democratic Peace Theory Reframed: The Impact of Modernity." *World Politics* 58 (1): 73–100.

Gates, Robert M. 2007. "Landon Lecture." Given at Kansas State University, November 26, http://www.defense.gov/speeches/speech.aspx?speechid=1199.

Gaubatz, Kurt T. 1999. *Elections and War: The Electoral Incentive in the Democratic Politics of War and Peace*. Stanford, CA: Stanford University Press.

Geis, Anna, Lothar Brock, and Harald Müller, eds. 2006. *Democratic Wars: Looking at the Dark Side of Democratic Peace*. London: Palgrave Macmillan.

Geis, Anna, and Wolfgang Wagner. 2011. "How Far is it From Königsberg to Kandahar? Democratic Peace and Democratic Violence in International Relations." *Review of International Studies* 37 (4): 1555–77.

Gelernter, David. 2004. "Another Vietnam?" *Weekly Standard*, October 11, 9–10.

Gerecht, Reuel Marc. 2004a. "Going Soft on Iraq." *Weekly Standard*, March 8, 27.

Gerecht, Reuel Marc. 2004b. "Not a Diversion." *Weekly Standard*, April 12 and April 19, 23–27.

Gershman, Carl. 1990. "Freedom Remains the Touchstone." *National Interest* 19: 83–86.

Ghosh, Peter. 2001. "Gramscian Hegemony: An Absolute Historicist Approach." *History of European Ideas* 27 (1): 1–43.

Gilovich, Thomas. 1991. *How We Know What Isn't So: The Fallibility of Human Reason in Everyday Life*. New York: Free Press.

Glaser, Charles L. 1996. "Realists as Optimists: Cooperation as Self-Help." *Security Studies* 5 (3): 122–66.

Gleditsch, Nils Petter. 1992. "Democracy and Peace." *Journal of Peace Research* 29 (4): 369–76.

Gleditsch, Nils Petter. 2008. "The Liberal Moment Fifteen Years On." *International Studies Quarterly* 52 (4): 691–712.

Goodin, Robert E. 1998. "Social Welfare as a Collective Social Responsibility." In *Social Welfare and Individual Responsibility: For and Against*, edited by David Scmidtz and Robert E. Goodin, 97–194. Cambridge: Cambridge University Press.

Gowa, Joanne. 1999. *Ballots and Bullets: The Elusive Democratic Peace*. Princeton: Princeton University Press.

Graham, Keith. 2000. "Collective Responsibility." In *Moral Responsibility and Ontology*, edited by Ton van den Beld, 49–61. Netherlands: Kluwer Academic.

Gramsci, Antonio. 1957. *The Modern Prince: And Other Writings*. New York: International Publishers.

Gramsci, Antonio. 1971. *Selections from the Prison Notebooks*. Edited and translated by Quintin Hoare and Geoffrey Nowell Smith. New York: International Publishers.

Gramsci, Antonio. 1992. *Prison Notebooks. Vol. I*. Translated by Joseph A. Buttigieg. New York: Columbia University Press.

Gramsci, Antonio. 1996. *Prison Notebooks. Vol. II*. Translated by Joseph A. Buttigieg. New York: Columbia University Press.

Gramsci, Antonio. 2007. *Prison Notebooks. Vol. III*. Translated by Joseph A. Buttigieg and Antonio Callari. New York: Columbia University Press.

Greenberg, Robert S., and Karby Leggett. 2003. "Bush Dreams of Changing Not Just Regime but Region." *Wall Street Journal*, March 2.

Gross, Allan G., and William K. Keith, eds. 1997. *Rhetorical Hermeneutics: Invention and Interpretation in the Age of Science*. Albany: State University of New York Press.

Guzzini, Stefano. 2000. "A Reconstruction of Constructivism in International Relations." *European Journal of International Relations* 6 (2): 147–82.

Guzzini, Stefano. 2001. "The Significance and Roles of Teaching Theory in International Relations." *Journal of International Relations and Development* 4 (2): 98–117.

Haas, Peter M. 1992. "Introduction: Epistemic Communities and International Policy Coordination." *International Organization* 46 (1): 1–35.

Haass, Richard N. 2000. "The Squandered Presidency: Demanding More from the Commander in Chief." *Foreign Affairs* 79 (3): 136–40.

Habermas, Jürgen. 1987. *The Theory of Communicative Action, Volume 2: Lifeworld and System*. Translated by Thomas McCarthy. Boston: Beacon Press.

Habermas, Jürgen. 1998. *Between Facts and Norms: Contributions to a Discourse Theory of Law and Democracy*. Translated by William Rehg. Cambridge, MA: MIT Press.

Hadar, Leon. 2009. "Who Lost the Middle East? The Collapse of the Neoconservative-led US–Israeli Hegemonic Project." In *Handbook of US-Middle East Relations: Formative Factors and Regional Perspectives*, edited by Robert Looney, 355–73. London and New York: Routledge.

Halper, Stefan, and Jonathan Clarke. 2004. *America Alone: The Neo-Conservatives and the Global Order*. Cambridge: Cambridge University Press.

Hansen, Lene, and Ole Wæver, eds. 2002. *European Integration and National Identity: The Challenge of the Nordic States*. London and New York: Routledge.

Hanson, Victor Davis. 2002. "Our Enemies, the Saudis." *Commentary* 114 (1): 23–28.

Haraway, Donna. 1988. "Situated Knowledges: The Science Question in Feminism and the Privilege of Partial Perspective." *Feminist Studies* 14 (3): 575–99.

Harding, Sandra G. 1991. *Whose Science? Whose Knowledge? Thinking from Women's Lives*. Ithaca: Cornell University Press.

Hartley, Thomas, and Bruce Russett. 1992. "Public Opinion and the Common Defense: Who Governs Military Spending in the United States?" *American Political Science Review* 86 (4): 905–15.

Hawkesworth, Mary E. 1996. "Knowers, Knowing, Known: Feminist Theory and Claims of Truth." In *Gender and Scientific Authority*, edited by Barbara Laslett, Sally G. Kohlstedt, Helen Longino, and Evelynn Hammonds, 75–99. Chicago: University of Chicago Press.

Hegel, Georg F. W. 1952. *Philosophy of Right*. Translated by T. M. Knox. Oxford: Clarendon Press.

Hegre, Håvard. 2000. "Development and the Liberal Peace: What Does It Take to Be a Trading State?" *Journal of Peace Research* 37 (1): 5–30.

Henderson, Gordon P. 2006. "The Public and Peace: The Consequences for Citizenship of the Literature of the Democratic Peace." *International Studies Review* 8 (2): 199–224.

Hobson, Christopher. 2009. "Beyond the End of History: The Need for a 'Radical Historicisation' of Democracy in International Relations." *Millennium: Journal of International Studies* 37 (3): 631–57.

Hobson, Christopher. 2011. "Towards a Critical Theory of Democratic Peace." *Review of International Studies* 37 (4): 1903–22.

How, Alan R. 2007. "The Author, the Text and the Canon: Gadamer and the Persistence of Classic Texts in Sociology." *Journal of Classical Sociology* 7 (1): 5–22.

Huntington, Samuel. 1989. "No Exit—The Errors of Endism." *National Interest* 17: 3–11.

Huntington, Samuel P. 1993. "The Clash of Civilizations?" *Foreign Affairs* 72 (3): 22–49.

Huntington, Samuel P. 1996. *The Clash of Civilizations and the Remaking of World Order*. New York: Simon & Schuster.

Huntington, Samuel. 2005. "The Great American Myth." Grano Lecture Series on American Empire, Toronto. February 10, http://www.aims.ca/library/huntington.pdf.

Hurka, Thomas. 2005. "Proportionality in the Morality of War." *Philosophy and Public Affairs* 33 (1): 34–66.

Hymans, Jacques E. C. 2004. "The Roots of the Washington Threat Consensus." In *Striking First: The Preventive War Doctrine and the Reshaping of U.S. Foreign Policy*, edited by Betty Glad and Chris J. Dolan, 33–45. New York: Palgrave Macmillan.

Ikenberry, G. John. 2002. "America's Imperial Ambition." *Foreign Affairs* 81 (5): 44–60.

International Science Shop Network. N.d. "Definition, Mission, and Criteria." http://www.scienceshops.org/new%20web-content/framesets/fs-about.html.

Ilani, Ofri. 2009. "Tel Aviv University honors Blair for Effort to Forge Solutions in Mideast." *Haaretz*, May 19.

Ish-Shalom, Piki. 2006a. "The Triptych of Realism, Elitism, and Conservatism." *International Studies Review* 8 (3): 441–68.

Ish-Shalom, Piki. 2006b. "Theory Gets Real, and the Case for a Normative Ethic: Rostow, Modernization Theory, and the Alliance for Progress." *International Studies Quarterly* 50 (2): 287–311.

Israel Ministry of Foreign Affairs. 2004. "Exchange of Letters between PM Sharon and President Bush." April 14, http://www.mfa.gov.il/MFA/Peace+Process/Reference+Documents/Exchange+of+letters+Sharon-Bush+14-Apr-2004.htm.

Israel Government. 2003. "Israel's Road Map Reservations." http://www.haaretz.com/hasen/pages/ShArt.jhtml?itemNo=297230.

Israel State Comptroller. 2004. *Annual Report No. 54B*. May 5 (in Hebrew).

Ives, Peter. 2006. *Gramsci's Politics of Language: Engaging the Bakhtin Circle and the Frankfurt School*. Toronto: University of Toronto Press.

Ivie, Robert L. 2005. *Democracy and America's War on Terror*. Tuscaloosa: University of Alabama Press.

Jackson, Patrick T., and Stuart J. Kaufman. 2007. "Security Scholars for a Sensible Foreign Policy: A Study in Weberian Activism." *Perspectives on Politics* 5 (1): 95–103.

Jackson, Patrick T., and Ronald R. Krebs. 2007. "Twisting Tongues and Twisting Arms: The Power of Political Rhetoric." *European Journal of International Relations* 13 (1): 35–66.

Jasanoff, Sheila. 1990. *The Fifth Branch: Science Advisers as Policymakers*. Cambridge, MA: Harvard University Press.

Jasanoff, Sheila. 2005. *Designs on Nature: Science and Democracy in Europe and the United States*. Princeton: Princeton University Press.

Jedlicki, Jerzy. 1990. "Heritage and Collective Responsibility." In *The Political Responsibility of Intellectuals*, edited by Ian Maclean, Alan Montefiore, and Peter Winch, 53–76. Cambridge: Cambridge University Press.

Jervis, Robert. 2003. "The Compulsive Empire." *Foreign Policy*, July–August, 83–87.

Joffe, Josef. 1992. "Bosnia: The Return of History." *Commentary* 94 (4): 24–29.

Jones, Ward E. 2006. "Philosophers, their Context, and their Responsibilities." *Metaphilosophy* 37 (5): 623–45.

Kagan, Robert. 1996a. "Clinton and Indonesia: The Real Scandal." *Weekly Standard*, November 4, 27–29.

Kagan, Robert. 1996b. "Harvard Hates America." *Weekly Standard*, December 9, 24–27.

Kaplan, Lawrence F. 1997. "The Selling of American Foreign Policy." *Weekly Standard*, April 28, 19–22.

Kaplan, Lawerence F. 1998. "Leftism on the Right." *Weekly Standard*, February 9, 29.

Kaplan, Lawrence F. 1999. "Dictatorship and No Standard." *Weekly Standard*, February 8, 27–29.

Kaplan, Lawrence F., and William Kristol. 2003. *The War Over Iraq: Saddam's Tyranny and America's Mission.* San Francisco: Encounter Books.
Kant, Immanuel. 1903. *Perpetual Peace: Philosophical Essay.* Translated by M. Campbell Smith. London: S. Sonnenschein.
Karsh, Ephraim. 2003. "Making Iraq Safe for Democracy." *Commentary* 115 (4): 22–28.
Katzenstein, Peter J., ed. 1996. *The Culture of National Security: Norms and Identity in World Politics.* New York: Columbia University Press.
Keck, Margaret, and Kathryn Sikkink. 1998. *Activists Beyond Borders: Advocacy Networks in International Politics.* Ithaca: Cornell University Press.
Kellner, Douglas. 2004. "Preemptive Strikes and the War on Iraq: A Critique of Bush Administration Unilateralism and Militarism." *New Political Science* 26 (3): 417–40.
Kingdon, John W. 1995. *Agendas, Alternatives, and Public Policies.* 2nd edition. New York: HarperCollins College Publishers.
Kirchheimer, Donna Wilson. 1989. "Public Entrepreneurship & Subnational Government." *Polity* 22 (1): 119–42.
Kirkpatrick, Jeane. 1979. "Dictatorships and Double Standards." *Commentary* 68 (5): 34–45.
Kissinger, Henry A. 1957. *A World Restored: Metternich, Castlereagh and the Problems of Peace, 1812–22.* Boston: Houghton Mifflin.
Kleiman, Ephraim. 2008. "Can 'Economic Peace' be the Solution?" *Haaretz,* December 10.
Klotz, Audie. 1995. *Norms in International Relations: The Struggle against Apartheid.* Ithaca: Cornell University Press.
Kratochwil, Friedrich. 1995. *Rules, Norms, and Decisions.* Cambridge: Cambridge University Press.
Krauthammer, Charles. 1989. "Universal Dominion: Toward a Unipolar World." *National Interest* 18: 47–49.
Krauthammer, Charles. 2001. "The Bush Doctrine." *Weekly Standard,* June 4.
Krauthammer, Charles. 2002. "Peace through Democracy." *Washington Post,* June 28.
Krauthammer, Charles. 2003a. "Iraq: A Moral Reckoning." *Washington Post,* May 16.
Krauthammer, Charles. 2003b. "Hoaxes, Hype and Humiliation." *Washington Post,* June 13.
Krauthammer, Charles. 2004a. "Democratic Realism: An American Foreign Policy for a Unipolar World." AEI Press, http://www.aei.org/docLib/20040227_book755text.pdf.
Krauthammer, Charles. 2004b. "In Defense of Democratic Realism." *National Interest* 77: 15–25.
Krauthammer, Charles. 2004c. "The Afghan Miracle: Why Isn't This Stunning U.S. Success Appreciated?" *Washington Post,* December 10.

Krauthammer, Charles. 2005. "Free to Dance in Iraq." *Washington Post*, February 4.
Kristol, Irving. 1990. "Defining Our National Interest." *National Interest* 21: 16–21.
Kristol, Irving. 1991. "Tongue-Tied in Washington." *Wall Street Journal*, April 15.
Kristol, William. 2003. "The End of the Beginning." *Weekly Standard*, May 12, 9.
Kristol, William. 2004. "The 9/11 Election." *Weekly Standard*, November 1 and November 8, 9.
Kristol, William, and Robert Kagan. 2000. "Introduction: National Interest and Global Responsibility." In *Present Dangers: Crisis and Opportunity in American Foreign and Defense Policy*, edited by Robert Kagan and William Kristol, 3–24. San Francisco: Encounter Books.
Kuhn, Thomas. 1962. *The Structure of Scientific Revolutions*. Chicago: University of Chicago Press.
Kupchan, Clifford. 2004. "Real Democratik." *National Interest* 77: 26–37.
Kurtz, Stanley. 2002. "The Terror of Islam." *Weekly Standard*, May 27, 38.
Marx, Karl. 1969. *The 18th Brumaire of Louis Bonaparte*. New York: International Publishers.
Lake, Anthony. 1993. "From Containment to Enlargement." Delivered at Johns Hopkins University School of Advanced International Studies, Washington, DC, September 21, http://www.mtholyoke.edu/acad/intrel/lakedoc.html.
Lane, Charles. 2000. "The Democracy Wave: Has It Crested?" *Weekly Standard*, January 17, 29.
Lane, Christopher. 1994. "Kant or Cant: The Myth of the Democratic Peace." *International Security* 19 (2): 5–49.
Lang, Anthony F., Jr. 2008. "Evil, Agency, and Punishment." In *Confronting Evil in International Relations: Ethical Responses to Problems of Moral Agency*, edited by Renee Jeffery, 89–114. New York: Palgrave Macmillan.
Latour, Bruno. 1987. *Science in Action: How to Follow Scientists and Engineers through Society*. Cambridge, MA: Harvard University Press.
Lepgold, Joseph. 1998. "Is Anyone Listening? International Relations Theory and the Problem of Policy Relevance." *Political Science Quarterly* 113 (1): 43–62.
Levi, Margaret. 1996. "Social and Unsocial Capital: A Review Essay of Robert Putnam's Making Democracy Work." *Politics and Society* 24 (1): 45–55.
Levy, Jack S. 1988. "Domestic Politics and War." *Journal of Interdisciplinary History* 18 (4): 653–73.
Levy, Jack S. 1989. "The Causes of War: A Review of Theories and Evidence." In *Behavior, Society, and Nuclear War. Vol. I*, edited by Philip E. Tetlock, Jo L. Husbands, Robert Jervis, Paul C. Stern, and Charles Tilly, 209–333. New York: Oxford University Press.
Levy, Jack S. 1994. "The Democratic Peace Hypothesis: From Description to Explanation." *Mershon International Studies Review* 38 (2): 352–54.
Lieven, Anatol. 2002. "The Wilsonian Veneer of US Foreign Policy." *Financial Times*, July 15.

Light, Margot. 2001. "Exporting Democracy." In *Ethics and Foreign Policy*, edited by Karen E. Smith and Margot Light, 75–92. Cambridge: Cambridge University Press.

Lindberg, Tod. 2004. "The Referendum on Neoconservatism." *Weekly Standard*, November 1 and November 8, 16–18.

Lindberg, Tod. 2007. "The Treaty of Democratic Peace: What the World Needs Now." *Weekly Standard*, February 12, 19–24.

Linklater, Andrew. 2000. *International Relations: Critical Concepts in Political Science. Vol. III*. London and New York: Routledge.

Lippmann, Walter. 1955. *Essays in the Public Philosophy*. Boston: Little, Brown.

Livni, Tzipi. 2008. "Address by F. M. Livni to INSS Conference: Security Challenges of the 21st Century." December 18, http://www.mfa.gov.il/MFA/Government/Speeches%20by%20Israeli%20leaders/2008/Address_FM%20Livni_INSS_Conference_18-Dec-2008.htm.

Livni, Tzipi. 2009. "World Will Not Accept 'Economic Peace' Alone." Tel Aviv University, December 31, http://blog.onevoicemovement.org/one_voice/2009/12/tzipi-livni-world-will-not-accept-economic-peace-alone.html.

Longino, Helen E. 2002. *The Fate of Knowledge*, Princeton: Princeton University Press.

Lowndes, Vivien, and David Wilson. 2001. "Social Capital and Local Governance: Exploring the Institutional Design Variable." *Political Studies* 49 (4): 629–47.

Lucas, J. R. 1993. *Responsibility*. Oxford: Clarendon Press.

Lukes, Steven. 2004. *Power: A Radical View*. 2nd edition. Basingstoke, England and New York: Palgrave Macmillan.

Lukes, Steven. 2005. "Power and the Battle for Hearts and Minds." *Millennium—Journal of International Studies* 33 (3): 477–93.

Lyne, John. 1998. "Rhetoric and Scientific Communities." In *Rhetoric and Community: Studies in Unity and Fragmentation*, edited by J. Michael Hogan, 265–83. Columbia: University of South Carolina Press.

MacMillan, John. 1995. "A Kantian Protest Against the Peculiar Discourse of Inter-Liberal State Peace." *Millennium—Journal of International Studies* 24 (3): 549–62.

Mandelbaum, Michael. 2001. "Bad Statesman, Good Prophet: Woodrow Wilson and the Post–Cold War Order." *National Interest* 64: 31–41.

Mandelbaum, Michael. 2002. *The Ideas that Conquered the World: Peace, Democracy, and Free Markets in the Twenty-First Century*. New York: Public Affairs.

Mannheim, Karl. 1968. *Ideology and Utopia*. London: Routledge and Kegan Paul.

Mansbridge, Jane J. 1970. *Beyond Adversary Democracy*. Chicago: University of Chicago Press.

Mansfield, Edward D., and Jack Snyder. 2005. *Electing to Fight: Why Emerging Democracies Go to War*. Cambridge, MA: MIT Press.

Maoz, Zeev. 1998. "Realist and Cultural Critiques of the Democratic Peace: A Theoretical and Empirical Re-assessment." *International Interactions* 24 (1): 3–89.

Maoz, Zeev, and Bruce Russett. 1992a. "Alliance, Contiguity, Wealth, and Political Stability: Is the Lack of Conflict among Democracies a Statistical Artifact?" *International Interactions* 17 (3): 245–67.

Maoz, Zeev, and Bruce Russett. 1992b. "Normative and Structural Causes of Democratic Peace, 1946–1986." Paper presented at the 33rd Annual Convention of the International Studies Association, Atlanta, Georgia, March 31–April 4.

Maoz, Zeev, and Bruce Russett. 1993. "Normative and Structural Causes of Democratic Peace, 1946–1986." *American Political Science Review* 87 (3): 624–38.

Marshall, Will. 2000. "Democratic Realism: the Third Way." January 1, http://www.ppionline.org/ppi_ci.cfm?knlgAreaID=128&subsecID=187&contentID=1123.

Marshall, Will. 2006. "Here Come the Realists." October 18, file:///G:/Documents/Democratic%20peace-book/PPI/Here%20Come%20the%20Realists%20by%20Will%20Marshall.htm.

Mattern, Janice Bially. 2005. "Why `Soft Power' Isn't So Soft: Representational Force and the Sociolinguistic Construction of Attraction in World Politics." *Millennium—Journal of International Studies* 33 (3): 583–612.

Mazarr, Michael J. 2003. "George W. Bush, Idealist." *International Affairs* 79 (3): 503–22.

McDonald, Patrick J. 2007. "The Purse Strings of Peace." *American Journal of Political Science* 51 (3): 569–82.

McDonald, Patrick J. 2010. "Capitalism, Commitment, and Peace." *International Interactions* 36 (2): 146–68.

McMahan, Jeff. 2006. "On the Moral Equality of Combatants." *Journal of Political Philosophy* 14 (4): 377–93.

Mearsheimer, John J. 1994–1995. "The False Promise of International Institutions." *International Security* 19 (3): 5–49.

Mearsheimer, John J. 2001. *The Tragedy of Great Power Politics*. New York: W. W. Norton.

Mearsheimer, John J., and Stephen M. Walt. 2002a. *Can Saddam Be Contained? History Says Yes*. Cambridge, MA: Belfer Center for Sciences and International Affairs, International Security Program Occasional Paper.

Mearsheimer, John J., and Stephen M. Walt. 2002b. "'Realists' Are Not Alone Opposing War with Iraq." *Chronicle of Higher Education*, November 15.

Mearsheimer, John J., and Stephen M. Walt. 2003a. "An Unnecessary War." *Foreign Policy*, January–February, 50–59.

Mearsheimer, John J., and Stephen M. Walt. 2003b. "Keeping Saddam Hussein in a Box." *New York Times*, February 2.

Megill, Allan, ed. 1994. *Rethinking Objectivity*. Durham, NC: Duke University Press.

Milbank, Dana. 2002. "A Sound Bite so Good, the President Wishes He Had Said It." *Washington Post*, July 2.

Milbank, Dana. 2004. "An Israeli Hawk Accepts the President's Invitation." *Washington Post*, November 23.
Miller, Benjamin. 1995. *When Opponents Cooperate: Great Power Conflict and Collaboration in World Politics.* Ann Arbor: University of Michigan Press.
Miller, David. 2001. "Distributing Responsibilities." *Journal of Political Philosophy* 9 (4): 453–71.
Miller, David. 2004. "Holding Nations Responsible." *Ethics* 114 (2): 240–68.
Miller, Steven E. 2006–2007. "The Iraq Experiment and the US National Security." *Survival* 48 (4): 17–50.
Monten, Jonathan. 2005. "The Roots of the Bush Doctrine: Power, Nationalism, and Democracy Promotion in U.S. Strategy." *International Security* 29 (4): 112–56.
Moses, Jeremy. 2010. "Liberal Internationalist Discourse and the Use of Force: Blair, Bush and Beyond." *International Politics* 47 (1): 26–51.
Mousseau, Michael. 2003. "The Nexus of Market Society, Liberal Preferences and Democratic Peace: Interdisciplinary Theory and Evidence." *International Studies Quarterly* 47 (4): 483–510.
Mousseau, Michael. 2009. "The Social Market Roots of Democratic Peace." *International Security* 33 (4): 52–86.
Mousseau, Michael. 2010. "Coming to Terms with the Capitalist Peace." *International Interactions* 36 (2): 185–92.
Mozgovaya, Natasha. 2010. "George Mitchell: U.S. Committed to Israel Security, Palestinian State." *Haaretz*, February 22.
Muravchik, Joshua. 1991. *Exporting Democracy: Fulfilling America's Destiny*, Washington, DC: AEI Press.
Muravchik, Joshua. 1992. "Conservatives for Clinton." *New Republic*, November 2, 2.
Muravchik, Joshua. 1993. "Lament of a Clinton Supporter." *Commentary* 96 (2): 15–22.
Muravchik, Joshua. 2001–2002. "Freedom and the Arab World." *Weekly Standard*, December 31–January 7, 15–16.
Muravchik, Joshua. 2002a. "The Bush Manifesto." *Commentary* 114 (5): 23–30.
Muravchik, Joshua. 2002b. "Hearts, Minds, and the War against Terror." *Commentary* 113 (5): 25–30.
Muravchik, Joshua. 2004. "The Richard Clarke Show." *Commentary* 117 (5): 32–41.
Murphy, Clare. 2005. "Bush's New Book for a New Term." January 21, http://news.bbc.co.uk/2/hi/americas/4195303.stm.
Mutz, Diana Carole. 2006. *Hearing the Other Side: Deliberative Versus Participatory Democracy.* Cambridge: Cambridge University Press.
Myrdal, Gunnar. 1969. *Objectivity in the Social Research.* New York: Pantheon Books.
Nadelmann, Ethan A. 1990. "Global Prohibition Regimes: The Evolution of Norms in International Society." *International Organization* 44 (4): 479–526.

Nell, Edward, and Willi Semmler. 2003. "The Economic Consequences of the Peace in Iraq." *Constellations* 10 (3): 425–36.
Nelson, John S., Allan Megill, and Donald N. McCloskey, eds. 1987. *The Rhetoric of the Human Sciences: Language and Argument in Scholarship and Public Affairs.* Madison: University of Wisconsin Press.
Nemeth, Thomas. 1980. *Gramsci's Philosophy: A Critical Study.* Brighton, England: Harvester Press.
Netanyahu, Benjamin, ed. 1987. *Terrorism: How the West Can Win.* New York: Avon Books.
Netanyahu, Benjamin. 1993. *A Place among the Nations: Israel and the World.* New York: Bantam Books.
Netanyahu, Benjamin. 1996. "Address by his Excellency, Binyamin Netanyahu, Prime Minister of Israel." July 7, http://www.gpo.gov/fdsys/pkg/CREC-1996-07-10/pdf/CREC-1996-07-10-pt1-PgH7160.pdf.
Netanyahu, Benjamin. 2002a. "Speech before the US Senate." April 10, http://www.netanyahu.org/netspeacinse.html.
Netanyahu, Benjamin. 2002b. "The Root Cause of Terrorism is Tyranny." *Wall Street Journal*, April 19.
Netanyahu, Benjamin. 2002c. "Fighting Terrorism: Eighteenth Annual John M. Ashbrook Memorial Dinner." May 3.
Netanyahu, Benjamin. 2002d. "Visions for Peace: Topple Arafat, then Talk Peace." June 13, http://www.netanyahu.org/visforpeacto.html.
Netanyahu, Benjamin. 2003. "At the Fourth Herzliya Conference." December 17, http://www.herzliyaconference.org/_Articles/Article.asp?ArticleID=1103&CategoryID=170.
Netanyahu, Benjamin. 2008. "At the Eighth Herzliya Conference." January 21, http://www.herzliyaconference.org/eng/?articleID=19878&categoryID=248.
Netanyahu, Benjamin. 2009a. "Incoming Prime Minister Benjamin Netanyahu's Speech at the Knesset Swearing-In Ceremony." March 31, http://www.pmo.gov.il/English/MediaCenter/Speeches/Pages/speechnetankness310309.aspx.
Netanyahu, Benjamin. 2009b. "Address by Prime Minister Benjamin Netanyahu Begin-Sadat Center at Bar-Ilan University." June 14, http://www.mfa.gov.il/MFA/Government/Speeches+by+Israeli+leaders/2009/Address_PM_Netanyahu_Bar-Ilan_University_14-Jun-2009.htm.
Newton, Kenneth. 2001. "Social Capital and Democracy in Modern Europe." In *Social Capital and European Democracy*, edited by Jan W. van Deth, Marco Maraffi, Kenneth Newton, and Paul F. Whiteley, 3–24. London: Routledge.
Norton, Anne. 2004. *Leo Strauss and the Politics of American Empire.* New Haven: Yale University Press.
Nossel, Suzanne. 2004. "Smart Power." *Foreign Affairs* 83 (2): 131–42.
Nozick, Robert. 1974. *Anarchy, State, and Utopia.* New York: Basic Books.

Nye, Joseph S., Jr. 1990. *Bound to Lead: The Changing Nature of American Power.* New York: Basic Books.
Nye, Joseph S., Jr. 2004. *Soft Power: The Means to Success in World Politics.* New York: Public Affairs.
Nye, Joseph S., Jr. 2007. "Smart Power." November 29, http://www.huffingtonpost.com/joseph-nye/smart-power_b_74725.html.
Nye, Joseph S., Jr. 2008a. "Public Diplomacy and Soft Power." *The Annals of the American Academy of Political and Social Science* 616 (1): 94–109.
Nye, Joseph S., Jr. 2008b. *The Powers to Lead.* New York: Oxford University Press.
Nye, Joseph S., Jr. 2009a. "The U.S. Can Reclaim 'Smart Power.'" January 21, http://www.latimes.com/news/opinion/commentary/la-oe-nye21-2009jan21,0,3381521.story.
Nye, Joseph S., Jr. 2009b. "Scholars on the Sidelines." *Washington Post,* April 13.
Nye, Joseph S., Jr. 2009c. "Obama's Nuclear Agenda." *Daily News Egypt,* October 13.
Nye, Joseph S., Jr. 2009d. "Testing Obama's Foreign Policy." *Business Daily,* December 15.
Nye, Joseph S., Jr. 2009e. "Smart Power." *New Perspectives Quarterly* 26 (2): 7–9.
Nye, Joseph S., Jr. 2010a. "An Alliance Larger Than One Issue." *New York Times,* January 6.
Nye, Joseph S., Jr. 2010b. "Is Military Power Becoming Obsolete?" *Korea Times,* January 13.
Nye, Joseph S., Jr. 2010c. "Davos: What's the Point?" *Washington Post,* January 26.
Nye, Joseph S., Jr. 2010d. "Smart Power Needs Smart Public Diplomacy." *Daily Star,* February 15.
Obama, Barack. 2004. "Keynote Address at the 2004 Democratic National Convention." July 27, http://www.pbs.org/newshour/bb/politics/july-dec04/obama-keynote-dnc.html.
Obama, Barack. 2005. "America's Nuclear Non-Proliferation Policy." May 26, http://obamaspeeches.com/017-America-Nuclear-Non-Proliferation-Policy-Remarks-Obama-Speech.htm.
Obama, Barack. 2007a. "The War We Need to Win." August 1, http://www.realclearpolitics.com/articles/2007/08/the_war_we_need_to_win.html.
Obama, Barack. 2007b. "Turning the Page in Iraq." September 12, http://www.presidency.ucsb.edu/ws/index.php?pid=77011.
Obama, Barack. 2008a. "The Past Versus the Future." January 30, http://www.presidency.ucsb.edu/ws/index.php?pid=77031.
Obama, Barack. 2008b. "The World Beyond Iraq." March 19, https://my.barackobama.com/page/content/fiveyearslaterspeech.
Obama, Barack. 2008c. "A New Strategy for a New World." July 15, http://www.realclearpolitics.com/articles/2008/07/a_new_strategy_for_a_new_world.html.

Obama, Barack. 2008d. "Election Night Victory Speech." November 4, http://edition.cnn.com/2008/POLITICS/11/04/obama.transcript.

Obama, Barack. 2009a. "News Conference by President Obama." April 2, http://www.whitehouse.gov/the_press_office/News-Conference-by-President-Obama-4-02-09.

Obama, Barack. 2009b. "Press Conference by the President." April 19, http://www.whitehouse.gov/the_press_office/Press-Conference-By-The-President-In-Trinidad-And-Tobago-4/19/2009.

Obama, Barack. 2009c. "News Conference by the President." April 29, http://www.whitehouse.gov/the_press_office/News-Conference-by-the-President-4/29/2009.

Obama, Barack. 2009d. "Remarks by the President on National Security." May 21, http://www.whitehouse.gov/the_press_office/Remarks-by-the-President-On-National-Security-5-21-09.

Obama, Barack. 2009e. "Remarks by the President on a New Beginning." June 4, http://www.whitehouse.gov/the_press_office/Remarks-by-the-President-at-Cairo-University-6-04-09.

Obama, Barack. 2009f. "Remarks by the President to the United Nations General Assembly." September 23, http://www.whitehouse.gov/the_press_office/Remarks-by-the-President-to-the-United-Nations-General-Assembly.

Odom, William E. 1995. "NATO's Expansion: Why the Critics Are Wrong." *National Interest* 39: 38–49.

Oneal, John R., and James Lee Ray. 1997. "New Tests of the Democratic Peace: Controlling for Economic Interdependence, 1950–85." *Political Research Quarterly* 50 (4): 751–75.

Oneal, John R., and Bruce Russett. 1997. "The Classical Liberal Were Right: Democracy, Interdependence, and Conflict, 1950–1985." *International Studies Quarterly* 41 (2): 267–94.

Oneal, John R., and Bruce Russett. 1999. "The Kantian Peace: The Pacific Benefits of Democracy, Interdependence, and International Organizations, 1885–1992." *World Politics* 52 (1): 1–37.

Oren, Ido. 1995. "The Subjectivity of the 'Democratic Peace': Changing U.S. Perceptions of Imperial Germany." *International Security* 20 (2): 147–84.

Oren, Ido. 2003. *Our Enemies and US America's Rivalries and the Making of Political Science*. Ithaca: Cornell University Press.

Oren, Michael B. 2002. "Build Strong Foundation and Peace Will Come." *Chicago Sun-Times*, June 5.

Organization for Security and Cooperation in Europe. 1999. "Charter for European Security." Istanbul, Turky, http://www.osce.org/documents/mcs/1999/11/4050_en.pdf.

Owen, John M., IV. 2005. "Iraq and the Democratic Peace: Who Says Democracies Don't Fight?" *Foreign Affairs* 84 (6): 122–27.

Pateman, Carole. 1970. *Participation and Democratic Theory*. Cambridge: Cambridge University Press.
Patten, Chris. 1999. "Speech at the Human Rights Discussion Forum." November 30.
Payne, Rodger A. 1996. "Deliberating Global Environmental Politics." *Journal of Peace Research* 33 (2): 129–36.
Payne, Rodger A. 2001. "Persuasion, Frames and Norm Construction." *European Journal of International Relations* 7 (1): 37–61.
Payne, Rodger A. 2007. "Neorealists as Critical Theorists: The Purpose of Foreign Policy Debate." *Perspectives on Politics* 5 (3): 503–14.
Perle, Richard. N. 2000. "Iraq: Saddam Unbound." In *Present Dangers: Crisis and Opportunity in American Foreign and Defense Policy*, edited by Robert Kagan and William Kristol, 99–110. San Francisco: Encounter Books.
Pielke, Roger A. 2007. *The Honest Broker: Making Sense of Science in Policy and Politics*. New York: Cambridge University Press.
Pelletiere, Stephen. 2004. *America's Oil Wars*. Westport, CT: Praeger.
Pipes, Daniel. 2002–2003. "The Scandal of U.S.–Saudi Relations." *National Interest* 70: 66–78.
Pipes, Richard. 1997. "The West and the Rest." *Commentary* 103 (3): 62–65.
Podhoretz, Norman. 2002a. "How to Win World War IV." *Commentary* 113 (2): 19–29.
Podhoretz, Norman. 2002b. "In Praise of the Bush Doctrine." *Commentary* 114 (2): 19–28.
Polachek, Solomon W. 1980. "Conflict and Trade." *Journal of Conflict Resolution* 24 (2): 55–78.
Polachek, Solomon W. 1997. "Why Democracies Cooperate More and Fight Less: The Relationship Between International Trade and Cooperation." *Review of International Economics* 5 (3): 295–309.
Pollak, Johannes. 2007. "Contested Meanings of Representation." *Comparative European Politics* 5 (1): 87–103.
Portes, Alejandro. 1998. "Social Capital: Its Origins and Applications in Modern Sociology." *Annual Review of Sociology* 24: 1–24.
Potter, Elizabeth. 2006. *Feminism and Philosophy of Science: An Introduction*. New York: Routledge.
Prelli, Lawrence J. 1989. *A Rhetoric of Science: Inventing Scientific Discourse*. Columbia: University of South Carolina Press.
Press-Barnathan, Galia. 2012. "Does Popular Culture Matter to International Relations Scholars? Possible Links and Methodological Challenges." In *Popular Culture and the State in East and Southeast Asia*, edited by Nissim Otmazgin and Eyal Ben-Ari, 29–45. London: Routledge.
Price, Richard M. 1995. *The Chemical Weapons Taboos*. Ithaca: Cornell University Press.

Price, Richard. 1998. "Reversing the Gun Sights: Transnational Civil Society Targets Land Mines." *International Organization* 52 (3): 613–44.

Progressive Policy Institute. 2003. "Progressive Internationalism: A Democratic National Security Strategy." October 30, http://www.ppionline.org/documents/Progressive_Internationalism_1003.pdf.

Project for a New American Century. 1997. "Statement of Principles." June 3, at http://www.newamericancentury.org/statementofprinciples.htm.

Project for a New American Century. 2000. "Rebuilding America's Defenses: Strategy, Forces and Resources for a New Century." September, http://www.newamericancentury.org/RebuildingAmericasDefenses.pdf.

Przeworski, Adam. 1999. "Minimalist Conception of Democracy: A Defense." In *Democracy's Value*, edited by Ian Shapiro and Casiano Hacker-Cordón, 23–55. Cambridge: Cambridge University Press.

Puddington, Arch. 2004. "Liberty for All." *Commentary* 118 (4): 72–75.

Putnam, Hilary. 2002. *The Collapse of the Fact/Value Dichotomy and Other Essays*. Cambridge, MA: Harvard University Press.

Putnam, Robert D. 1993. *Making Democracy Work: Civic Traditions in Modern Italy*, Princeton: Princeton University Press.

Putnam, Robert D. 2000. *Bowling Alone: The Collapse and Revival of American Community*. New York: Simon and Schuster.

Ray, James Lee. 1995. *Democracy and International Conflict: An Evaluation of the Democratic Peace Proposition*. Columbia: University of South Carolina Press.

Ray, James Lee. 1997. "The Democratic Path to Peace." *Journal of Democracy* 8 (2): 49–64.

Ray, James Lee. 2003. "A Lakatosian View of the Democratic Peace Research Program." In *Progress in International Relations Theory: Appraising the Field*, edited by Miriam Fendius Elman, 205–43. Cambridge, MA: MIT University Press.

Rawls, John. 1999a. *A Theory of Justice*. Revised Edition. Cambridge, MA: Harvard University Press.

Rawls, John. 1999b. *The Law of Peoples*. Cambridge, MA: Harvard University Press.

Reiter, Dan, and Allan C. Stam. 2002. *Democracies at War*. Princeton: Princeton University Press.

Reiter, Dan, and Allan C. Stam. 2003. "Identifying the Culprit: Democracy, Dictatorship, and Dispute Initiation." *American Political Science Review* 97 (2): 333–37.

Research Unit for Political Economy. 2003a. *Behind the Invasion of Iraq*. New York: Monthly Review Press.

Research Unit for Political Economy. 2003b. "Behind the War on Iraq." *Monthly Review* 55 (May): 20–49.

Ricoeur, Paul. 1991. "The Model of the Text: Meaningful Action Considered as a Text." In *From Text to Action: Essays in Hermeneutics, II*, translated by Kathleen

Blamey and John B. Thompson, 144–67. Evanston, IL: Northwestern University Press.
Riker, William H. 1986. *The Art of Political Manipulation*. New Haven: Yale University Press.
Riker, William H. 1996. *The Strategy of Rhetoric: Campaigning for the American Constitution*. Edited by Randall L. Calvert, John Mueller, and Rick K. Wilson. New Haven: Yale University Press.
Risse, Thomas. 2000. "'Let's Argue!': Communicative Action in World Politics." *International Organization* 54 (1): 1–39.
Risse, Thomas, Stephen Ropp, and Kathryn Sikkink, eds. 1999. *The Power of Human Rights: International Norms and Domestic Change*. Cambridge: Cambridge University Press.
Risse, Thomas, and Kathryn Sikkink. 1999. "The Socialization of International Human Rights Norms into Domestic Practices: Introduction." In *The Power of Human Rights: International Norms and Domestic Changes*, edited by Thomas Risse, Stephen C. Ropp, and Kathryn Sikkink, 1–38. Cambridge: Cambridge University Press.
Rosato, Sebastian. 2003. "The Flawed Logic of Democratic Peace Theory." *American Political Science Review* 97 (4): 585–602.
Rosen, Stephen Peter. 2003. "An Empire, If You Can Keep It." *National Interest* 71: 51–61.
Rosenblum, Jonathan. 2002. "Democracy—What a Beautiful Idea." *Jerusalem Post*, International Edition, July 5.
Rozen, Laura. 2009. "The Origins of 'Smart Power.'" January 14, http://thecable.foreignpolicy.com/posts/2009/01/14/the_origins_of_smart_power.
Rummel, Rudolph J. 1979. *Understanding Conflict and War*, Vol. 4, *War, Power, Peace*. Los Angeles: Sage.
Rummel, Rudolph J. 1981. *Understanding Conflict and War*, Vol. 5, *The Just Peace*. Los Angeles: Sage.
Rummel, Rudolph J. 1983. "Libertianism and Interstate Violence." *Journal of Conflict Resolution* 27 (1): 27–71.
Rummel, Rudolph J. 2009. "Why are we Fighting in Iraq?" http://democraticpeace.wordpress.com/2009/01/29/why-are-we-fighting-in-iraq/.
Russett, Bruce. 1988. "A Neo-Kantian Perspective: Democracy, Interdependence and International Organizations in Building Security Communities." In *Security Communities*, edited by Emanuel Adler and Michael Barnett, 368–94. Cambridge: Cambridge University Press.
Russett, Bruce M. 1993a. "A Post-Thucydides, Post-Cold War World." *Mediterranean Quarterly* 4 (1): 46–56.
Russett, Bruce. 1993b. *Grasping the Democratic Peace: Principles for a Post-Cold War World*. Princeton: Princeton University Press.

Russett, Bruce. 2005. "Bushwacking the Democratic Peace." *International Studies Perspectives* 6 (4): 395–408.

Russett, Bruce. 2010. "Capitalism or Democracy? Not So Fast, International Crises and the Capitalist Peace." *International Interactions* 36 (2): 198–205.

Russett, Bruce, and John R. Oneal. 2001. *Triangulating Peace: Democracy, Interdependence, and International Organizations.* New York: W. W. Norton.

Russett, Bruce, John R. Oneal, and David R. Davis. 1998. "The Third Leg of Kantian Tripod for Peace: International Organizations and Militarized Disputes, 1950–1985." *International Organization* 52 (3): 441–67.

Russett, Bruce, Barry O'Neil, and James Sutterlin. 1996. "Breaking the Security Council Restructuring Logjam." *Global Governance* 2 (1): 65–80.

Sakharov, Andrei. 1968. *Progress, Coexistence, and Intellectual Freedom.* Translated by the *New York Times.* London: Andre Deutsch.

Sakharov, Andrei. 1974. "Manifesto II." In *Sakharov Speaks,* edited by Harrison E. Salisbury, 98–114. London: Collins, Harvill Press.

Sakharov, Andrei. 1975. *My Country and the World.* Translated by Guy V. Daniels. London: Collins & Harvill Press.

Sakharov, Andrei. 1990. *Memoirs.* Translated by Richard Lourie. New York: Alfred A. Knopf.

Sarkees, Meredith Reid, and Phil Schafer. 2000. "The Correlates of War Data on War: An Update to 1997." *Conflict Management and Peace Science* 18 (1): 123–44.

Scanlon, T. M. 1998. *What We Owe to Each Other.* Cambridge, MA: Belknap Press, Harvard University Press.

Schafer, Mark, and Stephen G. Walker. 2001. "Political Leadership and the Democratic Peace: The Operational Code of Prime Minister Tony Blair." In *Profiling Political Leaders Cross-Cultural Studies of Personality and Behavior,* edited by Ofer Feldman and Linda O. Valenty, 21–35. Westport, CT: Praeger.

Schafer, Mark, and Stephen G. Walker. 2006. "Democratic Leaders and the Democratic Peace: The Operational Codes of Tony Blair and Bill Clinton." *International Studies Quarterly* 50 (3): 561–83.

Schimmelfenning, Frank. 2001. "The Community Trap: Liberal Norms, Rhetorical Action, and the Eastern Enlargement of the European Union." *International Organization* 55 (1): 47–80.

Schmitt, Gary. 2002. "A Case for Continuity." *National Interest* 69: 11.

Schneider, Gerald, and Nils Petter Gleditsch. 2010. "The Capitalist Peace: The Origins and Prospects of a Liberal Idea." *International Interactions* 36 (2): 107–14.

Schneider, Mark, and Paul Teske. 1992. "Toward a Theory of the Political Entrepreneur: Evidence from Local Government." *American Political Science Review* 86 (3): 737–47.

Schneider, Mark, and Paul Teske, with Michael Mintrom. 1995. *Public Entrepreneurs: Agents for Change in American Government.* Princeton: Princeton University Press.

Schumpeter, Joseph A. 1962. *Capitalism, Socialism and Democracy*. 3rd edition. New York: Harper Torchbooks.
Schwartz, Stephen. 2001. "Saudi Friends, Saudi Foes." *Weekly Standard*, October 8, 12–16.
Searle, John R. 1995. *The Construction of Social Reality*. New York: Free Press.
Sela, Avraham. 2005. "Politics, Identity and Peacemaking: The Arab Discourse on Peace with Israel in the 1990s." *Israel Studies* 10 (2): 15–71.
Shai, Nachman. 2009. "Knesset Speech," www.knesset.gov.il/plenum/data/00901809.doc.
Shai, Nachman. 2010. "Europe Can Help Israel's 'Smart Power.'" http://www.nachmanshai.co.il/?p=865.
Sharansky, Natan. 1988. *Fear No Evil*. Translated by Stefani Hoffman. London: Weidenfeld & Nicolson.
Sharansky, Natan. 2000a. "Who Will Speak the Truth?" *Washington Post*, October 12.
Sharansky, Natan. 2000b. "Only Democracy Brings Peace." *Wall Street Journal*, October 30.
Sharansky, Natan. 2000c. "Open Your Eyes, Mr. Prime Minister." *Jerusalem Post*, November 3.
Sharansky, Natan. 2001. "The Mistakes of Oslo." *Haaretz*, January 22.
Sharansky, Natan. 2002a. "Where Do We Go from Here?" *Jerusalem Post*, May 3.
Sharansky, Natan. 2002b. "Democracy for Peace," June 20, http://www.aei.org/papers/politics-and-public-opinion/democracy-for-peace/.
Sharansky, Natan. 2002c. "Free Palestine Can Become a Reality: A Plan for Peace and Democracy." *Wall Street Journal*, July 3.
Sharansky, Natan. 2002d. "Palestinian Democracy: Relevant and Realistic." *Haaretz*, July 18.
Sharansky, Natan. 2003. "Temple Mount Is More Important than Peace." *Haaretz*, October 16.
Sharansky, Natan, with Ron Dermer. 2004. *The Case for Democracy: The Power of Freedom to Overcome Tyranny and Terror*. New York: Public Affairs.
Shavit, Ari. 1996. "A New Middle East? What an Amusing Idea." *Haaretz Weekly Supplement*, November 22.
Shenhav, Shaul R. 2005. "Thin and Thick Narrative Analysis: On the Question of Defining and Analyzing Political Narratives." *Narrative Inquiry* 15 (1): 75–99.
Simon, Herbert W., ed. 1989. *Rhetoric in the Human Sciences*. London: Sage Publications.
Simon, Herbert W., ed. 1990. *The Rhetorical Turn: Invention and Persuasion in the Conduct of Inquiry*. Chicago: University of Chicago Press.
Singer, Peter. 1972. "Famine, Affluence, and Morality." *Philosophy and Public Affairs* 1 (3): 229–43.
Slaughter, Anne-Marie. 1995. "International Law in a World of Liberal States." *European Journal of International Law* 6 (1): 508–38.

Smith, Steve. 2004. "Singing Our World into Existence: International Relations Theory and September 11." *International Studies Quarterly* 48 (3) 499–515.

Smith, Tony. 2007. *A Pact with the Devil: Washington's Bid for World Supremacy and the Betrayal of the American Promise.* New York: Routledge.

Snyder, Jack. 2003. "Imperial Temptations." *National Interest* 71: 29–40.

Spiro, David E. 1994. "The Insignificance of the Liberal Peace." *International Security* 19 (2): 50–86.

Steele, Brent J. 2010. "Of 'Witch's Brews' and Scholarly Communities: The Dangers and Promise of Academic Parrhesia." *Cambridge Review of International Affairs* 23 (1): 49–68.

Strenger, Carlo. 2009. "Netanyahu Is Just a Mirror." *Haaretz*, March 26.

Stoll, Ira. 2002. "Israel's Reagan? Natan Sharansky Understands that Liberty Is the Only Guarantee of Peace." *Wall Street Journal*, December 13.

Szacki, Jerzy. 1990. "Intellectuals Between Politics and Culture." In *The Political Responsibilities of Intellectuals*, edited by Ian Maclean, Alan Montefiore, and Peter Winch, 229–47. Cambridge: Cambridge University Press.

Taheri, Amir. 2004. "After the Arab League." *Weekly Standard*, May 3, 20–22.

Tarrow, Sidney. 1996. "Making Social Science Work across Space and Time: A Critical Reflection on Robert Putnam's Making Democracy Work." *American Political Science Review* 90 (2): 389–97.

Taylor, Charles. 1985. *Philosophy and the Human Sciences. Philosophical Papers 2.* Cambridge: Cambridge University Press.

Tell, Davis. 1996. "Selling out to China." *Weekly Standard*, December 23, 9–10.

Tickner, J. Ann. 1992. *Gender in International Relations: Feminist Perspectives on Achieving Global Security.* New York: Columbia University Press.

Tickner, J. Ann. 2005. "What Is Your Research Program? Some Feminist Answers to International Relations Methodological Questions." *International Studies Quarterly* 49 (1): 1–21.

Tsygankov, Andrei P. 2003. "The Irony of Western Ideas in a Multicultural World: Russians' Intellectual Engagement with the 'End of History' and 'Clash of Civilizations.'" *International Studies Review* 5 (1): 53–76.

Tucker, Robert W. 1986. "Exemplar or Crusader? Reflections on America's Role." *National Interest* 5: 64–75.

Tucker, Robert W. 1992–1993. "Realism and the New Consensus." *National Interest* 30: 33–36.

Tyan, Maria. 2006. "Neoconservative Intellectuals and the Limitations of Governing: The Reagan Administration and the Demise of the Cold War." *Comparative American Studies* 4 (4): 409–20.

U.S. Department of State. 2002. *The Project for the Future of Iraq.* http://www.gwu.edu/~nsarchiv/NSAEBB/NSAEBB198/index.htm.

U.S. Senate. 1997. "Nomination of Madeleine Korbel Albright of the District of Columbia to be Secretary of State." January 22, http://www.c-spanvideo.org/videoLibrary/clip.php?appid=596936044.

von Hayek, Friedrich A. 1945. *The Road to Serfdom*. London: Routledge.
Wallenstein, Peter. 1973. *Structure and War: On International Relations 1820–1868*. Stockholm: Raben & Sjogern.
Wallerstein, Immanuel. 1979. *The Capitalist World-Economy*. Cambridge: Cambridge University Press.
Wallerstein, Immanuel. 1984. *The Politics of World-Economy: The States, the Movements and the Civilizations*. Cambridge: Cambridge University Press.
Walt, Stephen M. 1987. *The Origins of Alliances*. Ithaca: Cornell University Press.
Walt, Stephen M. 2005. "The Relationship between Theory and Policy in International Relations." *Annual Review of Political Science* 8: 23–48.
Waltz, Kenneth N. 1959. *Man, State and War: A Theoretical Analysis*. New York: Columbia University Press.
Waltz, Kenneth N. 1986. "Reflections on Theory of International Politics: A Response to My Critics." In *Neorealism and Its Critics*, edited by Robert O. Keohane, 322–45. New York: Columbia University Press.
Waltz, Kenneth N. 1997. "Evaluating Theories." *American Political Science Review* 91 (4): 913–17.
Weber, Max. 1949. *The Methodology of the Social Sciences*. Translated and edited by Edward A. Shils and Henry A. Finch. Glencoe, IL: The Free Press.
Weede, Erich. 1995. "Economic Policy and International Security: Rent-Seeking, Free Trade and Democratic Peace." *European Journal of International Relations* 1 (4): 519–37.
Weede, Erich. 2005. *Balance of Power, Globalization and the Capitalist Peace*. Berlin: Liberal-Verl.
Wehner, Peter. 2006. "The Wrong Time to Lose Our Nerve." *Wall Street Journal*, April 4.
Weizman, Steve. 2001. "Is Time on Our Side?" *Jerusalem Post*, International Edition, February 6.
Weldes, Jutta. 1996. "Constructing National Interests." *European Journal of International Relations* 2 (3): 275–318.
Wendt, Alexander. 1992. "Anarchy Is What States Make of It: The Social Construction of Power Politics." *International Organization* 46 (2): 391–425.
White House. 2002. "The National Security of the United States." September 17.
Widmaier, Wesley W. 2004. "Theory as a Factor and the Theorist as an Actor: The 'Pragmatist Constructivist' Lessons of John Dewey and John Kenneth Galbraith." *International Studies Review* 6 (3): 427–45.
Williams, Michael C. 2005. "What is the National Interest? The Neoconservative Challenge in IR Theory." *European Journal of International Relations* 26 (3): 307–37.
Wittes, Tamara Cofman, and Richard Youngs. 2009. *Europe, the United States, and Middle Eastern Democracy: Repairing the Breach*. Analysis Paper No. 18. Washington, DC: The Saban Center for Middle East Policy at the Brookings Institution.

Wolfson, Adam. 2004. "The Two Faces of Liberalism." *Weekly Standard*, October 18, 20–22.

Wurmser, Meirav. 2004. "Democracy Defended: Natan Sharansky Explains Why Democracy Makes the World Safer." *Weekly Standard*, December 6, 28–29.

Young, Iris Marion. 2004. "Responsibility and Global Labor Justice." *Journal of Political Philosophy* 12 (4): 365–88.

Young, Oran R. 1994. *International Governance: Protecting the Environment in a Stateless Society*. Ithaca: Cornell University Press.

Zakaria, Fareed. 1997. "The Rise of Illiberal Democracy." *Foreign Affairs* 76 (6): 22–43.

INDEX

Abu Ghraib, 147
Acton, Lord (Dalberg-Acton, John E. E.), 138, 226
Adelson Institute for Strategic Studies, 102
Adler, Immanuel, 15, 19, 57, 219, 220, 222
AEI World Forum, 105
Afghanistan, 106, 129–31, 136, 152
Africa, 164
Al Qaeda, 136
Albright, Madeleine, 81
America / American, 1, 8–9, 27, 34, 47, 50, 69, 73–157, 165, 189–91, 196, 206–7, 224, 227. *See also* United States
American Enterprise Initiative, 105
Angell, Norman, 109
Arad, Uzi, 223
Arafat, Yasser, 97, 98, 103, 106, 108
Arendt, Hannah, 227
Arens, Moshe, 93
Argentina, 95
Aristotle, 29
Armitage, Richard, 144–48
Ashley, Richard, 176–77
Asia, 78, 164
Australia, 158, 226
authoritarian, 55, 64, 73–74, 91, 95, 102, 108, 120, 129
autocracies / autocrats / autocratic, 57, 63–65, 90, 99, 106

Babst, Dean, 1, 7, 39, 45–46, 52, 156, 208
Bachrach, Peter, 226
Baghdad, 117, 195
Baker, James, 71–73
balance of power, 46–47, 94, 126, 131–34, 137
Balkans, 74, 120
Bar Ilan University (Netanyahu speech), 164
Barak, Ehud, 93, 105, 107, 224
Baratz, Morton, 226
Barber, Benjamin, 42

Barnes, Fred, 225
Barnett, Michael, 57, 222, 226
Bates, Thomas, 20–21
Baum, Thomas, 223
Beilin, Yossi, 102
Beit Hillel, 104
Bentham, Jeremy, 223
Berger, Peter, 179
Berlin, Isaiah, 47
Berman, Paul, 78, 87
Bin Laden, Osama, 105
Blair, Tony, 8, 69, 80–82, 167, 223
Blinken, Anthony, 145–46
Boot, Max, 35, 127–28, 139–40, 175, 185, 226
Botswana, 48
Boulding, Kenneth, 41, 44, 217
Bourdieu, Pierre, 29–30, 219
Britain, 82. *See also* England
Brock, Lothar, 50, 194, 219
Brown, Seyom, 41
Buchanan, Allen, 229
Bueno de Mesquita, Bruce, 40, 60, 62–65
Burke, Edmund, 112, 121
Burton, Michael, 223
Bush, George H. W., 71–73
Bush, George W., 1, 8–9, 35–36, 69, 75–87, 98, 101, 106–7, 110, 117, 121–23, 129–30, 136, 139–40, 145–46, 151–52, 184–85, 196
Bush administration, 8, 105, 114, 118, 127, 135–36, 140, 144–51, 169, 189, 206, 222, 226, 228
Bush doctrine, 9, 48, 80, 113, 115, 130–38, 154, 185, 195–96

Cairo Address / Cairo University speech, 149, 164
Camp David summit, 224
Canada, 41
capitalism, 20–21, 120, 122, 142, 155–60

259

capitalist peace, 10, 142–43, 154–70, 207, 226
Castlereagh, Robert Stewart, 133
Cato Institute, 158, 226
Cederman, Lars-Eric, 223
Center for Strategic and International Studies (CSIS), 144–54
Chalaby, Ahmed, 128
Checkel, Jeffrey, 15, 220
Cheney, Dick, 105–7
Chernoff, Fred, 212
Chicago Council on Foreign Relations, 81
China, 74, 78, 120, 132–33, 225
Christopher, Warren, 80–81
CIA, 119, 152
civil society, 11, 13, 20, 45, 78, 80, 125, 147, 150, 165, 173, 192–93, 202, 207–8, 215, 217, 228
Civil War, 130–31
Clarke, Jonathan, 70, 73–74, 117
Clinton, Bill, 1, 7, 8, 22, 68–87, 129, 144, 222–23
Clinton, Hillary Rodham, 146, 152–53, 169
Clinton administration, 8, 82, 144
Coady, C. A. J., 213
Coalition for a Realistic Foreign Policy, 190
Cobden, Richard, 159
Cohen, Raymond, 39, 93
Cold War, 7, 9, 16, 52, 69–73, 83, 106, 114–22, 132–33, 176
commonsense, 5–6, 7, 21, 24, 27, 37, 38, 68–69, 84, 87, 107, 133, 179, 180, 204–5
commonsensical descriptive vernacular, 6, 37–38, 205
Communism, 70–71, 106, 114, 116, 132
Connolly, William, 177–81, 189
consequentialism, 181, 212
conservatism, 7, 42–43, 67, 77, 87, 89, 94, 112–16, 120–28, 137–39, 220, 226
consolidated democracy, 1, 35–36, 44, 91, 95, 185
constructivism, 16, 18–21, 24–27, 197, 220
Creighton, Mandell, 226
Critical Theory, 2–4, 7, 34, 40, 176, 205, 212, 216–17, 226–27

CSIS Bipartisan Commission on Smart Power, 144–46, 154
Cyprus, 95

Dalberg-Acton, John E. E. (Lord Acton), 138, 226
Demenchonok, Edward, 228
democracy, 5–12, 25–29, 33–39, 42–207, 211, 215–29
    promotion of, 114–18, 122, 125–31, 137–38, 150, 206, 222, 225–26
democratic imperative, 161, 167, 171, 173, 190–97, 202, 217, 228
Democratic Leadership Council, 71, 79
Democratic Party, 71, 73, 79
Democratic Peace, 1–16, 28–29, 33–143, 148, 153–85, 189–91, 194–97, 202, 204–8, 213–29
    normative / cultural theories of democratic peace, 40, 53, 55–60, 66, 98, 123
    structural theories of democratic peace, 39, 53, 55, 60–66, 98–99, 103, 123–25
democratic realism, 79, 127
democratic theory, 42
    deliberative / participatory / normative theories of democracy, 7, 40–44, 50, 56–59, 65–66, 192, 214–17, 222
    structural / elitist / procedural theory of democracy, 42–43, 64, 66, 77, 89, 99, 104, 124–25, 128–30, 137–38, 215, 217, 229
democratization, 5, 8, 15, 28–29, 35–37, 42, 44, 69–137, 141, 150, 176–78, 185, 206–7, 218, 224–25
Denmark, 47–48
deontology, 213
Dermer, Ron, 107
Desert Storm, Operation, 71
de-Shalit, Avner, 42, 197, 216
Deutsch, Karl, 41, 44
Diamond, Larry, 79
dictatorship, 76, 79, 102–3, 106–8, 117, 124–26, 130, 137, 140, 160, 176
disengagement plan, 101. See also unilateral withdrawal
Dixon, William, 40, 57–60, 65, 67, 155, 211, 214
Dobriansky, Paula, 127–28

Donnelly, Tom, 128, 131
Doyle, Michael, 46, 48–51, 54, 221
Dryzek, John, 42
Duvall, Raymond, 226

Eastern Europe, 72
economic peace, 143, 155, 162–69, 207
Egypt, 94, 100, 123, 226
Ehrman, John, 70, 74, 117
Eldar, Akiva, 165, 167
Elster, Jon, 42
England, 77. *See also* Britain
epistemology, 13, 18, 33–34, 65, 188, 197–98
Etheridge, Eric, 226
Etzioni, Amitai, 135
Eurasia, 72
Europe, 82, 129, 133, 164, 219, 223, 225
European Security Strategy, 82
European Union, 82

Falkland Islands / Malvinas, 95
Farber, Henry, 39
Fayyad, Salam, 167
Fearon, James, 40, 60–65
Feldman, Nizan, 166–67, 227
feminism, 34, 221
Ferguson, Niall, 113, 225
Finlayson, Alan, 31 221
Finnemore, Martha, 15, 219
Fleurbaey, Marc, 177–78, 181–82, 198
Ford, Robert, 151
foundationalism, 13, 31–32
Fraser Institute, 226
Freeden, Michael, 4, 16–17, 23, 68, 219–20
Friedman, Thomas, 222–23
Frost, Mervyn, 228
Fukuyama, Francis, 70, 87, 114, 116, 120–22, 125–26, 131, 137, 225

Gadamer, Hans-Georg, 24
Gallie, W. B., 16
Gartzke, Erik, 10, 143, 157–62, 170, 180, 207–8, 226
Gates, Robert, 146, 152–53, 169
Gaza, 101–2, 163
Geis, Anna, 50, 219

Gerecht, Reuel Marc, 225
Gershman, Carl, 70, 73, 116–17
Giddens, Anthony, 180
Gilovich, Thomas, 221
Glazer, Nathan, 73
Gleditsch, Nils Petter, 69, 157, 221
Good Friday Agreement, 75
Goodin, Robert, 171, 182, 227
Graham, Keith, 228
Gramsci, Antonio, 4–7, 18–22, 25, 97, 193
Gramscian, 16, 19, 22, 73, 83, 145, 176, 194
Greater Israel, 94–96, 107–10
Greater Middle East and North Africa Project, 131
Greece, 29, 95
Gulf War, 117
Guzzini, Stefano, 15, 18

Haass, Richard, 74
Habermas, Jürgen, 42, 193–94
Habermasian, 32, 147, 220
Haiti, 74
Halper, Stefan, 70, 73–74, 117
Hamas, 154, 163
Haraway, Donna, 221
Harding, Sandra, 221
Hawkesworth, Mary, 34
Hayek, Friedrich A., 226
Hazony, Yoram, 94–95, 223
Hebron, 93
Hegel, Georg Wilhelm Friedrich, 137
hegemony, 5, 19–22, 25
Hegre, Håvard, 157
Heidegger, Martin, 24
Henderson, Gordon, 222
Herder, Johann Gottfried, 121
heresthetics, 29, 31
hermeneutical mechanism, 2, 4–5, 9–10, 14, 16, 18, 22–24, 27, 38, 40, 68, 143–44, 157, 160, 170, 204, 207
Herzeliya Conference, 162–63, 224
Hobbes, Thomas, 62
Hobson, Christopher, 219
How, Alan, 24
human rights, 72–78, 81–83, 96–97, 130
Human Rights Discussion Forum, 82

Huntington, Samuel, 114–16, 120–28, 131, 138, 225
Hurka, Thomas, 213
Hussain, Rashad, 151
Hussein, Saddam, 71, 116–19, 130

ideology, 3–5, 16–18, 24, 32, 65, 89–90, 108, 115, 125–26, 137, 142, 160, 184, 199, 219–20, 224
Ikenberry, John, 113
Institute for National Security Studies (INSS), 166
Institute of Public Affairs, 158, 226
International Science Shop Network, 228
Intifada, 101, 105, 227
Iraq, 36, 48, 71, 117–19, 130–31, 136–41, 149, 151, 153, 169, 185, 196, 207, 226
Iraq War / war in Iraq, 2, 9, 36, 79–82, 107, 117, 131, 134–36, 141, 146–52, 163, 172, 185, 189–96, 206, 227–29
ISA (International Studies Association), 193–94, 196
Ish-Shalom, Piki, 67, 137, 180
Islam, Muslim, 98, 105–6, 119–23, 163, 168, 225
Israel, 1, 2, 8, 15, 22, 35, 74, 85–117, 123, 143, 162–68, 172, 189, 197, 208, 219, 223–24
Israel Ministry of Foreign Affairs, 101
Israeli Government, 99, 101, 108
Israeli-Palestinian conflict, 74–75, 94–95, 104, 107, 166, 172, 206
Israeli Right, 8, 15, 28, 76, 85, 92, 94, 109, 117

Jackson, Patrick Thaddeus, 190, 220
Japan, 72
Jasanoff, Sheila, 219
Jedlicki, Jerzy, 227
Jerusalem, 99, 101, 107–9, 224
Jervis, Robert, 113
Jewish Agency for Israel, 102
Joffe, Joseph, 225
Jones, Ward, 189
Jordan, 94, 100

Kadima (political party), 168
Kagan, Robert, 74, 117, 225

Kant, Immanuel, 1, 29, 45–50, 54, 58–62, 86, 87, 90, 94, 98, 103, 111, 155–56, 159, 206, 223
Kaplan, Lawrence, 36, 74, 83, 87, 119, 127, 185
Katzenstein, Peter, 25
Kaufman, Stuart, 190
Kenya, 226
Kingdon, John, 220
Kirkpatrick, Jeane, 112
Kissinger, Henry, 132–33, 180
Kleiman, Ephraim, 166
Knesset (Israeli Parliament), 93, 101, 168, 224
Kratochwil, Freidrich, 15
Krauthammer, Charles, 70, 73, 79, 87, 116–19, 125, 127, 223–26
Kristol, Irving, 73, 116, 225
Kristol, William, 36, 73, 83, 87, 116–23, 127–28, 131, 185, 222, 225
Kuhn, Thomas, 34
Kurtz, Stanley, 122
Kuwait, 117
Kyoto, 130

Labor (Political Party), 93, 101
Lake, Anthony, 81–82
Lane, Christopher, 39, 81
Lang, Anthony, 220
Latour, Bruno, 219
Lebanon, 163, 226
Lepgold, Joseph, 174
Levy, Jack, 36, 52, 69
liberal peace, 48–51, 155–57, 162, 221
liberalism, 8, 42–51, 54–56, 67, 70, 74, 78–82, 87–89, 120, 133–35, 144, 148, 153, 155, 158–59, 185, 195–96, 216, 220–21
libertarian, 46–51, 112, 153, 159, 216
libertarian peace, 48
Lieven, Anatol, 100, 109
Likud (political party), 93, 101, 107
Linklater, Andrew, 81
Lipper, Tamara, 107
Lippmann, Walter, 42, 66, 229
Livni, Tzipi, 167
Longino, Helen, 219
Lucas, J. R., 177–78, 181, 198
Luckmann, Thomas, 179

Lukes, Steven, 144
Lyne, John, 31, 179

Mandelbaum, Michael, 78–79, 87
Mannheim, Karl, 34
Mansbridge, Jane, 42
Mansfield, Edward, 35, 225
Maoz, Zeev, 40, 51–60, 65–67, 93, 155, 211, 221
Marshall, Will, 79–80
Marx, Karl, 2, 20
Marxism, 120, 176, 220
Mattern, Janice Bially, 226
McDonald, Patrick, 157
McMahan, Jeff, 213
Mearsheimer, John, 9, 115, 131–36, 208, 226
Metternich, Klemens von, 133
Middle East, 15, 93–98, 102, 105–6, 114, 117–23, 129–31, 140, 167–69, 178, 207, 225–26
Milbank, Dana, 107
Mill, John Stuart, 159–60
Miller, David, 227
Miller, Steven, 113, 119
Mitchell, George, 167
Montesquieu, 159
Moravcsik, Andrew, 195
Morgenthau, Hans, 133
Morrow, James, 40, 60, 62, 65
Mousseau, Michael, 157
Müller, Harald, 50, 219
Muravchik, Joshua, 9, 70, 73–74, 82, 113, 116–18, 121–22, 222, 225
Musharraf, Pervez, 150
Mutz, Diana, 222
Myrdal, Gunnar, 228

National Security Strategy, 131, 139
NATO, 75, 219
neoconservatism, 1, 7–9, 15, 22, 28, 35–36, 68–83, 87, 94, 105, 112–51, 175, 178, 189, 195–96, 206, 222–25
neoliberalism, 195
Netanyahu, Benjamin, 1, 8, 10, 15, 33, 35–36, 86–87, 92–100, 106, 109–11, 115–18, 143, 154–55, 161–69, 185, 206–7, 223–25
neutrality, 34, 194, 197
Nicaragua, 95

1967 War, 94
9/11. *See* September 11, 2001
Nixon, Richard, 132–33
normative ethics of the social sciences, 11, 13, 198
North Africa, 131
Northern Ireland, 75
Nossel, Suzanne, 145–46
Nozick, Robert, 47, 50
Nye, Joseph, Jr., 10, 143–54, 168–70, 180, 207–8, 226

Obama, Barack, 10, 135, 143–53, 163–64, 167, 169
Obama administration, 143, 169, 207
objectivity, 6, 11, 13, 28, 31–34, 85–86, 90, 111, 129–30, 172–75, 183–89, 194, 197–203, 206, 209, 211–12
Oneal, John R., 155, 222
ontology, 188, 197–98
Operation Allied Force, 75
operationalization, 12, 55, 59, 66–67, 77, 88–89, 210–14, 217
Oren, Ido, 34, 39, 227
Oren, Michael, 223
Organization of the Islamic Conference, 151
Organization for Security and Cooperation in Europe (OSCE), 82–83
Oslo accords / negotiations / process / agreements, 8, 93, 96, 102–5, 116–17, 189
Owen, John M., 219, 228

Pakistan, 77, 150
Palestinians, 2, 8, 15, 75, 85–86, 92–110, 117, 123, 162–72, 191, 207–8
Palestinian Administrative Authority (PAA), 104
Palestinian Authority (PA), 95, 99–104, 107–8, 110, 117, 131, 164–67, 223
Pateman, Carole, 42
Patten, Chris, 82, 223
Payne, Rodger, 190, 220, 227
peace, 2, 5, 8, 35–59, 65, 69, 72, 76, 79–85, 91–110, 117–19, 124–25, 130, 153, 156–67, 178, 184, 191, 195, 199, 207–8, 211, 215, 217–19, 224–25

Peres, Shimon, 93
Perle, Richard, 74, 105
phenomenology, 24, 197
philosopher-king, 191, 193, 209
Pipes, Daniel, 120, 222
Pipes, Richard, 122
Plato, 191
Podhoretz, Norman, 122–23, 146, 222
Polachek, Solomon, 155–56
political avowal vernacular, 6, 37–38, 75–76, 80–83, 86–89, 96–97, 100, 106, 111, 131–35, 138–39, 147–48, 158, 161, 186, 191, 196, 205–7
political concepts / essentially contested concepts, 4–7, 12–18, 22–25, 38–42, 56, 60, 65, 68, 96–98, 144, 161, 178, 204–5, 209–12, 217, 220
political conviction, 5–18, 22, 27–28, 33, 36–38, 67, 75–76, 82–84, 87, 92, 95, 100, 109, 112–15, 125, 131–39, 149, 153–54, 157, 169, 204–6, 210–12
Portes, Alejandro, 29
positivism (scientific stance), 2, 13, 19, 31, 34, 56–57, 60, 90, 173, 176–77, 183, 188, 194, 197, 199–202, 214
postmodernism, 19, 28, 31
poststructuralism, 13, 31
Potter, Elizabeth, 221
power, 2, 3, 7, 14, 16, 24–27, 32, 39, 42–44, 47, 55, 60–61, 64, 70–71, 79, 88, 93, 99, 105–8, 113–18, 124, 127, 130, 132, 137–38, 176–80, 220
  hard power, 146–49, 152–54, 168
  smart power, 144–45, 148, 151–54, 169
  soft power, 10, 20, 80, 142–54, 168–70, 207, 226
pragmatism, 74, 140, 141
Press-Barnathan, Galia, 226
Progressive Policy Institute (PPI), 79–80
Project for the Future of Iraq, 226
Project for the New American Century, 118, 222
Przeworski, Adam, 42
public convention, 5–10, 14–18, 21–22, 25–29, 33–38, 67–88, 92, 96–97, 100–101, 105–15, 125, 127, 130–38, 154, 157–59, 169, 193, 200, 204–8, 212, 214, 224
Putnam, Hilary, 199
Putnam, Robert, 30, 180, 220–21

Quartet, 107, 167

Rabin, Yitzhak, 93
Rawls, John, 50, 195, 213–16, 229
Ray, James Lee, 52, 155
Reagan, Ronald, 71, 105, 222
realism, 9, 40–41, 44, 62, 69, 73–74, 94, 115, 122, 131–36, 138, 161, 176 , 213, 226–27
  classical realism, 226
  defensive realism, 134
  neoclassical realism, 226
  neorealism, 131, 176–77, 227
  offensive realism, 134
Realpolitik, 62
relativism, 13, 28, 31–32, 110–11, 114, 120, 123, 125, 128
Republican Party, 71, 73
republican peace, 39, 45, 90, 155
republicanism, 54, 90, 156
responsibility
  moral responsibility, 11, 171–73, 176–82, 195, 227
  political responsibility, 154, 161, 167, 171–73, 191–94, 227
  scholarly responsibility, 11, 171–73, 195, 202–3, 208–9, 215–16, 218
  social task responsibility, 11, 171–73, 182–83, 186, 189, 199–202, 218, 227–28
Reuel, Mark Gerecht, 119
rhetoric, 1, 14, 28–32, 71–75, 107–11, 147, 163–65, 220–21
rhetorical capital, 6–11, 15, 25–32, 36, 85–93, 102, 107, 110–11, 118, 154, 159, 161, 167, 168–73, 183–87, 193, 197–98, 202, 206–8, 220–21
Rice, Condoleezza, 107, 131
Ricoeur, Paul, 23
Riker, William, 29, 31
Roadmap (plan), 8, 85–86, 98–101, 106–10, 117, 119, 131

Rostow, Walt, 180
Rummel, Rudolph J., 46–51, 221
Rumsfeld, Donald, 152
Russett, Bruce, 37, 40, 51–60, 65–66, 155, 189, 194–95, 211, 221–22, 226
Russia, 72, 75

Sakharov, Andrei, 101–5, 224
Sartre, Jean Paul, 174
Saudi Arabia, 74, 119–20, 123, 222
Scanlon, T. M., 182–83
Schafer, Mark, 82, 223
Schmitt, Gary, 118
Schumpeter, Joseph, 42, 66, 229
Science and Technology Studies, 219
Searle, John, 187
second intifada, 101, 105, 227
security community, 41, 44, 57
security dilemma, 60–62, 157
Security Scholars for a Sensible Foreign Policy, 190
Segall, Shlomi, 228
September 11, 2001: 97, 105, 113, 116, 119–22, 129, 176, 222, 225
Shai, Nachman, 168–69
Shalem Center, 94, 102, 223
Sharansky, Natan, 1, 8, 15, 33, 78–79, 86–87, 92, 101–11, 115–19, 206, 224–25
Sharon, Ariel, 93, 97, 101, 104–5, 107, 110, 162
Shenhav, Shaul, 184, 223
Sikkink, Kathryn, 15, 219–20
Simon, Herbert, 31
Singer, Peter, 213
Siverson, Randolph, 40, 60–62, 66
Slaughter, Ann-Marie, 229
Smith, Adam, 159–60
Smith, Alastair, 40, 60–62, 66
Smith, Steve, 176
Smith, Tony, 72–74, 78, 135, 195–96, 219, 223, 227–29
Snyder, Jack, 35, 113, 225
Socialism, 42, 47–48
Somalia, 74
South Korea, 75, 226
sovereignty, 8, 41

Soviet Union / Soviet Block, 55, 75, 101–6, 116, 132–33, 224
stable peace, 41, 44, 94, 99–100, 163, 215–17
Stalin, Joseph, 103, 106
Steele, Brent, 219, 228
Stoll, Ira, 117, 224
Strauss, Leo, 113
Straussian, 121, 123
structural realism, 226
Sweden, 47–48
Syria, 96, 151
Szacki, Jerzy, 174, 227

Taliban, 129
Taylor, Charles, 212
terrorism, 71, 75, 78–82, 93, 97–100, 105–6, 113–14, 119–21, 129, 131, 135–36, 139, 146, 154, 164, 168, 185, 222–25
theoretical construction, 5–18, 22–27, 33, 36–40, 60, 65, 67–70, 73–76, 84, 92, 97, 100, 113, 115, 118–19, 125–27, 130–36, 157, 204–17
theoretical explanatory vernacular, 5, 36–38, 100, 134, 148, 161, 186–87, 205
theoretical imperative, 171–73, 190, 194–97, 202
theoretician-citizen, 11, 13, 161, 167, 173, 187, 190–93, 200–202, 208–9, 217–18
Tickner, J. Ann, 221
totalitarian, 73, 98
Trinidad and Tobago, 151
truth, 2, 22, 31–37, 48, 83, 88, 91, 120, 122, 127, 132, 149, 185, 188, 198, 213, 223
Tucker, Robert, 118
Tunis, 102

unilateral withdrawal, 108, 162–63. *See also* disengagement plan
United Nations, 93, 104, 116, 146, 150
United States, 8, 35, 41, 72, 74, 77–80, 85, 93–99, 105–10, 117–32, 138–58, 163, 175, 185, 191, 208, 219, 222, 225–26. *See also* America

U.S. Congress, 82, 95, 110, 144
U.S. Senate, 97, 101

Vietnam, 135
Vietnam War, 118

Walker, Stephen, 82, 223
Wallerstein, Immanuel, 176–77
Walt, Stephen, 9, 115, 131–36, 208, 226
Waltz, Kenneth, 40, 177, 194, 198, 217
war, 1, 9, 36, 39, 40–45, 48, 50–66, 69–81, 87–88, 91, 95, 98, 100, 103, 105–6, 110, 113–14, 119, 125, 127, 129, 130–36, 140, 146, 156–57, 160–63, 166, 178, 185, 199, 208, 211, 213, 217, 223, 225, 228
Washington, D.C., 93, 144
Weber, Max, 189
Weede, Erich, 157
Wehner, Peter, 127–28

Weldes, Jutta, 20, 25, 220
West Bank, 102, 108
Western Europe, 72
White House, 131, 138, 163
Widmaier, Wesley, 189
Williams, Michael, 117
Wilson, Woodrow, 125
Wolfowitz, Paul, 105, 107
World Trade Organization (WTO), 74
World War II, 45

Yistael B'Aliyah (political party), 101
Young, Iris Marion, 227
Yugoslavia, 75

Zakaria, Fareed, 221
Zerilli, Linda M. G., 34
Zionism, 108
"zooming in, zooming out," 12, 204, 210–16